Secondary Schools

━◆ A REFERENCE HANDBOOK

CONTEMPORARY EDUCATION ISSUES

Secondary Schools

➤ A REFERENCE HANDBOOK

Leila E. Villaverde

A B C 🟤 C L I O

Santa Barbara, California • Denver, Colorado • Oxford, England

Library of Congress Cataloging-in-Publication Data
Villaverde, Leila E.
    Secondary schools : a reference handbook / Leila E. Villaverde.
        p.   cm — (Contemporary education issues)
    Includes bibliographical references (p.) and index.
    ISBN 1-57607-981-3 (hardcover : alk. paper)
    ISBN 1-57607-982-1 (e-book)
    1. Education, Secondary—Aims and objectives—United States.
2. High schools—United States—History.   I. Title.   II. Series.

LA222.V55 2003
373.73—dc22

                                                            2003015197

07 06 05 04 03   10 9 8 7 6 5 4 3 2 1

This book is also available on the World Wide Web as an e-book. Visit abc-clio.com for details.

ABC-CLIO, Inc.
130 Cremona Drive, P.O. Box 1911
Santa Barbara, California 93116-1911

This book is printed on acid-free paper ∞.
Manufactured in the United States of America

To my parents, Jose Luis and Elba,
who teach by example, flawlessly merging history,
education, and wisdom

⚡ Contents

◆ Series Editor's Preface

The Contemporary Education Issues series is dedicated to providing readers with an up-to-date exploration of the central issues in education today. Books in the series will examine such controversial topics as home schooling, charter schools, privatization of public schools, Native American education, African American education, literacy, curriculum development, and many others. The series is national in scope and is intended to encourage research by anyone interested in the field.

Because education is undergoing radical if not revolutionary change, the series is particularly concerned with how contemporary controversies in education affect both the organization of schools and the content and delivery of curriculum. Authors will endeavor to provide a balanced understanding of the issues and their effects on teachers, students, parents, administrators, and policymakers. The aim of the Contemporary Education Issues series is to publish excellent research on today's educational concerns by some of the finest scholars and practitioners in the field while pointing to new directions. The series promises to offer important analyses of some of the most controversial issues facing society today.

Danny Weil
Series Editor

● Preface

This books attempts to serve as a compendium and a chronology of secondary education in the United States. It maps some of the social and cultural movements as they relate to the construction of secondary schools and adolescence. This book extends from the historical foundations to the contemporary conceptualizations of secondary education, also focusing on the different types of secondary schools available and their purposes. Legislation and policy that pertains to the construction and improvement of secondary schools will be documented as well to further understand the direction and intent of secondary education. It is pertinent to look into and study the different types of schools, target audiences, goals, accessibility, admissions, assistance, and so on. Both the standardization and commercialization of secondary schools are crucial to include in this reference resource of secondary schools given the increasing use of standardized tests and corporate sponsors. Last, various resources and organizations are annotated for further research, reading, and information.

I want this book to chart and inform the conceptualization, construction, and execution of secondary schools in their various forms and intents. This book investigates the purpose of secondary schools throughout history and today. In addition it will serve as a resource in the understanding of policy, legislation, and reform. My hope is that this is a useful tool for all involved in and committed to secondary education.

Leila E. Villaverde

Chapter One

•◦ Introduction and History

As the United States developed as a nation, the desire and motivation to educate youth promptly evolved. In this chapter secondary education is defined and traced through the history of education in this country, as well as through references to global influences on the American curriculum.

ORIGINS OF SECONDARY SCHOOLS

Institutions of secondary education in early America were influenced in some part by ancient Greece, Egypt, Babylonia, China, England and Rome (French 1967). Each country's educational system presented different models, some emphasizing the mind (development of the intellect), body (development of manual abilities and physical attributes), or both in the education of young males. It was common practice to provide greater educational opportunities for young men than for young women. Further distinctions were made based on class and location (where students came from in the country), which determined the type and quality of education male students would receive. During the Middle Ages secondary curriculum was divided into two parts: the trivium (grammar, rhetoric, and logic) and the quadrivium (arithmetic, geometry, astronomy, and music). These curricular designs focused mainly on the liberal arts. The Renaissance also greatly influenced curriculum for secondary education as it shifted studies to the classical literature of Athens and Rome. Classical literature and languages such as Latin and Greek were regarded as a means to an end, a way to unlock vast knowledge. There was a significant reliance and dependency on curriculum content and slightly less emphasis on method in early America. This by no means implies method was unimportant; on the contrary, rigor and discipline were unconditionally expected as paths for success, actualization, and for some, salvation. Nonetheless there was an almost mystical belief in study itself. This curriculum was standardized over time and lost much of its passionate purposes and intents. (This cycle remains a rather common curricular practice, as new ideas lose some of their liberatory tendencies or are interpreted in formalized and static ways.) As the study of science gained popularity so did its methodology, stressing the discipline of the mind and the development of reason. This chapter contextualizes what the United States inherited as the colonies developed and secondary education was established.

Next we move to the developing New World where we discuss the different types of schools created on the American shores after the English settled on the East Coast and moved westward.

FOUR TYPES OF SCHOOLS

The Latin Grammar School

The Latin Grammar School was the first type of secondary school to be established in Boston in 1635. These were modeled after the schools in England that aimed to prepare young men for college. Shortly after the schools were developed, Harvard College was established in 1642 and later renamed Harvard University. Harvard's course of study was largely theological: reading scriptures and understanding Christ as the foundation of knowledge. Students needed to exhibit a mastery of advanced study in Latin. By 1647, school was made compulsory by the "old deluder" law (legislation and policies will be discussed in greater detail in Chapter 2). This law was not uniformly respected or upheld; it varied greatly by location and the priorities placed on formal education. Even though the Latin Grammar School was designated as "public," parents were asked to pay or contribute what they could for these services. The original plans for the colonies' first Latin Grammar School were made as early as 1621 in Virginia, but that never came to fruition as a result of a Native American uprising (also known as the Indian Massacre of 1622) (Koos 1927; French 1967; Douglass 1964). This revolt was evidence of the strained relationship between settlers and Native Americans and their resistance to convert to Christianity. History is riddled with tensions and the development of secondary education is not without them as ideas of schooling, curriculum, and student potential are debated.

Soon after 1647, with the establishment of the first grammar school other schools were opened in Massachusetts, Connecticut, New Hampshire, and Rhode Island. Most of the larger towns had established this type of comprehensive system of secondary education. Other colonies instituted modifications to the grammar school. In 1689 William Penn ordered Philadelphia to open grammar schools. New York opened such schools after 1700. This is the earliest evidence of the institutionalization of secondary schooling in the colonies. A more expansive view of education and learning would warrant documentation and discussion of informal learning that has occurred throughout history, not just with the European settlers. It would be important to understand what learning practices and schooling structures Native Americans, blacks, and Mexicans (since most of the Southwest was still part of Mexico at this point in history) had established prior to 1635. These practices and institutions may have focused on agricultural knowledge and social and cultural understanding that informed the way one survives as opposed to a dependency on text as the only source of developing one's intellect. In today's society describing learning as living is a commonly understood practice, yet not as commonly implemented in schools.

The curriculum of the Latin Grammar School consisted of anywhere from four to seven years of Latin and Greek taught by a schoolmaster who delivered the college-preparatory curriculum. Latin was studied first and Greek followed, always through scripture and literature, paying close attention to language (reading, writing, spelling), grammar, and rhetoric. As time passed, other subjects were incorporated into the curriculum, but never displaced the importance of Latin or Greek. In 1789, the curriculum was officially shortened to four years. This seems to be where the high school as we know it originated. Students were expected to have command of English grammar before entering the four-year cycle.

The South, according to French (1967), had few organized schools. Plantation owners instead hired tutors educated in New England's secondary and higher education systems. Inherent in this history is the foundational difference between the North and the South.

Most teachers were clergymen or sons of clergymen trained primarily for religious services. These practices and expectations transferred to the schools where the relationship of student to knowledge was rigidly constructed and not subject to negotiation or question. Other individuals employed as teachers taught without specific training in education. Some received training either emphasizing content at the expense of methodology or vice versa. In the grammar schools the methods implemented were based on rote memorization, translation, repetition, and examination. This methodology was one way to standardize or account for the varying degrees of teacher preparation. The focus was not necessarily on student learning, and the quality of student comprehension is uncertain. Students' reflections of their learning note a stress on memorization rather than understanding all of the grammatical structures and guidelines (Koos 1927). At that time the field of child psychology had not made its presence known and any modifications to the curriculum based on students' cognitive abilities were not institutionalized. Many teachers, regardless of scientific studies or theories, modify instruction when they get to know their students better. These practices are largely individualized and informal (and this type of modification is more common now that cognitive psychology and child psychology have heavily influenced what is taught when and to whom).

The Latin grammar schools (some, not all) gave way to the "academy" as a structure for schooling. The need to make schooling and learning more practical was the impetus to change secondary education.

The Academy

As the political and social climate changed in what would soon become the United States, democracy took stronger hold and Latin grammar schools held stronger ties to England than was desired by new citizens. Businesses relying on increased trade also demanded different knowledge, such as accounting, surveying (for westward expansion), foreign languages (other than Latin and Greek), and science as crucial to understanding the world. Many young men were already learning these through apprenticeships and private venture schools that were established in local residences. Tuition was charged for this type of education. These schools were considered "public," as defined by their openness to whoever could pay the tuition. By the 1730s, students were being schooled to go to college, take part in government, become businessmen or teachers, or continue to further their studies. Much like private schools today, the academies were free to create and modify curriculum as they wished or for the needs of young men.

Benjamin Franklin saw these schools as great opportunities for the reformation of secondary education. Franklin proposed the first formal academy in 1749, and it was created in 1751 as the Philadelphia Academy and Charitable School. Franklin was very interested in practical studies and thought these were more fitting of the times. The curriculum involved three areas of study: classical, English, and mathematical-scientific. Students also had the opportunity to learn other foreign languages. The major difference in addition to orientation was that students had a choice of what they preferred to study or what they would find useful (most times these were the same). The curriculum had two intentions as the academy movement was popularized, training for life and preparation for college. These curricular orientations retain their popularity in secondary education throughout various decades, tracking youth for one or the other.

Franklin instituted a board of trustees to help in all school matters. The academy never truly embodied Franklin's proposal exactly, but when he was asked to serve abroad as colonial agent the trustees made other curriculum decisions. The trustees reformed the curriculum, extracting the practical component that was at the heart of Franklin's vision. As the model for the academy spread and more schools all over the nation (including the South and Midwest) were established, other changes took place. Religion was more broadly defined, students of all classes attended, and, eventually, both male and female students were educated there. (It was not until 1784 that the first coeducational academy was founded.) All of the academies had their own board of trustees, and in organization and curriculum they mirrored the colleges of the time. Some of the academies were funded by tuition, endowments, or land grants. The labels for the academy changed from school to school; some were institutes, colleges, or seminaries. But this type of schooling was responsible for the quickest surge of secondary education throughout the nation, not just in the Northeast. Many Latin grammar schools added practical studies to their curriculum or revamped their mission entirely. Some of the academies acted as extended elementary schools due to the learning conditions the students had in common schools. The academies varied in scope, purpose, organization, and funding, yet their common theme was to educate one way or another in more accessible ways than the population of the United States had known before. By 1875 most academies streamlined their curriculum to more stringent college preparatory courses (French 1967; Koos 1927). During this time the study of character development and faculty psychology (a branch of psychology that regards the mind as a muscle best exercised through education, particularly drills, repetition, and memorization) were prevalent; consequently the curriculum sought to address ways in which academic content could positively transform an individual's character and increase his or her intelligence as well.

Similar methods to the grammar school were employed with greater emphasis in training the mind and developing good character, rectifying any lazy tendencies or moral deficiencies (the same with more fervor would motivate vocational education). Again it is important to understand the variances possible from headmaster to headmaster in the delivery of teaching and learning. Other types of academies were created for different sectors of the population, particularly Native Americans and African Americans. Before we turn to the discussion of these schools, one more pedagogical model common during the early 1800s needs to be included in this trajectory, the Lancasterian system.

Joseph Lancaster came to the United States in 1818 and developed a hierarchal system of schooling for poor white boys, usually referred to as "paupers." In this type of classroom "the teacher sat far above his students and assistants on a raised platform or stage. The assistants or monitors, themselves older unpaid students, marched up and down the long rows of younger students conveying the instructions of the teacher and maintaining absolute order" (Nasaw 1979, 20). Every day, students' positions within the classroom changed according to their performance. The worse the student performed, the further from the teacher he was. Everybody was ranked and the main instructional strategy was dictation or lecture. This system insisted on using extreme means of control and discipline to reform these "deficient" students. The Lancasterian schooling system was considered highly successful in institutionalizing mandatory education for the poor. The public concern and attempt was to "save" poor youth, mainly boys, but in essence the presence of these "idle" young men presented a threat to safety in the public's consciousness. In the end these boys needed to be dealt with and turned into productive citizens before they became a greater burden to the developing society.

Academies and Schools for Others

In the creation of academies mainly for white boys and some for white girls, educational and societal leaders of various racial and ethnic backgrounds saw a need to also create academies and schools for Native American children. The academies for "other" children were created for very different reasons, such as assimilation, redemption, and civilization. These academies and schools, mostly boarding schools off the reservations, sought to convert students to Christianity, whiteness, and civilization. Students were removed from their families and given new names, religion, customs, language, and literacy. Some well-known schools were the Carlisle Indian Industrial School, Chilocco Indian School, and Choctaw Academy. These boarding schools and day schools represent an unheard story in American education encompassing highly questionable ethical and racial practices in the name of education.

An interesting exception to these academies and schools was the Bloomfield Academy, later renamed the Carter Seminary (still in operation today as a boarding school for Native Americans), which was founded by the Chickasaw Nation in 1852, with the help of missionaries, for Chickasaw girls (boys were admitted after 1949). This school's purpose was twofold, assimilation and self-preservation. The missionaries who envisioned this school were the Reverend John Harpole Carr (who also built the school himself and grew all the food supply) and his wife, Angelina (who planned the school's curriculum and schedule), of the Methodist Episcopal Church (Cobb 2000). Missionaries, the Chickasaw

Nation, and the federal government, each reigning at different time periods, directed school administration. Each administration had a slightly different agenda, yet the curriculum was heavily based in academic literacy, social literacy, religious literacy, and domestic literacy (Cobb 2000). Each administration placed more emphasis on the type of literacy they privileged, which modified the purpose of the school and the type of student they sought or desired. "Literacy, for the Chickasaws, was a way to control their own transformation; it was not a practice of freedom but a practice of control—a way to create an acceptable place for themselves in a different world" (Cobb 2000, 37). As a result boarding schools and day schools were seen as an opportunity to increase the ways in which the Chickasaw could become agents of their own future. Assimilation was a means to an end, not an end to tribal culture and knowledge.

During the first administration of the academy, mission work was the entire focus of the curriculum. The Reverend Carr focused on religious literacy as the main objective of education. Learning scripture and Christian tenets was required of every student, as well as the mastery of the English language. Students were not allowed to speak their native language at all and they were expected to choose Bloomfield as a new way of life. The Civil War closed the academy for several years and also ended the missionary administration. This afforded the Chickasaw an opportunity to gain administrative control of the Bloomfield Academy. The new literacy agenda was in place from 1865 to 1907, and this era was called the Golden Age of the academy. In 1868 Mrs. Murray (a member of a prominent Chickasaw family) and her husband took over the administration of the school (Cobb 2000). In 1870 Professor Robert Cole became superintendent and established the high school grades, and it was not until five or six years later that a law was established by Governor Overton making Bloomfield Academy a female seminary (Cobb 2000). Shortly thereafter the superintendents were all Chickasaw. The main objective of the school was to provide equality for Native American children. The curriculum became more rigorous and provided more advanced-level courses. The majority of students at Bloomfield were biracial, "mixed-blood," which meant one of the parents was white and English was that parent's native language. These students usually were already English literate by the time they entered the seminary. According to Cobb Johnson, one of the Chickasaw superintendents, there was a concerted effort to enroll full-blood students. He also offered financial assistance for families who would relocate into the area and enroll their daughters in the seminary. Bloomfield was one of the only institutions allowed to issue diplomas for their graduating students. Their curriculum was so advanced it compared to the junior college's curriculum. This opened many opportunities for Native American women during this period and this quickly became quite a prestigious institution. The young women who graduated from Bloomfield were seen as advocates and negotiators for their families in the ever-looming presence of white society. This institution, its administration, its students, and its philosophy could be considered feminist under today's discourse. The institution never used that terminology to my knowledge, but the focus on empowerment and seeing these young women as agents of social change certainly affected the political and social roles of Native American women in that arena.

The arts were considered central to the curriculum, so during the Golden Age, students had a wide variety of options in areas of study and excellence. It was a deliberate curricular reform that Bloomfield students did not study domestic literacy. The administration considered domestic literacy a counterproductive measure in securing equality. These young women became quite adept at code switching (the ability to use two languages, cultural values, or norms interchangeably) and negotiating both the white world and Chickasaw Nation. In present times these young women would be considered "border crossers" by cultural theorists. Unfortunately the Golden Age came to a close when the government took over the school in the early 1900s. Again the curriculum changed, but the school continued. Overall the Chickasaw Nation controlled thirteen day schools, four academies, and an orphan's home (Cobb 2000). There was no doubt of the immense influence Chickasaws had over defining their own identity. Such self-sufficiency and autonomy raised concern in the government and many attempts were made to recapture control and reinstitute subservience to the government. The government proceeded to break many treaties that were signed with Indian nations. Tremendous racial discrimination and inequity ensued.

As a direct consequence of the Economic Opportunity Act of 1965 a new school was created, the Demonstration School, on the Navajo Reservation in Arizona. This act reinstated Native American participation and control, thereby changing the direction in educational decisionmaking. The school was established on June 27, 1966, and was controlled by a five-member Navajo school board. This is an important shift in thinking toward members of a much suppressed group in the history of the United States and in secondary education.

Bishop Richard Allen also recognized the importance of education to the future of the African American community. In 1795 he opened a day school for sixty children and in 1804 founded the Society of Free People of Colour for Promoting the Instruction and School Education of Children of African Descent. By 1811 there were approximately eleven black schools in the city of Philadelphia (http://earlyamerica. com). Some of the first black schools in the late 1770s were created from and affiliated with local churches.

Independent black churches in the South grew in the latter part of the nineteenth century. These churches were founded in the North and helped finance and build new churches and schools in the South, increasing literacy considerably. Literacy, again, was defined as being able to read and master scripture. This institutionalized religion relied mainly on text and not as much on oral traditions. Much like the missionary schools for Native Americans, the church-related schools for African Americans were regarded as quite successful in educating their students (http://docsouth.unc.edu/church/introduction.html).

By 1867 Howard High School was founded in Delaware by the Society for the Improvement of Morals of the People of African Descent. Howard High School became a historic institution, given its central role in the education of African Americans in this country. Its principal was a woman, Edwina B. Kruse, who served from 1871 to 1922. In Delaware and nationally, Howard High School was a pillar of excellence in academics, athletics, and the arts. In 1975, the Howard Comprehensive High School became the Howard Career Center (www.whispersofangels.com).

As early as 1787, New York African Free Schools were created by different organizations whose sole purpose was to grant free black males and females the right to learn basic academic skills and industrial skills. Philadelphia; Providence, Rhode Island; Baltimore; and Pittsburgh soon followed, opening schools during the first half of the nineteenth century. Northern philanthropists contributed finances for black education throughout the North and South. Black educators were vocal about retaining curricular control and challenged some of the hidden agendas and conditions of the support. Many of their demands were the employment of black teachers and curriculum diversification. Their objective was to provide equal education to black children and youth, not an inferior curriculum motivated by discriminatory racial ideologies. Ohio was ahead of the times in regard to African American education and an advocate for African American suffrage. Two colleges—Oberlin, established in 1833, and Wilberforce, established in 1856—admitted both black and white students. Wilberforce University was considered an African American university. For years African Americans developed their own educational systems through churches and in private homes. At times these attempts at educating the young met much resistance. African Americans endured many racist practices to continue with quality education for their children and youth. Mission schools, similar to the mission schools for Native Americans, were developed. Black and white educators were employed at these schools. By the 1870s, classrooms were designated for secondary education and more schools were needed for the increase in student population. A new school was built in 1886 in Oxford, Ohio, that created much controversy. Black residents objected to a law passed that prohibited the new school from allowing black students to attend; as a result black students walked over to the new school to be enrolled on September 14, 1887 (Rousmaniere 2003). Again students and family met great physical resistance. Parents filed suits against the Board of Education and the court ruled in their favor—not necessarily because they wanted to uphold equal rights for black Americans, but rather because school boards could not make any decisions that contradicted the state legislature. Oxford schools were obligated to admit students without distinct discrimination on the basis of race to any public school (Rousmaniere 2003). History repeated itself several decades later with the court ruling to desegregate schools in *Brown v. Board of Education* in 1954.

Boarding schools also existed for African Americans. Among the most notable are the Piney Woods County Life School in Mississippi, Redemption Christian Academy of Troy in New York, Lauringburg Institute of Lauringburg in North Carolina, and Pine Forge Academy of Pine Forge in Pennsylvania. These schools were founded in the early part of the twentieth century. At one point in history there were over eighty such schools, yet as integration was implemented many closed. A few are still in existence today. The Piney Woods School was founded by Laurence C. Jones, who graduated from the University of Iowa in 1907. This school, similar to the Chickasaw-run Bloomfield Academy, is extremely important historically because it was founded and run by an African American. Jones started teaching local children informally. He then used a sheep shed to create a school where more students could get a well-rounded education. Shortly after he taught at the Utica Institute (an industrial school), he moved to Mississippi where he developed the Piney Woods School. Many of the above boarding schools are still run by African Americans and offer comprehensive curricula, some from K–12 and postgraduate, others 9–12, and offer the possibility of being a day student or a boarding student during the week or through the weekend. Despite segregation, unavailable funds, and incredible discrimination, persons of color persevered—believing in the transformative power of education. This was quite subversive, particularly in the South where several decades prior to that time fines and imprisonment were inflicted on those who tried to educate blacks.

Another wrinkle in unknown schooling history is the collaboration between African Americans in the South and Julius Rosenwald in Illinois, a self-made, early partner of Sears, Roebuck, and Company. He was one of the wealthiest men in the nation and helped finance construction for approximately 5,300 rural schools in fourteen southern states from 1912 to 1932, educating more than 25 percent of African American youth (Zeitz 2003). Rosenwald provided matching funds for the $4.7 million raised by African Americans. After reading Booker T. Washington's work, Rosenwald decided to join forces with Washington to start the rural-school construction project through the Rosenwald Fund. Other funds were pivotal in the construction of black schools, such as the Peabody Education Fund, John Slater Fund, Anna T. Jeans Foundation, and Phelps-Stokes Fund. Students would walk for miles sometimes to get to school and back. The desire for education and self-sufficiency was greater than any obstacles placed in the way by southern racial politics. The Rosenwald Fund provided much needed resources in the path to democratic access. Rosenwald insisted that African Americans be involved in the construction and design of their education. Critics construe Rosenwald's initiatives as part of white northern attempts to keep blacks as a subordinate working class (Zeitz 2003). Given the incredible positive impact his initiative had throughout the South, one has to carefully weigh the amount of lives that were bettered by his financial assistance and the support it provided for a growing community. There are only a few of the Rosenwald schools left. These are now considered national historic sites in need of preservation. The National Trust for Historic Preservation is trying to preserve the schools that are left in North Carolina, Alabama, and Louisiana.

Almost a century after the first African Free Schools opened, additional independent black schools were created. Some of the most often discussed are also Muslim schools. The first independent black Muslim school opened in Detroit in 1932, and another one opened in Chicago around 1934. Today these schools, in particular, have a rigorous academic curriculum and students often outscore other schools in standardized tests. Philosophically these schools differ tremendously from public or other religiously oriented schools. Many parents (from various socioeconomic classes) seek these schools when possible in order to give their children a better education, one that does not underestimate their children's ability because of race or class. In the 1960s and 1970s more parents and communities sought control over schools, and the modern independent black school movement gained strength again in New York and New Jersey, forming the Council of Independent Black Institutions (CIBI) in 1972, Black Independent Schools (BIS), and the Institute for

Independent Education (IIE) following closely thereafter (www.ascac. org/papers/whyourownschools.html). These schools have provided and can continue to provide an important alternative in education for students who are often poorly served by public schools. Independent black schools focus on dealing with African American culture as the basis for curriculum development and assessment. Parents, educators, and community members are often disheartened by the achievement gaps between races in the present educational system. Concerned individuals with educational visions for every student regardless of race, culture, or gender oftentimes become the greatest advocates for educational reform. These in particular intend to provide the type of education that works to diminish the socioeconomic differences in U.S. society.

Another type of institution developed and transformed many of the academies and existing schools; these were called public high schools.

Public High Schools

Parents were hesitant to pay extra for tuition if they were already being taxed for local schools. A lot of students switched to public high schools from the academies. The first public high school, known as the English Classical School, was instituted in Massachusetts in 1821 (Koos 1927). By 1824 it had moved and changed its name to the English High School. Other states followed Massachusetts's lead, with high schools opening as far south as South Carolina in 1839. The first female high school is documented in Worcester in 1824, and Boston is recognized as having one in 1826, which closed two years later and reopened approximately two decades later. Massachusetts was the first to establish a state system of public secondary education as a result of a state law in 1827 (Koos 1927). The struggle was to make secondary education free, much as had been done for "common schools," which served as elementary schools for "all," and the same was hoped for high schools, particularly in the early nineteenth century after the U.S. republic was created (French 1968).

It is important to note that the school movement was more popular in larger towns than in rural areas. Some families could not dispense with the labor that children supplied, so public high schools were for the middle classes, as the upper classes still sent their children to the academies or private institutions.

Based on several court cases, secondary education schools, particularly free public high schools, were now considered part of the common schools and were given the right to levy property taxes for the schools. This was an important achievement as it gave every child the right to be educated in the basics or fundamentals and in the specialization of the secondary school. Yet, as with more contemporary decisions or institutions, the ideals or conceptualizations vary greatly from the actual practice. The high schools were free and public, but had admissions requirements, such as multiple entrance exams delineating literacy levels. The cost of books or supplies, transportation, lack of child labor laws, no attendance requirements beyond age fourteen, and theoretical inclinations (not appealing to some) seemed to pose problems as well. As they do today, high schools varied tremendously in resources and accessibility. The curriculum was subject-centered, emphasizing the acquisition and retainment of knowledge and not the application of it. Also, as more women had access to education and college preparation, the number of female teachers increased. Teaching was designated a respectable career for a woman but she was usually paid less than her male counterparts. All of these things, in addition to attempts at standardizing the curriculum, quickly transformed secondary education.

The course of study ranged from three to five years, with most schools preferring four years. The curriculum covered traditional and classical subject matter and more general/practical courses. Toward the end of the nineteenth century vocational education and commercial studies were also incorporated into the public high school curriculum. Also at this point, the Committee of Ten was assembled and their report was presented in 1893. The Cardinal Principles of Secondary Education came more than two decades later (these two reports will be discussed in Chapter 2).

Extended Secondary School

The extended secondary school marks the changes made to high schools, elementary schools, and higher education. The last two years of elementary school were redesigned into the junior high school and the high school was extended by two more years. The high school extension became the junior college. These curricular and structural changes were instituted to provide transitional spaces in which to extend the knowledge acquired through schooling. These changes started quite informally as each school attempted to suit the needs of their students. By the early 1900s both the junior high school and junior college started in the West and Midwest, as follows: Berkeley, California, 1909; Los Angeles, California, 1910; and Joliet, Illinois, 1902. (Private junior colleges also existed during this time, yet these were not considered direct extensions from the high school.) During the first decade of the twentieth century, studies on child development, adolescence, and psychology simultaneously encouraged and supported the need for this reconfiguration and particularly the establishment of the junior high school. The result was three institutions of learning before higher education: elementary school, junior high school, and high school.

REORGANIZATION OF THE HIGH SCHOOL

For the most part educational systems in the United States consisted of eight elementary school grades and four high school grades. Some schools in New England offered a nine/four arrangement and schools in the South offered a seven/four arrangement. The impetus to change the grade-level structure started in the colleges and universities (Anderson and Gruhn 1962). Suggestions were made to start college preparatory courses in the upper elementary grades. Restructuring became more serious after the Report of the Committee of Ten in conjunction with the child study movement: it was concluded that developmental milestones, which prepared youngsters for advanced study earlier, occurred in seventh grade, not ninth. What we see here is the concern for an appropriate transition from elementary school to high school. Another concern was the time male students spent with female teachers (largely as a response to Stanley Hall's studies on adolescence and child development, which are discussed further in the section on adolescence), so the initiative was made to transition male students into secondary education more quickly.

The proposal for reorganization attempted to allocate equal time between elementary and secondary education, creating a six/six structure (six years in elementary education, three of the following six years in junior high school, and three in high school). Schools in California and Ohio in 1910 were the first documented to reorganize and institute the junior high school starting with seventh grade (some accounts discuss junior high schools as early as the late 1890s [Koos 1927]). With more youth going to school, part of the need to build or create junior high schools was to alleviate the overcrowded elementary and secondary schools. The junior high school would also facilitate curriculum differentiation, allowing students to remediate and excel in different subjects without having to fail the entire grade. One purpose that is consistent with today's is to provide a place where curriculum, structure, teaching, and learning would suit the specific needs (psychological, cognitive, physical, emotional, and social) of the young adolescent.

The junior high school was called the little high school because its structure and curriculum replicated those of the high school. Educational leaders were dissatisfied with this classification given that many by the first decade of the twentieth century started to see the potential of junior high schools as something very different. Some junior high schools were seventh and eighth grades only; others were from seventh to ninth. A list in the 1920s was compiled to express the purposes of middle-level schooling (Messick and Reynolds 1992). The list stressed meeting individual differences, prevocational exploration, guidance, developing good citizenship, profitable self-activity, retention of students, introduction of new subjects, college preparation, economy of time, providing completion for those not going to college, and stimulating educational advancement (16–17). These multiple purposes did not exactly provide a clear vision of the need and intent of junior highs. It seems as if with this institution U.S. education was trying to fix all ills in the span of two to three years. The impossibility of the task soon became reality.

As changes in society prioritized different educational purposes, junior high schools emphasized college prep courses less and became more creative about curriculum integration and scheduling. Several concepts were initiated that still are a part of today's schooling, such as homeroom, block scheduling, core classes, and electives. In 1957 with the launching of Sputnik, education became the subject of great debate. There was a concerted shift in curriculum to an attempt at rigor in mathematics and science. The feeling was the United States needed to compete and schools were the institution in which to train individuals for the future. The focus of schooling became the teaching and learning of math and science, and later the addition of reading and language arts. Disciplines were favored over integration or creativity. A decade and a half later, new studies and thinking emerged about adolescence and schooling.

Efforts to change the junior high came with much resistance. Teachers who taught at the junior high level were originally trained to be high school teachers; consequently it was evident teachers needed to be educated on early adolescence and the curriculum innovations for middle-level schooling. Yet educational leaders persisted in believing that the little high school was not an appropriate structure for eleven- to fourteen-year-olds. By 1973 the National Middle School Association (NMSA) was founded and insisted schools for this age group needed to have a different structure and curricular program. In 1977 the association issued a set of goals for middle-level education, which stressed that every student should be well-known by at least one adult who provides guidance, be helped to achieve skills and continued learning, have ample experiences to develop decisionmaking and problem-solving skills, acquire fundamental knowledge, and have opportunities to explore interests (Messick and Reynolds 1992). The school structure was reorganized so that sixth through eighth grades were considered middle school and ninth grade would be freshman year in high school. The middle school is also characterized by the curricular structure known as curriculum integration or interdisciplinary curriculum. These two curriculum models are not the same but are often used interchangeably. Curriculum integration (less common) requires a complete infusion of separate disciplines as one studies, researches, and experiences concepts or themes. James Beane provides a clear philosophy and examples in his book *Curriculum Integration.* What is known as interdisciplinary, or multidisciplinary, curriculum integrates curriculum along any theme, big idea, concept, or skill but maintains each discipline. Students for the most part still move from class to class, yet they study a unit where knowledge is threaded and integrated for maximum comprehension. Usually a team of teachers work and plan together on the unit and provide sometimes a seamless learning experience for students. These teams sometimes are looped for the entire three years students are at the middle school so students have a consistent core of teachers with whom they can develop strong relationships. The NMSA later issued characteristics of excellence for middle schools. At the core of these characteristics was the concern for the physical, intellectual, social-emotional, and moral needs of the early adolescent, as well as including most of the purposes issued earlier. In addition the association expressed the need to educate teachers specifically for middle school instruction and the need to involve parents in the school.

The middle school then became a great site for educational reform. Several reports published during the 1980s had significant impact on schooling, especially secondary education (these will be discussed in detail in Chapter 2). One of particular significance was *Turning Points: Preparing American Youth for the Twenty-first Century* (1989) by the Carnegie Council on Adolescent Development, which again showed that social and economic needs shape and influence schooling and learning, as well as collective assumptions about youth. Middle school in recent years has been a source of great initiatives and creativity. Some educators feel that given its position, literally in the middle, it has great potential and leeway for curriculum, teaching, and students.

VOCATIONAL EDUCATION

An important part of the development of secondary education in the United States is vocational education, with its inception in 1876 at the

Philadelphia Centennial exposition (Kliebard 1999). The different versions of secondary education above do not specifically address the incredible influence on both schooling and society vocational education had. The Industrial Revolution forced into view different conceptions of education and how members of this society were prepared to contribute economically and socially. Vocational education started as an alternative to apprenticeships, and it was first called mechanistic arts. John D. Runkle opened the School of Mechanic Arts adjacent to a preparatory school in Massachusetts. Runkle was concerned with the educative process as opposed to the product. At this point an academic curriculum still existed in conjunction with the mechanical arts curriculum. There was great motivation to incorporate this new curriculum into the public high schools and strong pride in the worth of "good work" as well as the need to reinsert value in labor. Given the emphasis on classical education and other modifications of academic schooling, there was a great divide in how society viewed learning and people's worth. Runkle's inclinations seemed to express a passion for craftsmanship and the art of being involved in this work, as opposed to a direct tracking and reproduction of the status quo. Quickly things changed— Calvin Woodward joined forces with Runkle and created an image for mechanical training as inherent to being an American and a good worker. He created a picture of strength and invincibility playing on the need to recapture the good values of hard work. The core objectives of manual training became evident and lasting: manual training as moral regeneration, as pedagogical reform, and as preparation for the workplace in the industrial society (Kliebard 1999).

Large cities created technical schools; others incorporated such training into the existing public schools. There was great debate in regard to when vocational education should be introduced into the curriculum and what should serve as a prerequisite. Yet the arguments in support of vocational education, given the times, prevailed. There were certain sections of the population that were targeted for this type of schooling; they were African Americans, Native Americans, and the poor. It was "believed to have curative powers for immigrants as well as for various ethnic and racial minorities" (Kliebard 1999, 13). It was seen in much the same ways as common schools, as a means to socialize and Americanize. Black intellectuals embraced this idea for different reasons, mainly as a way to solidify self-sustenance. Booker T. Washington was a student in the Hampton Institute (set up by Samuel Armstrong). He later developed the Tuskegee Institute where he employed African American teachers from Hampton and Fiske University and provided a curriculum centered on skills training to foster and support an independent class of black artisans. Washington desired economic independence. W.E.B. Du Bois disagreed with Washington's approach and preferred a classical curriculum (to exercise the intellect) so as to not reify stereotypes of African Americans as inferior. He believed that the future leaders of his people, "the talented tenth," would be short-changed if they received solely manual training. Both Washington and Du Bois contributed greatly to the education of African Americans during and after the Industrial Revolution. Both argued significant points. The important synthesis is that a holistic or comprehensive education needs both the intellectual and practical strand to be successfully integrated in curriculum. Unfortunately vocational education has not shed its stigma of somehow being an inferior type of education.

More modifications took place in the curriculum, moving from manual training to vocational training. National organizations rallied around vocational training to support its centrality in the curriculum and the workforce. The labor force was involved in evaluating the curriculum as they had a vested interest in producing competent workers.

Women were another group that in the long run fared well in vocational education as a result of commercial education. Initially women's education consisted of domestic skills. Here again there were distinct divisions in terms of race and ethnicity. Cooking was one of the first of the domestic arts to make its way into the Milwaukee public school curriculum. The emphasis was on making cooking and housekeeping as economical as possible with proper nutrition and hygiene. There were separate trade schools for boys and girls. In retrospect, through Selden C. Menefee's report in 1938, clerical education by far seemed most successful, as the young women trained in commercial programs remained in professions or jobs that were closely aligned with what they studied.

Continuation Schools

Under vocational education, continuation schools existed to afford youth, mainly fourteen to sixteen years old who were no longer in schools, a place to further their training. The Milwaukee Vocational School was set up as a continuation school. The school extended its audience to the working class in order to further their skills. A curriculum for part-time working students was implemented with teachers who were familiar with the particular industry taught. More details on the curriculum and influences on vocational education are discussed in Chapter 4.

Transformation of the High School

After the Great Depression and World War II, the labor market left few opportunities for youth. Schools saw increased enrollments and sought federal aid, yet were met with much political red tape from social scientists and New Deal (a campaign for federal aid for vocational education) leaders. The struggle remained that of making the secondary school central in youth's lives given the change in the economy and society. Schools needed to change. They had been strictly academic, strictly vocational, essentially about life adjustment, and unsatisfying to the bulk of American youth. This and the change in the labor market created what historians call "the youth problem," which included delinquency, promiscuity, political activism, and alienation. Schools, as a result of retrenchment, were unequipped to deal with increased enrollment. The schools were in crisis. The government created two agencies (Civilian Conservation Corps, CCC, and National Youth Administration, NYA) to help youth transition from adolescence to adulthood, mainly with securing employment. The controversy continued as the federal agencies used money otherwise allocated for schools, and older adolescents in particular were being "lured" from education. Both of these agencies employed youth to work in national parks, forests, and other social or ecological projects. They focused on providing both work-study programs and post–high school employment.

Education associations and professional educators criticized these programs extensively, largely due to the loss of funds. Not much was discussed on the merit of these social and public endeavors and the experiences youth might benefit from. Commissions were drafted to attack these programs and to reinstitute the public high school as the universal education for youth. Schools became sites for curriculum experiments in order to assess best practices for the diversity of the student body. The purpose of the high schools changed more or less to holding tanks for adolescents, a purposeful alienation from the adult world and in most respects society. Educators claimed the population was very different, less talented. And here I must alert you to the use of language: students were *more diverse,* meaning the numbers of minorities and women increased, and therefore the assumption by some educators of decreased talent and ability. As a result tracking surged, although it was not labeled as such; instead it was a concern "to provide different educational programs for students with varying abilities" (Angus and Mirel 1999). Vocational education was losing its popularity, not because of educational initiatives, but as a result of the labor market and the assurgency of semiskilled positions. Life education was pervasive in the general curriculum. Heavy criticism came from educators, parents, and communities that this trend was antidemocratic. Life-adjustment education was seen as another way to reify class structure and elitism in U.S. society.

As the 1960s and 1970s ignited great social, cultural, and political debates, the education of American youth came under scrutiny. National defense was of concern, youth were seen as the future, and little faith was placed on their abilities. Adolescence became this abstract vacuum of all sorts of possibilities, the majority with great negativity impending. Schools were not adequately engaging youth and providing hope for productive futures that felt fulfilling for students. Adult, family, and economic values were imposed on adolescents and education became a flimsy bridge from youth to adulthood. The curriculum once again was transformed with a desperate focus on math and science to compete on a global scale.

Much unrest lay at the center of these two decades: America was finding and solidifying its true identity as it wrestled with democratic ideals and unfulfilled practices. Schools were at the center of youth activism and political movements from all sectors of society. Educational reform was demanded and the social climate embraced it. As with all movements the possibility always exists for other groups to appropriate visions and goals for other means. Part of the objectives of the Civil Rights movement and the women's movement was to provide equal educational opportunities inclusive of curriculum that represented minorities and women in abundant and positive roles, opened rigorous academic classes to minorities and women, and revisited knowledge from multiple perspectives. Education was a much contested and struggled-over social space. Fortunately curriculum expanded and gave way to some of these demands. Unfortunately these same demands were used to rationalize tracking and differentiated curriculum. There was still a central, mainstream curriculum unencumbered by the marginal social strife. Status quo remains today even after significant curricular transformation.

As education was more and more complicated by governmental policy, business paradigms, bureaucracy, and standardization, alternatives surged all over the nation. The 1980s and 1990s were simultaneously parallel tunnel visions of economic reproduction and education alternatives. Charter schools, vouchers, and home schooling were seen as viable solutions to public schools. (Each requires a layered discussion that will be addressed in Chapter 4 and in other parts of the book.) It is crucial to understand both the sequence of change and the content of change in the American secondary school. The implications of these changes are substantial to the growth and development of youth in our society in addition to the education of educators and educational activists.

General Educational Development (GED) Testing Service

The GED test is the equivalent of a high school diploma. Many individuals choose to take the GED test instead of continuing in high school for a variety of reasons. The tests were first created in 1942 for military personnel whose educational careers had been shortened by war. The tests initially were named the Veteran's Testing Service. During the following decades there was an increased demand to offer the test to nonmilitary personnel to obtain a document validating high school-level skills necessary for work. Since 1942 there have been three more editions (1978, 1988, and 2002) of the test. The academic content areas assessed on the test are English/language arts (literature/reading), social studies, science, and mathematics. These are based on the proficiencies high schools require for graduation around the nation (see Chapter 3). The different editions of the test have changed as secondary education has been reformed. Major changes concentrate on shifts from rote and recall knowledge to application and interpretation of knowledge. In the 2002 edition, individuals must write a timed essay. The test also includes calculator and noncalculator math sections and analytical problem-solving test items in science and social studies. The changes in the test also reflect a changing society and a changing use of the test. The test is no longer just used for employment requirements, but also as admissions criteria for colleges and universities. In the age of technology there are numerous virtual ways to complete not only the GED test but high school courses as well.

ADOLESCENCE

Adolescence is at the heart of much educational debate. Throughout time adults have been concerned about the future of youth and the country. The two go hand in hand as educational institutions are charged with preparing youth for work and society. Particular focus also is necessary for the way children and adolescents develop and mature. The advances in adolescent psychology heavily influenced secondary education, its structure, content, and evaluation. The findings from researchers such as Hall, Jean Piaget, Erik Erikson, and Lawrence Kohlberg shaped how educators, parents, physicians, and communities viewed and treated youth. Adolescent development was seen as something that was crucial to curriculum sequence and content, how schools were organized, how students were grouped and tracked, and ultimately what type of education was offered to whom. How adolescence is defined and constructed is then necessary to further investigate and discuss. Based on the literature, age markers were placed on where childhood and adolescence began and ended, which subsequently determined who was allowed to go to junior high or high school. Paths to adulthood were not similarly paved, with some having more access to longer schooling and others to work. These incongruencies and changes in developmental psychology and educational philosophy are pivotal markers in the construction of secondary education.

In understanding secondary education, it is of most import to also comprehend the construction and development of adolescence. During the inception of secondary education the concept of childhood and adolescence changed dramatically, from the lack of child labor laws, to creating schools and training, to the development of "adolescence" and the child study movement in the late nineteenth and early twentieth centuries. Stanley Hall is said to be the leader of the child study movement, "which aimed to utilize scientific findings on what children know and when they learn it to understand the history of human life" (Lesko 2001, 54). He was a proponent of recapitulation theory in which the stages of evolution are paralleled to the development of a child. Hall thought adolescence was the pinnacle of human development. Much as for Piaget, adolescence represented the height of cognitive ability. For Hall the study of adolescence would give him insight into the human race. Adolescence, mainly for Hall, became a time for extreme monitoring and caring for the essence of masculinity—particularly for white males, who were considered superior genetic specimens.

In adolescence one could become developed and superior or fixed in an inferior stage. Education, the process by which one was civilized, was extremely important. Hall was concerned with health and physical education, particularly in doing the right amount to release anger, but restraining excessive expressions, which would interfere with a young man's overall strength. Health was characterized by rationality; in fact civilization, the future of the race, rested on the ability to develop reason. Education, he believed, needed to take place in single-sex institutions for fear of feminization of the boys, and tracking was to differentiate boys with various future possibilities. He pushed for studies on pedagogy that promoted social efficiency perspectives and advocated for engagement in the world as young males were removed from it (Lesko 2001).

Hall's work was seminal in its influence on curriculum as the education of boys and girls was delineated drastically for over a century, and his psychology defined the differences between races and opportunities. Lesko also attributes the influence of Hall's psychology to the taxonomy of labels and the practice of naming to depict the superior as the norm, in contrast to the inferior, which was anything else. This culture of creating stages and rigid structures for being establishes a universal timeline through which all children are supposed to grow and develop. The dangers of such universalization are the strict guidelines for what is deemed normal and abnormal and how these conclusions affect the real lives of youth and the consequences they may produce.

In general, child psychology and developmental theories must be studied carefully and assessed for their appropriateness given the time and population. Theorists like Les Vygotsky offer developmental theories more accepting of the student's culture and personal development. The work of psychologists has influenced education greatly; therefore it is essential to understand the available theories as well as to question their appropriateness for the given era.

Adolescence is a time of potential change and transformation, great discovery, challenge, and risk. There is a constant struggle between intimacy and independence, particularly at this time. In addition to the physical, psychological, and cognitive growth that occurs, school structure changes. Students move from elementary school to middle school or junior high to high school. The transition between elementary school and middle school or junior high can be of great significance. Helping students cope with the transition so that they can maximize their learning opportunities needs to be a central concern of secondary educators. School reform can be motivated by the changing needs of adolescents as learning is offered in ways that capitalize on the challenges presented to students at this time of their lives. It is also a time to secure student curiosity and engagement instead of perpetuating alienation from learning and success. Cottle (2001) discusses the development of adolescent consciousness in a culture of distraction. He affirms that the culture that we live in fosters distraction and overstimulation, making it difficult for anyone to focus on one task. Yet he advocates for adolescents (as well as educators) to take advantage of these opportunities to engage in critical self-reflection in order to improve the meaning in one's life. Through this self-reflection students have the ability to develop awareness and consciousness. Learning then goes beyond school grounds while simultaneously being at the core where a student's uses of memory, thinking, intellect, and emotion are intertwined so learning makes sense and is made applicable to life, whether immediate or not. Cottle's work is useful in secondary education because he stresses the exploration and improvement of self in a school system that provides skills and knowledge for sustenance in society. The two emphases provide a holistic education for secondary students and teachers. The larger point is that we cannot ignore the individual student in the collective sociopolitical, historical, cultural, and economic aspects of schooling and learning.

Adolescence is almost a mythical space where stories and theories are constructed about the ages from thirteen to nineteen, although for some adolescence begins as early as age ten. There is significant documentation of physical, emotional, psychological, cognitive, and social changes that affect the adolescent. How or when the changes occur or the consequences of these changes are more inconclusive. There may be patterns that adolescents similarly experience, but I want to caution any secondary educator to always challenge what is read by one's experience with adolescents. Some are not in great psychic turmoil or suffering from raging hormones. The growth process can be as collective as it is individual. It's crucial for educators, principals, parents, and the community at large to know well the literature on child psychology and human development and to allow for their students, sons, daughters, and young members of society to share with them their experiences. Most important, we need to validate students' perspectives on their learning and lives as they are challenged to take an active part and exercise their responsibilities.

PURPOSES OF SCHOOLING

Last but not least is the need to discuss the general purposes of schooling in the United States since the inception of its institutionalization. The larger purpose of schooling in the "new land" and throughout our history has been to assimilate and acculturate immigrants into a unified culture that was distinctly American. There was a concerted effort to standardize education, even though resources were unequal. As waves of immigrants settled in the United States, so did the myriad of customs, cultures, religions, and languages. Initially there was a strong effort to convert people to Christianity, and then other religions and beliefs entered the landscape. The important thing to understand is that the existence of plurality was never intended to displace the Eurocentric perspective. This is evident later in history when other languages are dropped from the curriculum and English is made central, often at the expense of native languages. The process of assimilation oftentimes put tremendous faith in the educational system as the possible solution for society's ills. This sometimes blind faith is very much alive today. The point is that no educational system on its own will resolve anything, but the people willing to understand its history and potentials have the greater advantage in being able to truly suit the needs of students, schools, communities, and the nation.

Broudy, Smith, and Burnett (1964, 3) state, "In an older conception, education was regarded as a process whereby the individual became a 'true person' whose innate capacities for a life of virtue, justice, and wisdom were expressed and refined. . . . Salvation, too, was seen as contingent upon schooling." The process of schooling has always been seen and used as a mechanism for socialization and discipline. The intent is to use a social institution to shape the future generations, unify the population, and prepare for national needs. The total thirteen years or so spent in school not including trade school, college, or institute are a major force in a young person's life. Some may perceive secondary education as a crucial element in the future of youth; as young people grow and develop through school and other agencies (including family and peers) they formulate visions and possibilities for their future. More important, their academic and social experiences can solidify an adolescent's self-worth and self-efficacy. It seems that schooling in general is an important venue for human growth and development, given the different agendas in school formation; it is unfortunate that groups of students and individual students' potential are compromised for these agendas.

School as a designated means to culturally reproduce the capitalist economic system (Apple 1990) can also reproduce distinctive insights conducive to more human interaction, as well as empowering experiences. Schools may not only reproduce but also produce new hybrid ideas and possibilities. I give great credence and hope to actual experience in the classroom and the relationship developed with teachers and subject matter that could truly transform a student's life as well as a teacher's. Particularly in secondary education—where the propensity for dropping out may be high or the apathy already solidified from elementary school—junior highs, middle schools, and high schools have the opportunity to be the point of pivot toward a greater sense of meaning and direction for one's life.

In the next chapter, we will look at the policies, acts, reports, and legislation that have shaped secondary education and the lives of those involved with the schools.

REFERENCES

Anderson, Vernon E., and William T. Gruhn. 1962. *Principles and Practices of Secondary Education.* New York: Ronald Press Company.

Angus, David L., and Jeffrey E. Mirel. 1999. *The Failed Promise of the American High School, 1890–1995.* New York: Teachers College Press.

Apple, Michael. 1990. *Ideology and Curriculum.* New York: Routledge.

"Archiving Early America." http://earlyamerica.com. Accessed January 2003.

The Association for the Study of Classical African Civilizations. "Atlanta Declaration." www.ascac.org/papers/whyourownschools.html. Accessed January 2003.

Beane, James. 1998. *Curriculum Integration: Designing the Core of Democratic Education.* New York: Teachers College Press.

Broudy, Harry S., B. Othanel Smith, and Joe R. Burnett. 1964. *Democracy and Excellence in American Secondary Education: A Study in Curriculum Theory.* Chicago: Rand McNally.

Cobb, Amanda J. 2000. *Listening to Our Grandmother's Stories: The Bloomfield Academy for Chickasaw Females, 1852–1949.* Lincoln: University of Nebraska Press.

Cottle, Thomas. 2001. *Mind Fields: Adolescent Consciousness in a Culture of Distraction.* New York: Peter Lang Publishing.

Douglass, Harl R. 1964. *Secondary Education in the United States.* New York: Ronald Press Company.

French, William M. 1967. *American Secondary Education.* New York: Odyssey Press.

Henretta, James. "Richard Allen and African-American Identity: A Black Ex-Slave in Early America's White Society Preserves His Cultural Identity by Creating Separate Institutions." http://earlyamerica.com. Accessed January 2003.

Kliebard, Herbert M. 1999. *Schooled to Work: Vocationalism and the American Curriculum, 1876–1946.* New York: Teachers College Press.

Koos, Leonard V. 1927. *The American Secondary School.* Boston: Ginn.

Lesko, Nancy. 2001. *Act Your Age! A Cultural Construction of Adolescence.* New York: Routledge/Falmer.

Maffly-Kipp, Laurie F. 2001. "An Introduction to the Church in the Southern Black Community." University of North Carolina at Chapel Hill. http://docsouth.unc.edu/church/introduction.html. Accessed January 2003.

Messick, Rosemary G., and Karen E. Reynolds. 1992. *Middle Level Curriculum in Action.* New York: Longman Publishers.

Nasaw, David. 1979. *Schooled to Order: A Social History of Public Schooling in the United States.* New York: Oxford University Press.

Rousmaniere, Katie. "School Segregation in Oxford, Ohio: The Perry Gibson Case of 1887." Department of Educational Leadership, Miami University, Ohio (January). www.units.muohio.edu/eduleadership/FACULTY/KATE/Oxford/deseg.html. Accessed January 2003.

Vygotsky, Les V. 1997. *Educational Psychology.* New York: CRC Press.

Whispers of Angels. "A Story of the Underground Railroad." www.whispersofangels.com. Accessed January 2003.

Zeitz, Joshua. 2003. "Rosenwald's Gift." *American Legacy: The Magazine of African American History and Culture* 9, no. 1: 23–29.

Chapter Two

Chapter Two

● Chronology

LATE 1630s AND 1640s

Shortly after the first documented legislation for secondary education dictating compulsory education is passed (and the Boston Latin Grammar School opens its door in 1635), Harvard College is established in 1636. The rules and course of study of Harvard College are important to discuss briefly since they will heavily influence what happens in secondary schools (particularly grammar schools and academies). Some of the settlers are educated in Cambridge and Oxford and want a similar structure and curriculum for Harvard (Willis et al. 1994). The main purpose of the original curriculum is theological, consistent with the Act of 1647. Some of the curriculum includes the humanities and the sciences, and the methods of instruction are mainly lecture, recitation, and debate. Learning is of great concern for the settlers in both image and as security for the future. Rigor and discipline are considered two means in which to achieve productive learning.

The colonial legislature creates a mandate to establish public Latin schools. This law, Old Deluder Satan Act of 1647, is meant to protect men from Satan by instituting places, schools, and curriculum where young men and boys can read scripture. Through this form of learning students can be, in essence, more intelligent and moral, better equipped to ward off temptation. This law orders that every town with fifty or more households create a school and appoint a schoolmaster. In these schools students are to learn how to read and write. Tuition is paid by parents, masters, or the entire town. In the case that the town has one hundred households or more, they are instructed to establish a grammar school to prepare students for university. If towns neglect to do this, they incur a fine (French 1967; Koos 1927; Anderson and Gruhn 1962).

Despite the fines for not complying, many towns do not endorse or enforce the law. There are towns, even in Massachusetts, by the early 1700s that do not have secondary grammar schools. An important distinction is that elementary schools are to teach children to read scriptures, fulfilling the need for religious values, and the secondary schools are to prepare them for college, so students can fulfill secular functions demanded by society. There may have been many other reasons (as there are today) for not privileging the knowledge students learn in school over what they learn in real life through experience and work. Both elementary and secondary schools are tuition based; many parents cannot afford tuition or do not think to spend money on education when there are more pressing issues and needs in the household. It is unclear exactly how many schools are available for girls or for children who are poor, Native American, black, or Latino (primarily the indigenous, Mexican, and Indian peoples settled in the West, which used to be Mexico).

LATE 1740s

In 1740 the Moravian School is founded for girls and by 1785 it is opened to non-Moravians. The late 1700s and early 1800s mark the popularity and establishment of private schools for white girls and young women, usually called female academies or seminaries.

Benjamin Franklin founds the first academy in 1751, called the Public Academy, in the city of Philadelphia. The importance of his proposal, *Proposals Relating to the Education of Youth in Pennsylvania, 1749,* is both his critique of the grammar schools and the presentation of a different vision for education and society. This academy is designed specifically for American youth and offers a three-part curriculum: Latin, English, and mathematics. The emphasis shifts to practical education, which foreshadows the split between vocational and academic education. The curriculum provides studies in things ranging from penmanship to classical literature, with more inclusion of English authors and works and less Greek or Latin (but these are still part of the curriculum). The academy in its structure and proposal offers a different vision of education where potentially more of the population could benefit, especially those who desire vocational preparation (and are not college- or ministry-bound). The larger issue though is an economic one. The academies are largely private, with tuition requirements and a board of trustees. Documentation exists of provisions being made for students who could not afford tuition, but it is not clear how pervasive this practice was.

The proposal as a document and plan broadens what is considered a respectable education and what is worthy of study. In its popularity it widens access for both boys and girls to get a more comprehensive education. There is a particular concern for youth, their development, and engagement in learning (Anderson and Gruhn 1962). Not all academies take on the exact mission; they vary greatly in curriculum and population. Even though the academies take on different forms from what Franklin proposes, his vision and contribution are crucial to what we define as secondary education today.

1779

Georgetown, Washington, D.C., establishes its own private schools and George Town College opens its doors in 1791.

1785

Boston and Rhode Island open their first private female academies by Susanna Rowson and Mary Balch respectively.

LATE 1780s

During 1785 and 1787, federal ordinances are established to provide public land for common schools. These ordinances also dictate that the lands be free of slavery or involuntary servitude, as well as maintain good relationships with Native Americans and provide religious freedom for common schools (Deboer, Kaulfers, and Metcalf 1966). These ordinances reinforce schooling as a public responsibility.

1799

A girls' school in Georgetown, Washington, D.C., is incorporated and renamed the Academy of the Visitation in 1828 by Congress. The Billings School around this time period enrolls both white and black students. It is forced to close and reopen as a black-only school.

EARLY 1800s

Charity schools are founded by financial elites in order to rehabilitate or remove unruly, poor children from their parents. The Irish are considered to be the most problematic group at this time (Nasaw 1979).

Military and naval academies are established, which are significant in their influence of secondary schools.

EARLY 1810s

The Lancaster School Society of Georgetown founds a school supported by the Corporation of Georgetown. This school offers free education to both boys and girls, including African Americans. This is the starting point of public education for girls and African Americans in the District of Columbia. As time goes on, both girls and African Americans are able to get a better and better education.

1814

Emma Willard opens the Middlebury Female Seminary in response to the local college's refusal to admit women. Brimming with confidence over the success of her seminary, the graduates, and her own teaching techniques, Willard moves to Troy, New York, and opens the Troy Female Seminary in hopes of attracting public funding opportunities.

1818

Lancaster comes to the United States to start a model school for poor white boys. It is considered too expensive to also educate girls since at this time girls and boys need to be in different and separate buildings (Nasaw 1979).

Sunday schools become more popular. These schools are not necessarily always religious, but their main objective is to assimilate every student into the Protestant ethics and civil society. By 1830 these schools receive public funds in the Northeast.

1819

The Indian Civilization Fund Act legislates Protestant missionaries to establish Native American schools in order to offer religious education and other academic subjects. This solidifies the formal relationship between the United States government and the intent to "civilize" others in the nation. Being civilized usually requires a conversion to Christianity.

1822

Brooklyn Collegiate Institute for Young Ladies is built in Brooklyn, New York. Its comprehensive curriculum consists of six years of Latin, grammar, arithmetic, poetry, music, geography, mythology, theology, history, philosophy, female biography, composition, economics, and a variety of foreign languages (these courses vary throughout the years). This is considered a very fashionable boarding institute.

1823

Miss Lydia English's Female Seminary, a school for upper-class girls, and the Mount Zion Episcopal Church Academy, an all-black school, are founded.

1824

Catherine Beecher opens a private school for girls in Hartford, Connecticut, known as the Hartford Female Seminary, which teaches the higher branches of learning. She, her father, and her sister organize the Western Female Institute in Cincinnati, which prospers until 1837, and later organizes the Ladies Society for Promoting Education in the West. She is also involved in the founding of women's colleges at Burlington, Iowa; Quincy, Illinois; and Milwaukee, Wisconsin.

LATE 1820s

The Massachusetts Law of 1827 is the first to mandate high school throughout the state. This law dictates that every city, town, or district with five hundred or more families must provide a schoolmaster (competent and with good morals) to instruct in elementary subjects and a curriculum similar to the one found in the academies (history of the United States, bookkeeping, geometry, surveying, rhetoric, Latin, Greek, logic, and so on) (Koos 1927). This law, in effect, takes the Act of 1647 to the next level in requiring a state system of secondary education. The mandated high school opens up possibilities for the tax support of education.

AFTER 1830

A new genre of child-guidance books is published to remedy the effects of urbanization and family disintegration. Obedience and respect for authority are emphasized. These books charge the mother with the sole responsibility for the child's future (Nasaw 1979).

1833

Oberlin College is the first to enroll women. Many young women and pioneer wives open private female schools in their homes for extra income. Some of these schools accept a small number of male students.

EARLY 1850s

The 1850s see an increase of private female academies all over the nation. In 1852 the Bloomfield Academy is founded by the Chickasaw Nation with the aid of missionaries. This is a federally run boarding school in Pennsylvania. (It is renamed the Carter Seminary in 1932.) This institution marks an uncommon occurrence of Native Americans exercising great control over the school and the education of their children.

The Union Free School Act of 1853 is passed in New York to establish academic departments within the schools under the state's supervision. In New York specifically the state always had a strong involvement in the education of its youth. With the involvement of the state the schools are forced to be free and public, and are supported by taxes from the public and state. This law also allows for the creation of boards of education elected by legal voters (French 1967).

LATE 1850s

The Reverend E. C. Chirouse opens a school in 1857 for Native American boys and girls. At this and similar missionary-run schools, traditional religious and cultural practices are strongly discouraged and instruction in the Christian doctrines takes place utilizing pictures, statues, hymns, prayers, and storytelling

(Marr). Missions receive federal funds during this time and the Tulalip Mission School is said to be the first contract Native American school. This contract provides federal funds for structural maintenance and the church provides school supplies, clothing, housing, and medical care. By 1905 a larger school is opened as a result of the Point Elliot Treaty with Native Americans. The acquisition of lands for development is not always achieved through equitable practices.

1862

The first Morrill Act authorizes public land grants to the states for the establishment and maintenance of agricultural and mechanical colleges. The second Morrill Act is issued in 1890, extending monies for instruction in these colleges.

LATE 1860s

The Department of Education for the United States is established in 1867. (In 1980, under Public Law 96-88, it becomes a cabinet-level department.) This office solidifies the federal government's involvement in education.

1868

The Taunton Commission issues a report in 1868 revealing what parents want from secondary education.

1869

The University of Michigan in 1869 undertakes a program (the Michigan Plan) of admissions based on observations and evaluations of educators in secondary education (Kliebard 1999). This is a way to prepare future applicants to the university.

1872

In 1872 the Kalamazoo case is put before the Supreme Court and the decision is in favor of the Michigan voters. This case establishes the right of Michigan's citizens to create a free high school with taxes levied from property and to elect a superintendent. (The right to secondary education per se is not mentioned in the constitution, but it does provide for common schools and a university.) This case is not alone; similar cases are tried with similar outcomes throughout the states. The importance is the right of people to create school districts and pursue established institutions of secondary education with public funds. At this point common schools include both elementary and secondary schools.

LATE 1870s

During this period vocational ideas begin to take hold on the educational landscape of the United States. In 1877 Runkle's Report of Mechanic Arts to the Massachusetts Board of Education is presented. This is the first report presented to a board of education seeking approval to incorporate mechanical arts education in public high schools. Great care is taken to present the need for manual training not only for the sake of society, but to show the value of taking pride in good work. As vocational education becomes more popular, national organizations use federal legislation such as the Morrill Act of 1862 and the Hatch Act of 1887 to lobby for federal resources. The Davis Bill includes provisions for agricultural education, and the Paige Bill supports industrial education and home economics.

1879

Women are first admitted to Columbia College in New York.

Captain Richard Pratt opens the Carlisle Indian Industrial School in Pennsylvania. As at the Hampton Institute in Virginia, students are sent to Carlisle to learn trades that would afford them integration into white society. Often this education is counterproductive given the prejudice and discrimination students experience. Schools like Carlisle also separate students from their families and culture, usually marginalizing them from the reservations. (Pratt was an advocate of using education to assimilate "others" into white society. He required students to wear uniforms, have short hair, and take new names; students were not allowed to speak their native language.)

1892

The National Educational Association appoints the Committee of Ten, and Charles W. Elliot, president of Harvard University, accepts the chairmanship. The Committee of Ten Report evaluates the whole field of secondary education and recommends further action for the academies and public high schools. There are ten men appointed to this committee from different colleges, universities, and schools. The committee asks approximately two hundred schools to share detailed information on their curriculum; only forty respond by the time they meet. They evaluate what subjects are taught, where, and for how long. Their intent is to create a document that standardizes the secondary curriculum in order to ensure quality and equal preparation across the nation. After deciding on a core of subjects they select a nine-person committee for each subject (a total of sixty-nine people are present at the meetings) and supply them with the exact questions to structure the pedagogical suggestions and evaluations of the subject and students. The questions ask for the subcommittee to decide when the particular subject should be introduced, for how many hours a week, for how many years, how the subject might be portioned, how the subject should fare in college admissions, whether it should be taught the same for college- and noncollege-bound students, what methodology and evaluation would best suit the subject matter, and so on. An interesting outcome is that all involved in these deliberations agree the curriculum should be taught the same regardless of the student's future career plans (college or not). Compiling information and suggestions from all the subcommittees, they outline a course of study for the twelve years any student is supposed to be in school. From that they more carefully design the high school curriculum.

This high school curriculum consists of four years, each year progressively more complicated. The first year consists of Latin; English (literature and composition); German or French; algebra; history of Italy, France, and Spain; and applied geography (each taught for a minimum of four periods a week). In the second year, if French is not studied in the first year it is to be taught, geometry, botany or zoology, and English history are added. During the third year, rhetoric, physics, U.S. history, astronomy, and meteorology are added. During the fourth year, grammar, trigonometry, higher algebra, chemistry, civil government, geology or physiography, anatomy, physiology, and hygiene are added. During the second and third year, students have an option of taking bookkeeping and commercial arithmetic instead of algebra. The report does allow individual schools to offer more or slightly less than what is suggested, as well as to evaluate what strengths and weaknesses students possess when they start secondary education in order to best suit their population. In short the report presents a set of criteria, standards, or guidelines for quality secondary education.

The implications of this report also affect the education and preparation of teachers, as they would need to meet the ability to teach this curriculum. By default this report influences the curriculum of teacher preparation in universities and colleges. Important to note is the omission of the arts and physical education (as well as other foundation courses) from the four-year curriculum. The committee's intent, as stated in the report, is to leave these courses to the discretion of local authorities on how to implement them. Nobody on the committee or subcommittees is a representative of these courses or disciplines. One can conclude that the arts and physical education held only a peripheral position in the development of youth in the United States in the latter part of the nineteenth century. The report makes other suggestions regarding smaller class sizes or the availability of teacher's assistants, as well as Saturday morning science laboratories. The Committee of Ten wishes to create collaborations between colleges and universities with secondary schools in order to continue the improvement of secondary education and potential admissions into higher education for students who desire that track. James H. Baker, president of the National Council of Education, attaches a letter to the report with some critiques to the language used and omissions of subject matter that help develop the relationship between objective and subjective knowledge with the ability to discern between the two. His letter sheds light on the complex nature and importance of developing curriculum. Regardless of what the committee states, the curriculum devised is largely dependent on what would be necessary for college admission.

1895

By 1895 more universities (the University of Illinois and the University of Wisconsin) adopt the program to prepare future applicants to the university by evaluating secondary education. This approach creates the North Central Association, the body who accredits secondary schools that meet the standards.

1896

The Supreme Court decision *Plessy v. Ferguson* sets the standards for "separate but equal" educational facilities for different races. But for decades the overwhelming majority of African American citizens are reduced to second-class citizenship under the "Jim Crow" segregation system. Schools are separate, yet never equal. There is great disparity between schools in structural conditions and schooling supplies.

LATE 1890s

Missionary schools are common on Native American reservations. Religiously oriented schools are designed to "reform" Native Americans with a particular focus on elevating moral character and instilling Christian values.

EARLY 1900s

Schools for Hispanics operate in Texas and around the nation where the population garners it.

1904

Stanley Hall writes *Adolescence*, an influential work in the child-study movement stressing empirical psychological studies on what marks youth development. His work strongly affects conceptions of masculinity and the secondary education of both boys and girls.

Mary McLeod Bethune founds the Daytona Normal and Industrial Institute for Girls, at Daytona Beach, Florida. The institute merges with Cookman Institute for men, located in Jacksonville, in 1923 to form Bethune-Cookman College. She is president of the college until 1942, by which time the school has grown from its original five members to over 1,000. In 1935 she founds the National Council of Negro Women. She also advises President Franklin D. Roosevelt on minority affairs. She is the vice president of the NAACP and heads the McLeod Bethune Division of Negro Affairs of the National Youth Administration (Schugurensky).

Also in 1904 Margaret Haley, a school teacher from Chicago, presents a paper at the National Educators Association (NEA) convention in St. Louis on "Why Teachers Should Organize." Haley discusses democracy, equity, citizenship, and the importance of teachers' autonomy and professionalism (and the deskilling of teachers). She criticizes state subsidies to corporations, budget cuts to education, the routinization of teaching and learning, the corruption of the press, the deterioration of teachers' salaries, the subservience of elected politicians to lobbies, and the push toward commercialism in public schools. She advocates progressive education, a more fair distribution of wealth, and a strong unionism encompassing white-collar and blue-collar workers. The teachers whom Haley attempts to organize are primarily young females who are usually forced to resign after marriage. She seriously questions the lack of professional treatment these young teachers receive and salaries that are lower than their male counterparts'. Within their classrooms, they often have the task of educating more than sixty students with little support (Schugurensky). This highlights the conditions teachers deal with early in the twentieth century.

1905

Hazings as initiation practices are first documented in 1905 within high schools for both sororities and fraternities. They continue at the high school level until 2002.

In 1905 W.E.B. Du Bois and twenty-seven other men create the Niagara Movement, an organization of black intellectuals calling for full political, civil, and social rights for black Americans (in the manifesto only men are mentioned as receiving these liberties). This organization sets out to oppose Booker T. Washington's *Atlanta Compromise* of 1895. After the race riot of 1908 in Springfield, Illinois, white liberals join with the Niagara Movement.

1909

In 1909 the Committee of Forty is initiated to address the atrocities that are occurring against African American men and women. This committee includes both female and male notable figures of the times, including Ida Wells-Barnett. This committee and the Niagara Movement start the National Association for the Advancement of Colored People (NAACP), a national civil rights organization.

In 1909 Ella Flagg Young is the first woman superintendent of a major school district, Chicago, Illinois. She is a high school math-ematics teacher prior to becoming a principal of the largest school in the city and then superintendent. (When she was fifty-five years old she pursued a doctoral degree under John Dewey.)

1910s

Early in the 1900s several attempts and initiatives reorganize the high school, paving the way for the junior high school and the extended secondary school. This discussion and reorganization continues until the present day.

The Emma Willard School, built between 1910 and 1927, is recog-nized as the country's first secondary school for females. This is another representation of Willard's commitment to the education of females.

In 1912 Franklin Bobbitt takes Gary, Indiana, schools as his model of social efficiency. The schools mirror the operation of a factory as he adapts the work of Frederick Taylor to education. The impact of Bobbitt's work for secondary education is exten-sive and still in effect today.

The Committee on Economy of Time in Education is appointed by the National Education Association in 1905 and a report is pro-duced in 1913. This report suggests that secondary education be reduced to two years. During this time social efficiency is at its high point, so economizing on time and resources is a prime con-cern and desire. Essentially, the report states, efficiency is achieved by improving teaching methods, eliminating nonessentials, and organizing curriculum to fit human development (Willis et al. 1994). The report stresses common knowledge defined as "habits, skills, ideals, ideas, information, and prejudice" (136). The ques-tion looms of how common was "common," yet the intent is to fit into the existing social structure as opposed to questioning, chal-lenging, or transforming it. At the heart of the social efficiency movement in education is scientific methodology used to both evaluate and produce curriculum.

The Committee of Nine on the Articulation of High School and College is established at this time as well. The task of this com-mittee is to report and define a well-organized high school with three years of two major subjects and two years of one minor subject. Some of the subjects necessary in this type of high school are English, foreign language, mathematics, social science, natural science, and some electives. The organization and chosen subject matter are always in preparation for college. There is no significant change from the Committee of Ten's report.

Throughout this time vocational education continues to develop and grow.

The Smith-Hughes Act is first introduced in 1914, then reintroduced in 1915, and passes in 1917. The United States is just entering World War I and the need for industrial productivity and training is very high. This act promotes vocational education over other educational initiatives of the time. It secures matching federal funds for vocational, agriculture, trade, industrial education, and home economics (Kliebard 1999). This act also specifies guidelines for the acquisition of funds through the establishment of a vocational board to develop plans detailing financial management. As a result of the act, home economics enrollments soar, but so do racial, ethnic, and class differences (Kliebard 1999). Other acts in the late 1920s and 1930s follow this one, securing federal funds for vocational education.

1918

The Vocational Rehabilitation Act of 1918 provides grants for veterans from World War I to reintegrate into society through vocational training. In 1920 the Smith-Bankhead Act provides grants to states for these vocational rehabilitation programs. Given the popularity of vocational education and the assumed benefits, there is strong federal support for this type of education.

Bobbitt writes *The Curriculum;* this book sets the stage and defines social efficiency as a theory of curriculum for secondary education.

The Seven Cardinal Principles of 1918 is another report commissioned by the National Education Association. Although the report of the Committee of Ten promotes a subject-centered approach to secondary education, the Cardinal Principles emphasize a student-centered approach. This report discusses "the reorganization of secondary education; the goals of education in a democracy; the role of the secondary school in achieving these objectives; the interrelation of the various objectives of secondary education; education as a process of growth; the need for explicit, immediate values as contrasted with deferred values in secondary education; articulation of the elementary, secondary, and higher branches; the need for dividing the six years of secondary education into junior and senior sections; the need for relating the curriculum to the expressed objectives of education; the specializing and unifying functions of secondary education; advocacy of secondary education for all youth; and the need for a comprehensive high school with different curricula to meet the individual needs of a heterogeneous school population" (French 1967). This is deemed the declaration of independence for secondary education.

The report acknowledges the changing needs of schools, society, and students. The NEA committee sees this as natural in the development of a democratic society. The report also suggests that like any institution secondary education is resistant to change, so modifications are slow. Human development is discussed as a lifelong process; consequently the report sees the need to better articulate and organize the relationship between elementary school and high school. The report points out the desire to educate the individual and further the quality of relationship with the self, his or her work, and society. Therefore the recommended seven principal objectives for secondary education are health, command of the fundamental processes, worthy home membership, vocation, citizenship, worthy use of leisure, and ethical character (French 1967). This report undoubtedly influences how we perceive and what we expect of secondary education and education as a whole. The shift to a more student-centered perspective infuses a sense of humanity and respect for minors that was not common before.

1920s

The Federal Indian policy changes its philosophy from the automatic removal of children from their families, forced enrollment in boarding schools, and indoctrination into the mainstream to a curricular reform that includes different Native American cultures in the areas of study. But change is slow and the objective to assimilate and reform remains.

1922–1923

Edward L. Thorndike administers intelligence tests to over 8,000 high school students to determine which courses are more conducive to increasing mental ability and intelligence.

1923–1924

George S. Counts conducts a study of high school curriculum and the differentiation that exists at the time. He reports eighteen different courses in California and fifteen in Massachusetts (Kliebard 1995).

1929

The George-Reed Act of 1929 raises federal funds for vocational education.

EARLY 1930s AND 1940s

The Progressive Education Association (Commission) initiates an eight-year study in 1933 to determine what subjects are essential to success in college. Results from the study support high schools in taking greater liberties with curriculum since both groups studied (the traditional and experimental curriculum) had equal success in college. The results indicate there are no inherent values in certain subjects that make them essential for college (Douglass 1964). Yet the high school curriculum is geared for college admissions regardless of what would be appropriate for the adolescent population. This is problematic and therefore the commission states two purposes: "1) to establish a relationship between school and college that would permit and encourage reconstruction in the secondary school; 2) to find, through exploration and experimentation, how the high school in the United States can serve youth more effectively" (quoted in Willis et al. 1994).

Standardization and accreditation become important at this time. The Cooperative Study of Secondary School Standards involves the major accrediting associations who work on developing new standards for accreditation of secondary schools. The standards developed intend to liberalize secondary education through democratic and qualitative practices. An evaluation of what high school students are studying, what educational tracks they are in, and how many students are enrolled is conducted. A resolution is proposed in 1945 to attend to the 60 percent of students who do not receive adequate life adjustment education, which advocates life skills (Douglass 1964).

In 1933 H. H. Ryan, principal of Wisconsin High School on the campus of the University of Wisconsin, initiates a special experimental curriculum for a segment of the high school. He argues for the curriculum to reflect more directly vital social functions (Kliebard 1995). This is one effort among many in the 1930s to produce a hybrid curriculum that would more accurately prepare youth for living. Schools across the states experiment with curriculum integration, accelerated programs, block scheduling, life issues, and joint planning between teachers and students.

From 1934 to 1956 the League of United Latin American Citizens works diligently to improve educational conditions for thousands of Mexican American youth in the Southwest.

The George-Deen Act of 1936 extends federal funds for commercial studies in secondary schools.

1938

The Essentialist Committee for the Advancement of American Education presents its beliefs through two books, Boyd H. Bode's *Progressive Education at the Crossroads* and John Dewey's *Experience and Education*.

1940

A special committee on secondary school curriculum prepares *What High Schools Ought to Teach* for the American Youth Commission. This report traces the growth of education in the United States, as well as the subjects taught. Different types of secondary education are also highlighted.

1942

In 1942 the GED test is designed (revised again in 1978, 1988, and

2002). The test is originally used for military personnel, but as it gains popularity the test is made available to civilians. In 2003 it is used by hundreds of thousands of people across the United States and Canada. The different versions of the test reflect changes in secondary education and society. Like other standardized tests the use of critical thinking, knowledge application, and technology are among the newest revisions. The GED test in general marks an important departure from a traditional structure of schooling and advancement.

1949

In 1949 Ralph Tyler conceptualizes the *Basic Principles of Curriculum and Instruction*, otherwise known as the Tyler rationale. This rationale, which originated in a course syllabus, outlines the structure of a curriculum and stresses objectives, procedures, sequence, and evaluation. This is quickly adopted and used as the guidelines for a teacher's lesson plan. This curricular structure strongly affects secondary education, particularly how learning is organized and offered to adolescents.

1950s

This decade sets important precedents for education, its quality, and inclusivity. In 1954 *Brown v. Board of Education* revokes the "separate but equal" doctrine and desegregates public schools. The consequences and effects of this decision are still debated today. Another issue is neighborhood zoning, which dictates who goes to what school and specifies different property taxes. This influences the quality of education and resources available for a school or schools in the area.

Starting in 1957, students can take college credit in high school through advanced placement offerings. This allows students to accumulate college credit while still in high school. Advanced placement courses require an examination at the end of the course and a score of 3 or above to get college credit. This continues the emphasis of a college education. High schools extend college credit to their students in order to compete and "prepare" adolescents for the college environment.

After World War II the nation has a preoccupation with global competition and defending the nation. An education act in the late 1950s provides funds and resources for schools and individuals to improve on the study of science, mathematics, foreign languages, and technology. The concern is for the maintenance of and preparation for the national defense of the United States. The act addresses the lack of opportunities for those who want to study these subjects and cannot afford training. The act stresses the need to equalize access to these disciplines. By 1964 reading, geography, history, and English are added to the list of disciplines. Loans are made available for nonprofit institutions and for graduate studies. Many individuals become teachers with this support.

The National Defense Education Act of 1958 (Public Law 85-864) provides assistance to state and local school systems for strengthening instruction in designated subjects. It also provides improvement of state statistical services; guidance, counseling, and testing services; and training institutes. Another interesting outcome of this act is the experimentation and dissemination of information on the more effective utilization of television, motion pictures, and related media for educational purposes, and vocational education for technical occupations necessary for the national defense.

The late 1950s are also important for special education. A special provision in 1959 is made for students with a variety of disabilities and for preparing teachers to meet the needs of students. Gifted education is also given attention. Media is used here as well for educational purposes and assistance of special needs children.

1960s

The Civil Rights movement influences every aspect of society. This initiates a host of programs dealing with desegregation and economic inequality. The Elementary and Secondary Act of 1965 authorizes grants for elementary and secondary school programs for children of low-income families; school library resources, textbooks, and other instructional materials for schoolchildren; supplementary educational centers and services; strengthening state education agencies; and educational research and research training. This act extends funds to elementary and private schools, even parochial ones. A number of titles delineating different provisions are housed in this act. In 1968, amendments are made to this act, modifying existing programs and providing more support for the education of students with special needs. Support is authorized for regional centers for education of handicapped children, model centers and services for deaf-blind children, and recruitment of personnel and dissemination of information on education of the handicapped. Education in rural areas, dropout prevention programs, and bilingual education also receive support and funds at this time.

In keeping with all the curricular reforms, a model secondary school for the deaf is established by Gallaudet College in 1966.

The National Advisory Council on Vocational Education is created.

In 1965, the National Advisory Council on Indian Education (NACIE) is formed. The council is established to advise the secretary of education and Congress on funding and administration of programs with respect to Native American youth or adults. A year later President Johnson appoints a Native American, Robert Lafollette Bennett, as the first commissioner of Indian affairs. Two years later the National Council on Indian Opportunity (NCIO) is established to facilitate participation in U.S. government decisionmaking concerning Native American policy.

Also in 1965 the Economic Opportunity Act is passed, affording Native Americans the opportunity to participate in, and control, their own programs. The United States provides the funds to administer programs for Native Americans. Other federal programs have significant Native American participation, including Headstart, Upward Bound, Job Corps, and Vista. The Economic Opportunity Act creates "Community Action Programs," which involve 105 Indian reservations in seventeen states by the end of the 1960s. An initiative for a new design of Native American education called the Rough Rock Demonstration School on the Navajo Reservation in Arizona is spearheaded by the Office of Economic Opportunity. Rough Rock becomes a symbol for participation and control, thereby becoming a forerunner of Native American participation in educational decisionmaking. The school is established June 27, 1966, and controlled by a five-member Navajo school board (www.k12.wa.us/indianedu/curr_self/cp.asp).

The Bilingual Act of 1968 provides federal funding to encourage local school districts to try approaches incorporating native-language instruction. Most states follow the lead of the federal government, enacting bilingual education laws of their own or at least decriminalizing the use of other languages in the classroom (www.rethinkingschools.org/Archives/12_03/langhst.htm). Funds are also provided for preservice and in-service training of teachers for these programs.

In 1969 the Kennedy Report, titled "Indian Education: A National Tragedy, A National Challenge," states, "the dominant policy of the federal government toward the American Indian has been one of coercive assimilation" and the policy "has had disastrous effects on the education of Indian children" (www.aiefprograms. org/history_facts/history.html#1776). Much awareness is developed and effort put forth to reform the dehumanizing educational initiatives of the past. A significant amount of work remains to be done in the twenty-first century.

1970s

Both elementary and secondary schools are encouraged to start and maintain environmental programs. Teacher training is also provided. Drug awareness and prevention is another educational focus for this decade, as well as developing and implementing programs to keep elementary and secondary students in school.

The Title IX Educational Amendment of 1972 states that nobody can be excluded from or subject to discrimination in education, jobs, rights, and status based on gender.

The Indian Education Act of 1972 and 1974 amendments provide Native Americans with aid to establish and conduct educational programs and services such as bilingual and bicultural enrichment programs, reading programs, guidance services, transportation, parental involvement, and teacher training.

It is mandated during this time that all handicapped children are educated in the least restrictive environment based on their specific needs, in addition to receiving all services necessary.

In 1973 *Lau v. Nichols* rules that public schools must provide a comprehensible education to students with limited English-language proficiency. This court decision initiates a national concern in educational equity for students for whom English is a second language. Policymakers respond to the special needs of this growing population. In the mid- and late 1970s, legislation is passed to force schools to provide programs for these students.

Employment training programs for youth are established in 1977 through schools as work study. A variety of possibilities exist for secondary students, yet the objective is to give students hands-on work experience while getting school credit. Career education is popular and programs are developed for both elementary and secondary schools.

In 1975 Public Law 94-142 is passed to ensure that all children with disabilities have available to them a free, appropriate public education that emphasizes special education and related services, meets their unique needs, and prepares them for employment and independent living.

1980s

Four reports are published in 1983 illustrating the state of education in the United States, yet *A Nation at Risk* gets the most notoriety. The National Commission on Excellence in Education requests papers, test scores, and discussions on student and school performance. The results do not paint a rigorous or productive picture of student achievement and teacher performance. This report generates much discussion about its dismal conclusions. As a result of this report massive movements to standardize learning and return to some basic content drastically change curriculum. Following is the report *Action for Excellence: A Comprehensive Plan to Improve Our Nation's Schools*, commissioned by the Education Commission, which discusses curricula and evaluates states' standardized scores. Two other reports, *High School: A Report on Secondary Education in America* by Ernest Boyer and *A Place Called School: Study of Secondary Education in America* by John Goodland, are field studies of fifteen to thirty-eight schools where substantial observation, interviews, and curricula are analyzed and discussed. These two reports provide different and more in-depth evaluations and syntheses of our schools during this time, yet these two reports, given their qualitative nature, are largely pushed to the periphery of the educational conversation. The country as a whole reacts to the portrait of *A Nation at Risk* perhaps too hastily without further investigating some of the conditional factors in the nation.

The 1980s are a period of conservative initiatives in education with more support for the sciences, mathematics, and reading. Vocational education also receives additional funds through the Perkins Act, yet this is not necessarily a priority. To close the decade another report of great importance is issued, *Turning Points: Preparing American Youth for the Twenty-first Century*, commissioned by the Carnegie Council on Adolescent Development. The task force authoring the report consists of seventeen distinguished members from a variety of recognized institutions. The report focuses on reorganizing and restructuring middle schools with particular attention to adolescent development and curriculum. Adolescents are discussed as "youth adrift" needing to be directed into productive lives. The vehicle for this direction for the most part is the schools. The report begins with early adolescence at ten years old and terminates middle school age at fifteen. The report in general continues to look at adolescence from a deficit model and looks to education to remedy the problems. The suggestions on curriculum and school organization are intended to provide more meaningful learning for the adolescent. Their suggestions include smaller communities of learning and curriculum focusing on health and critical thinking. The Carnegie Council also commissions another report on adolescents, *Great Transitions: Preparing Adolescents for a New Century.* This report takes further care to question conceptualizations of adolescents needing to be fixed and in turmoil by raging hormones; nonetheless there is still significant stress on health education, especially on cultivating "good, proper, and moral" behavior. Both reports stem from a positivist paradigm of human development and education. In carefully reading these reports it is important to critically question some of the assumptions, as well as recognize the contributions to secondary education.

During the 1980s home schooling becomes more popular. It has been in existence for centuries, yet it hasn't been recognized. With the advent of compulsory education, any other type of education was relegated to the margins. Significant strides were made in the 1960s and 1970s toward a more "organized" home schooling alternative, but it isn't until the 1980s that more and more families choose this type of education.

In 1988 the Augustus F. Hawkins–Robert T. Stafford Elementary and Secondary School Improvement Amendments (Public Law 100-297) reauthorizes, through 1993, major elementary and secondary education programs including Bilingual Education, Math-Science Education, Magnet Schools, Impact Aid, Native American Education, Adult Education, and other smaller education programs. Also at this time the Technology-Related Assistance for Individuals with Disabilities Act provides financial assistance to states to develop and implement statewide programs of technology-related assistance for persons of all ages with disabilities. This allows schools to further suit the needs of students with disabilities.

1990s

The Americans with Disabilities Act is amended and ensures against the discrimination of persons with disabilities. Assistive technology needs are addressed for students with disabilities, and more attention is given to agencies and programs to ensure students, parents, and schools are getting the services they need.

More emphasis is placed on the prevention of high school dropouts, as well as an improvement of basic skills programs. *Goals 2000* is developed during the 1990s, an attempt to nationalize curriculum and educational goals with the intent to make the United States more competitive on a global scale. Science, math, and geography are heavily emphasized in the curriculum. Several panels and councils develop out of this initiative to provide states and local communities with support in aligning their standards and curricula. School-to-work initiatives are revamped and formalized so that states and local communities can provide consistent work training, work-based learning, school-based learning, as well as certificates or diplomas for specified skills. Violence prevention programs come into the schools to provide conflict resolution and peer mediation. Amendments to the Elementary and Secondary Education Act modify provisions and initiatives for Native American education in particular.

In 1990 the Native American Languages Act provides grassroots support for Native American heritage.

The discussion of vouchers really started in the 1950s, yet it isn't until the 1980s and 1990s that the concept becomes more organized and actual policies and monies are afforded for privatization of schooling. In the early 1990s, voucher programs start in the Midwest and quickly spread all over the country. Foundations generate millions of dollars for vouchers, known as national private scholarships.

In 1994 roughly ten thousand college students, high school students, and teachers protest proposed cuts to education in New York City. Many such protests are seen in other major cities faced with similar economic cuts.

In 1999 private school taxes appear at the federal level and the governor of Florida passes the first statewide school voucher program. This generates much criticism as some argue it violates the first amendment, the separation of church and state, and the commitment to public schooling accessible to all. Debates for vouchers and privatization of schooling use language to disguise intents to educate some at the expense of others.

The 1990s see charter schools move to the forefront of educational debates with the increasing concern for accountability and failing schools. Again we see the 1980s as a catalyst for alternatives, particularly charter schools. Policies (with funding) are drafted around the nation to support the development and operation of charter schools. By the end of the decade over a thousand charter schools have opened.

EARLY 2000s

The No Child Left Behind Act is President George W. Bush's main educational initiative of 2001. This reenacts the Elementary and Secondary Act of 1965 with significant amendments. I feel it is necessary to review this particular policy in great detail given the proposed impact it will have for secondary education and the learning community in general.

The No Child Left Behind Act redefines the federal role in K–12 education and purports to close the achievement gap between disadvantaged and minority students and their peers. It is based on stronger accountability, increased flexibility and local control, expanded options for parents, and teaching methods that are proven to work (www.ed.gov). The main change is the reliance on assessment at the national, state, and local levels. Particular attention is given to the assessment of mathematics and reading through standardized tests. The purpose of this new policy is stated as providing fair and accurate measurement of student achievement and reporting trends in math, reading, and other specified subjects. (Close attention should be paid to the frequent use of "fair," "valid," "reliable," and "accurate" in this policy as it pertains to evaluation.) A national assessment of reading and math in all schools, both private and public, should occur every two years in grades 4 and 8. Twelfth grade is the only grade in high school that is targeted for national evaluation in reading and math. The policy also suggests that students be tested every year and in each subject for developmental analysis until the assessment tools are proven to produce high-quality data that are valid and reliable.

It is clearly stated in the policy that data from the assessment shall not be used by the federal government to rank, compare, or otherwise evaluate individual students or teachers or provide rewards or sanctions to individual students, teachers, schools, or local agencies (www.nagb.org/about/plaw.html). In addition it states the data shall not be used to influence standards, assessments, curriculum, and instructional materials. However, in practice, the tests heavily influence what is taught and how it is taught, since the results are tied to available funds and resources for each school. Participation is said to be voluntary and only with parental consent, yet further in the act participation seems to be only voluntary in subjects other than math and reading. The standards that the tests are based on seem vague and rhetorical:

In general, such levels shall be determined by identifying the knowledge that can be measured and verified objectively using widely accepted professional assessment standards; and developing achievement levels that are consistent with relevant widely accepted professional assessment standards and based on the appropriate level of subject matter knowledge for grade levels to be assessed, or the age of students, as the case may be. (www.nagb.org/about/plaw.html, *under* participation)

The repeated use of "widely accepted professional assessment standards" leaves the origin of these standards unnamed, as well as by whom they are widely accepted. What profession? What does this have to do with cognitive academic evaluation? How are they measured and verified? What constitutes "objectively"? How is the "appropriate level of subject matter knowledge" determined? The preceding questions only point to the lack of specificity in discussing the exact criteria that students will be evaluated on. This is problematic since these assessment practices are to be exercised on a national level. Up to this point there have not been serious initiatives to nationalize the curriculum or means of evaluation. The federal government has stayed out of education since the Constitution does not authorize it to do so. *Goals 2000* attempts to initiate national priorities by putting math and science at the forefront of educational concern and endeavors, but the discussions never make it into the classrooms in any consistent or uniform manner.

Toward the end of the policy there is a "prohibition against bias," which states: "The Board shall take steps to ensure that all items selected for use in the National Assessment are free from racial, cultural, gender, or regional bias and are secular, neutral, and non-ideological" (www.nagb.org/about/plaw. html). The reader must question how and under what methodology this prohibition will take place. How will bias be assessed and evaluated? How is it possible to create standardized test items that are truly neutral when the knowledge base they are derived from may not be? It is important for the state of secondary education (and for education in general) that the public and the educational sector carefully read and question the policies, which influence learning and teaching in today's society. The quality and quantity of information students receive are crucial to their future decisionmaking. Standardizing curriculum and assessment may not bring about the results that the federal government is after because of the ways in which teachers and students must also standardize the ways they teach, learn, and study.

This law has received both support and criticism from Republicans, Democrats, and others. The major support comes as a result of its focus on accountability, teacher quality, high standards, consequences for schools that fail, improving literacy, and rewards for closing the achievement gap. These are also the source for its criticism, along with the role of the federal government and the excessive use of standardized testing. On the one hand, the public is right to demand higher-quality education, yet on the other hand, the means to this end can be highly questionable. The prevalent use of standardized tests to assess student achievement has an incredibly limiting effect on classroom instruction and learning. Teachers are pressured to teach to the test and students are pressed to learn through rote memorization and deductive reasoning. Schools use tests as measures of promotion and retention. Teachers are limited to what and how they can teach, and many (teachers, students, administrators, parents, community) are alienated from the transformative potential of schooling and education.

At this point let us turn to the educational blueprint of the act itself in order to get a better sense of its premise. According to this blueprint, the act proposes to:

→ Increase accountability for student performance: States, districts and schools that improve achievement will be rewarded. Failure will be sanctioned. Parents will know how well their child is learning, and that schools are held accountable for their effectiveness with annual state reading and math assessments in grades 3–8.
→ Focus on what works: Federal dollars will be spent on effective, research-based programs and practices. Funds will be targeted to improve schools and enhance teacher quality.
→ Reduce bureaucracy and increase flexibility: Additional flexibility will be provided to states and school districts, and flexible funding will be increased at the local level.
→ Empower parents: Parents will have more information about the quality of their child's school. Students in persistently low-performing schools will be given a choice. (www.ed.gov/offices/OESE/esea/nclb)

Each major component has several subinitiatives that specify in greater detail accountability, assessment, consequences, reading instruction, funds for technology, bonuses and rewards, school reports, school choice, research-based practice, focus on math and science, safety, and character education. Although these may seem agreeable necessities, there is an underlying behavioral structure to the reform policy. In other words there is

positive reinforcement for desired results and negative reinforcement for not achieving these. When monetary and resource
rewards are linked to test results, the potential exists for the
importance of the process to shift from increased learning to
securing funds. Another concern is research-based practices in
which teacher quality is measured strictly quantitatively and
scientifically. A lot of what teachers do in the classroom—that
which imprints their expertise and caring—may not be easily
quantifiable, nor fit into what is privileged by research stressing
decontextualized classroom instructional strategies and classroom management. In the measures to standardize teaching
excellence, individual creativity may find its way out of the
classroom.

The key to this policy's success or demise will undoubtedly
be its implementation. There has been considerable discussion
and concern with the ability to construct the assessment tools
necessary to begin the necessary testing and initiatives. Some
schools are worried that they will not meet desired results and
funds will be cut as a result. Struggling schools will continue to
struggle instead of finding a reprieve and a path to successful
reform. For some, more testing will only compound the problems
they have with current testing and student achievement.

With respect to school choice, some say competition for
public schools strengthens them; others believe this policy will
only cover limited expenses for parental choice and will create
further deficits for public schools. Title I, which provides federal
funding to states and school districts for disadvantaged students,
seems to be positioned as conditional money if and only if high-
poverty schools improve annually. Curriculum development will
narrow as schools meet the demands of the tests. One must also
question where the funds are coming from to create the assessment tools and "quality" teacher programs. Of general concern is
the apparent reversal of the federal government's role and the
rhetoric of local control and the reluctance to withdraw funds
from states and districts.

States like Vermont are discussing refusing federal education money in order to avoid the testing requirements. The discussion examines the cost of test implementation as exceeding
the amount of allotted federal money (www.rethinkingschools.
org). Organizations opposing the testing movement may find
their greatest project yet.

2002

The Bilingual Education Act of 1968 under Title VII of the Elementary and Secondary Act expires in 2002. As No Child Left Behind enters the stage, the Bilingual Act leaves, but a transformation takes place as it becomes the English Acquisition Act. Bilingual education and English acquisition may be components of each other, but for the most part the development and maintenance of native language skills are seen as unimportant. The focus is strictly on English acquisition skills, yet much research has proven (Krashen 1996) that literacy skills in a native language transfer over to English: if one is neglected, it will have a negative correlation to English acquisition. Although the end of an act and its replacement may seem like semantic wordplay to some, it has incredible significance for students in need of these services, for teachers preparing for licensure, and for school communities needing to test at certain levels.

The Supreme Court in June 2002 rules school vouchers can be used for religious schools, putting into question the separation of church and state. Yet the government contends it does not provide state sponsorship for religious schools. Miner (2002) states, "In its school voucher decision, the U.S. Supreme Court laid out a blueprint for constitutional voucher-type programs that fund religious institutions. First, the money must pass through an individual who makes a 'true private choice' to use that money at a religious institution, and second, there must be an array of religious and nonreligious choices. In the Cleveland case, the 5–4 Court majority ruled that even though more than 99 percent of Cleveland vouchers go to religious schools, parents have an array of educational options, including traditional public schools, magnet schools, and charter schools. Thus, the court reasoned, the voucher program does not favor religion. And because the vouchers go to parents, not directly to a religious school, they aren't a government endorsement of religion" (www.rethinkingschools. org/special_reports/voucher_report/Box171.shtml).

Other issues will certainly surge as the No Child Left Behind Act unfolds and vouchers, as well as charters, are forced into the spotlight as public schools are mandated to adopt various initiatives. The only option is to stay informed in order to make the best collective and individual decisions.

REFERENCES

American Indian Education Foundation. www.aiefprograms.org/history_facts/ history.html#1776. Accessed March 2003.

Anderson, Vernon E., and William T. Gruhn. 1962. *Principles and Practices of Secondary Education*. New York: Ronald Press.

Deboer, John J., Walter V. Kaulfers, and Lawrence E. Metcalf. 1966. *Secondary Education: A Textbook of Readings*. Boston: Allyn and Bacon.

Douglass, Harl R. 1964. *Secondary Education in the United States*. New York: Ronald Press.

French, William M. 1967. *American Secondary Education*. New York: Odyssey Press.

Georgetown, Washington, D.C. www.georgetowndc.com/schools.php. Accessed January 2003.

Kliebard, Herbert M. 1999. *Schooled to Work: Vocationalism and the American Curriculum, 1876–1946*. New York: Teachers College Press.

Kliebard, Herbert M. 1995. *The Struggle for the American Curriculum: 1893–1958*. 2nd ed. New York: Routledge.

Koos, Leonard V. 1927. *The American Secondary School*. Boston: Ginn.

Krashen, Stephen D. 1996. *Under Attack: The Case Against Bilingual Education*. Burlingame, CA: Language Education Associates.

Marr, Carolyn J. "Assimilation Through Education: Indian Boarding Schools in the Pacific Northwest." http://content.lib.washington.edu/aipnw/marr/page2.html. Accessed March 2003.

Miner, Barbara. 2002. "Keeping Public Schools Public: Voucher Decision Opens Pandora's Box." *Rethinking Schools* (Fall). www.rethinkingschools.org/special_reports/voucher_report/Box171.shtml.

Nasaw, David. 1979. *Schooled to Order: A Social History of Public Schooling in the United States*. New York: Oxford University Press.

National Assessment of Educational Progress. www.nagb.org/about/plaw.html. Accessed September 2002.

National Education Association. 1893. Report of the Committee of Ten.

Newman Library. http://newman.baruch.cuny.edu/digital/2001/beecher/catherine.htm. Accessed January 2003.

Office of Superintendent of Public Instruction. www.k12.wa.us/indianedu/curr_self/cp.asp. Accessed March 2003.

Rethinking Schools. www.rethinkingschools.org. Accessed August 2002.

Schugurensky, Daniel. *Selected Moments of the Twentieth Century*. Department of Adult Education, Community Development and Counseling Psychology, Ontario Institute for Studies in Education of the University of Toronto (OISE/UT).http://womenshistory.about.com/gi/dynamic/offsite.htm?

sitez=http://fcis.oise.utoronto.ca/%7Edaniel%5Fschugurensky/
assignment1/1904haley.html. Accessed April 2003.

U.S. Government. "No Child Left Behind Policy." www.ed.gov/offices/OESE/
esea/. Accessed October 2002.

Willis, George, William H. Schubert, Robert V. Bullough Jr., Craig Kridel, and John
T. Holton. 1994. *The American Curriculum: A Documentary History.*
Westport, CT: Praeger.

Chapter Three

☙ Curriculum in Secondary Schools

In the early twenty-first century, secondary school curriculum retains the spirit of the Committee of Ten report of 1893 with college preparatory requirements dominating the daily schedule of most students, but there are many derivations of this curriculum for high school and middle school. The middle school has branched out since the 1970s into a completely different structure of academic knowledge production. This chapter discusses the various structures of curriculum for the secondary school student and its content, scope, and intent. In addition this chapter introduces the reader to the various movements in curriculum, how each is defined and applied through curricular practices, the effects it has on schooling and students, and the influences on the larger society. Certain curricular movements and key theorists are mentioned to provide readers with resources and points for further study. The history of curriculum is extremely complex and rich, with much relevance to today's practices. I invite further investigation and the creation of many pedagogical possibilities.

Throughout the history of secondary education, textbooks have been integral to curriculum construction and teaching; therefore this chapter will also delineate how influential textbooks have been. The main goal of this chapter is to further investigate curriculum. The following questions will be addressed: What is curriculum? What knowledge is of most worth and to whom? What is the importance of curriculum? As Chapter 1 explains, there was significant debate and deliberation over what students should learn in an organized institution strictly dedicated to preparing youth for work, sustenance, and contribution to society. High schools are supposed to be comprehensive institutions offering a variety of coursework and preparation. Curriculum is not as neutral as suspected and it can have great influence on a student's abilities and enjoyment for learning in and out of school.

TEXTBOOKS

Ever since the commencement of schooling in the United States, textbooks have guided curriculum, learning, and teaching practices. The textbook industry was not what it is today. It was not standardized, uniform, or abundant. In the 1820s this changed with technological advances and more economical publishing. Many critics argued against the overdependence on texts as they thought it stunted true teaching. However, books became central to teaching and learning. Reese (1995) states, "Northern educators usually regarded common reading materials as a major educational advance, if not a panacea. Textbooks presumably democratized knowledge, making specialized learning available to everyone" (104). Reese also references William T. Harris as privileging standard texts for making authoritative knowledge more accessible (104). Standard texts were exactly that: a presentation of uniform ideas about the subject matter being studied. Textbooks also provided an efficient method to promote ideological ideas, values, and practices. These textbooks and ideas began to monopolize instruction and created canons of knowledge in every discipline. The majority of the books written by male theorists (largely professors) and some practitioners dictated curriculum and instruction. Instruction was riddled with memorization, repetition, and recall. As society became divided by economic classes, different educational needs appeared primarily for more practical and useful learning. Thus began the debates over classical, scientific, social, vocational, life adjustment, child study, and other movements and reform in curriculum. Curriculum and instruction were seen as a way to train the mind and discipline the body. The sciences were thought to be helpful in mastering nature and the socially constructed environment. English was said to help students master bodies of knowledge and afford a sophisticated ability to communicate. Schooling objectives expanded in service of the state and of the prevailing moral values of the times and leaders.

CURRICULUM AND HUMANISM

Humanism during the 1800s influenced curriculum greatly as it promised to secure an appreciation of life and betterment of society through classical literature and high culture. Kliebard (1992, 3) states that humanism

has come to be associated with a set of subjects, a segment of the school curriculum, believed to have the power to stir the imagination, enhance the appreciation of beauty, and disclose motives that actuate human behavior. From its early association with the study of Latin and Greek, humanism has gradually been expanded to the study of language generally as a distinctive possession of human beings, and with the arts—music, painting, sculpture, poetry—as the highest forms of expression by which human beings convey their experience and their aspirations.

The humanistic curriculum was said to prepare the mind in order to control the environment. The mind set the individual apart from anything else; therefore it needed to be developed through rigorous academic courses of study. In addition to training the mind, the humanistic curriculum was intended to enrich and expand intellectual capacities, to allow the mind to reach new possibilities in memory, reasoning, and imagination. This curriculum intended to facilitate aesthetic expressions full of sophistication and promise. There were many interpretations of this type of curriculum and toward the end of the nineteenth century it was closely aligned with faculty psychology (a branch of psychology using drills, memorization, and repetition as educational strategies to exercise the mind as a muscle). This made a strong case for offering traditional disciplines as the subject matter for secondary education, usually with few or no electives. Many of the courses of study included Greek, Latin, classical literature, science, pure mathematics, philosophy, theology, and the arts.

As the curriculum turned to focus on the need for social control, the humanistic influence was losing ground. The academy as an elite institution would soon be transformed by popular access to education. The influences of humanism have been constantly pushed out of the curriculum and subsequently reinstated. The ongoing struggle continues today, as any type of education that cannot be standardized and tested is usually removed from the classroom. Humanism was the core of curriculum in the academies until the public high school emerged in the United States. At that same time, the population's need and desire to attend secondary schools increased immensely. The nation was growing and the need to educate immigrant youth was assessed as crucial. Basic erroneous assumptions about the ability of youth in general and of immigrants, the poor, people of color, and even those of different religious beliefs led educational leaders and reformers to implement changes in the curriculum. Many decided the intellectual trend and classical inclination of humanism were ill suited for the populace. The school needed to be the primary agent in socializing the young into society, and the curriculum was the vehicle through which to shape and construct the desired product.

CURRICULUM AND THE CHILD STUDY MOVEMENT

The essence of this curricular movement was the child, that is, the student in the school system. The major figures of this movement, William Torrey Harris, John Dewey, and Stanley Hall, had distinctly different approaches to the child study curriculum.

Harris believed the interests of the child were important, but they should not dictate the course of study or the direction of society. He understood every child had a particular inclination and he saw the purpose of education as shaping these inclinations in the search for truth, beauty, and good. His philosophy demanded literacy in order to enter the five windows—arithmetic, geography, history, grammar, and literature—which would ensure great human learning. Harris believed these windows provided the main structure of curriculum, and other subjects would make up a second tier of curricular studies.

Hall supported a scientific pedagogy where a child's natural impulses would determine what was taught. Hall strongly believed in culture-epochs, stages in the development of the human race, which would parallel the development of the child, really a combination of the educational philosophy of John Frederick Herbart (stressing the development of moral social character through the study of history and literature correlated with the evolution of the human race) and Darwinian theory. Curriculum was aligned to the particular stage of human development the children were at. Hall and his constituents saw this correlation as a perfect way to suit the needs of the student. He was an advocate for curriculum differentiation and even creating separate schools for those students with specific cognitive skills and for the sexes. He believed that girls and boys needed to be separated throughout school, as he was extremely concerned with preserving young men's masculinity. Adolescence was regarded as the pinnacle of the human race, and Hall closely scrutinized the high school curriculum to ensure a race of superior men.

Dewey questioned the exclusive use of science and its direct relationship to curriculum reform and design. "Dewey seemed to be making the case for a child as a striving, active being capable of intelligent self-direction under proper circumstances" (Kliebard 1995, 48). Dewey critiqued Hall's combination of overly scientific and mystical inclinations, and differed from Harris as well. His ideas flourished with his appointment to the University of Chicago and his development of the Laboratory School in the late 1890s. While in Chicago, Dewey worked with Ella Flagg Young and Jane Addams to further the type of education that would positively affect individuals from all socioeconomic and ethnic backgrounds.

Dewey organized the curriculum of the Laboratory School in three sections: manual training, history and literature, and science. The inclusion of manual training for Dewey was essential as a way to provide concrete experiences for the theoretical lessons students were learning. For example Dewey saw carpentry or cooking as means through which students could learn, use, and apply mathematical computations and environmental understandings of the ingredients and materials used for these types of work. His attempt at curriculum integration meshed life and curriculum in order for students to maximize their learning experiences in the school. Dewey saw the possibilities of learning mathematics, chemistry, physics, and geography through the practical exposure of different occupations. One of Dewey's major concerns was to find curricular ways in which the child was engaged in his or her learning and not separated from it. Ultimately Dewey believed the curriculum is the conduit for socializing individuals into the existing culture and society. Reading, writing, and arithmetic, the cornerstones of any type of education, were not taught as separate subjects, in isolation from context or assignment. Students learned how to read, write, and do math through actual assignments and tasks in the integrated curriculum. Dewey believed this would lead to true mastery of these skills.

The School and Society (Dewey 1901) further describes the curriculum theory Dewey tried to exemplify in the Lab School. Contrary to popular understanding of Dewey's work, his intent was neither to focus simply on hands-on approaches nor to allow the child to do as he or she pleased. His version of the child study movement integrated application of knowledge and study of knowledge in curricular units of instruction that would further an individual's understanding of self and society. When he left the University of Chicago in the early part of the twentieth century the Lab School curriculum was modified continuously and many of Dewey's ideas were left behind. He became a professor of philosophy at Columbia University in New York and did not continue any attempts to bring his curriculum theory to life as he had done in Chicago. His influence on education and philosophy is still discussed in schools and by teachers around the country, yet its effects on practice are not as evident.

SOCIAL EFFICIENCY AND THE CURRICULUM

Social efficiency is perhaps the most influential of curricular movements and certainly the most lasting throughout different time periods. The social efficiency movement focused on exact scientific measurement of educational outcomes and control of the social order. The school was seen as an agent of social control and as a means of producing workers for society. The school was also utilized as a site to ensure obedience to society's laws. Educators were incredibly influenced by Frederick W. Taylor, the father of scientific management. One educator of particular interest to this discussion is Franklin Bobbitt, who took Taylor's ideas and practices in factories and applied them to schools, most often to high schools. Bobbitt's book, *The Curriculum* (1918), marks the beginning of the field of curriculum for some. Bobbitt saw great promise for his ideas as exemplified in Gary, Indiana, schools. Superintendent Wirt, of Gary, Indiana, schools, ordered an ongoing use of the schools throughout the day in order to maximize time, space, and resources. Wirt's focus was not curricular but structural and economic. He wanted to make schools efficient 100 percent of the time; therefore school was in session all day long and students attended in shifts. More students could be served this way and school resources would be maximized. Even though most schools would not adopt this format, the ideas of efficiency were adopted and practiced, and soon schools across the nation were managed and rearranged for maximum task performance and accountability. Bobbitt advocated for schools to become community centers providing leadership and recreation (including the arts) for the public. Bobbitt wanted to extend the use of schools to increase their efficiency and purpose. The idea of schools as community centers was sparingly discussed. Schools are usually staples in the community or neighborhood they are in; consequently using them as community centers could actually serve the community in numerous ways. Today "full service schools" offer medical, social, and physical services for students. The idea of community centers as places to develop different interests out of leisure and desire is yet to be fully enacted. Such centers were more common at the turn of the twentieth century.

Bobbitt extended task analysis and managerial control to the school curriculum. He believed students were the raw materials that would be shaped and molded to produce a finished product ready to serve or fit into particular class structures and occupations in society (Kliebard 1995). He believed students needed to be taught differently depending on who they were and what they were assumed to become. Girls and boys received different types of education. Likewise, curricular differentiations were in place for various socioeconomic classes. The use of a scientifically based curriculum appealed to many educators who were seeking some assurance in turning schools around and securing a means in which to educate the masses. There was also great concern during this time period for youth to become contributing and productive citizens. Using schools to train them for the workforce was an important promise of the social efficiency movement. There is an assumed security, consistency, and legitimacy associated with scientific measurement. It is of no surprise why this particular movement gained such support. Scientific management offered to provide effective goals, procedures, and outcomes. Taylor coined "task idea" as "the most prominent single element in modern scientific management. At least one day in advance, management must provide workmen complete instructions regarding each detail of the task to be performed the following day" (Pinar et al. 1995, 95). This is quite similar to the lesson plans required of teachers by administrators. The ideas of tasks and time on task have become central elements in successful teaching and learning in addition to classroom management strategies. These tasks are usually outlined through numerous procedures to ensure success. The compartmentalization seen in tasks is also evident in the fragmentation of subject matter in the schools. Fields of study and disciplines are studied in parts to master each step or section. The whole is not necessarily of concern, just mastery of the part or task. The accumulation of completed tasks is then equated to success and high cognitive ability without ever investigating the depth of understanding, application, or integrating the parts into a whole. Through social efficiency, "curriculum became the assembly line by which economically and socially useful citizens would be produced. Social utility, for these reformists, became the sole value by which curriculum would be judged (Pinar et al. 1995, 95–96).

Curriculum, according to Bobbitt, needed to be defined by the tasks required of an adult in society. Students needed to be prepared for the world of work. Through the standardization of tasks and objectives, the scientific analysis and development of curriculum, learning, and schooling changed. Academic tracks grew in popularity as educators saw a need to separate students by cognitive ability and future placement in society. Curriculum was predetermined and not developed through its interaction with both student and teacher. Educational outcomes were heavily analyzed in search of the most efficient methods of instruction. Once successful methods were found, content was not the priority, but how it was taught. During this time period an important shift occurred: the overreliance on methods and instruction to secure learning and a de-emphasis on content. This remains true today as many textbook companies and educational programs will try to sell a particular method of instruction as the "one method" that achieves test or academic results. The emphasis on methods over content, or the need to separate the two aspects of learning, produces yet another fragmentation in the learning process for both students and teachers. This emphasis has the potential of frustrating teachers, students, and administrators as they buy into false claims of improvement or success. One method is not applicable to all subject matter, one method does not suit the needs of all students, and one method does not allow teachers to bring their experience and expertise to the instructional arena.

The social efficiency movement created curriculum experts, people designated to help districts and particular schools achieve results. The educator was no longer seen as the expert. The power of educational decisions was slowly taken away from teachers, students, administrators, and parents. This created another avenue for the commercialization of schools. With this curriculum orientation, schools were treated as businesses, and evaluated on the rate of production (graduation), the quality of the scientific curriculum, and the method of instruction used. The factory model was more popular than ever. This type of curriculum was regarded as having the highest promise for socially controlling youth and subsequently society. Schools were used as agents of social control and class stratification.

The education field has never truly let go of the desire to control learning with the exactitude of science. The popular assumption is that schools should prepare students for the workforce and have a great impact on society. Toward the middle of the twentieth century Ralph Tyler inadvertently developed the Tyler rationale and to some extent continued the educational mission of the social efficiency movement. The Tyler rationale (1949) consists of four questions:

1. What educational purposes should the school seek to attain?
2. What educational experiences can be provided that are likely to attain these purposes?
3. How can these educational experiences be effectively organized?
4. How can we determine whether these purposes are being attained? (1)

These questions were derived from a course syllabus Tyler was teaching. This framework became so popular it quickly was regarded as "the" method to construct curriculum and was adopted as a model for lesson plans. Many have critiqued this rationale as antitheoretical, ahistorical, and apolitical. It basically requires educators to state the educational objectives, tasks, procedures, and means of evaluation. Tyler did not intend for his rationale to be adopted without question in the manner that it was. The Tyler rationale is closely aligned with the social efficiency movement as a result of its impact on standardizing curriculum and instruction, in addition to its procedural nature, bureaucratic interests, and scientific reliance. Tyler is said to have expanded Bobbitt's two-step method of defining educational objectives and devising learning experiences (Pinar et al. 1995). The fundamental belief for the social efficiency movement was the transfer of academic skills to other venues, primarily the workforce. The main objective of this movement was to industrialize the curriculum to fit the business industry. The Tyler rationale was one way of structuring instruction and learning through particular tested categories. The effects of the social efficiency movement are evident today as the school systems and educational leaders press toward a more technocratic system. The overuse of standardized testing is also a consequence of this movement. Turning to standardized tests over any other evaluation mechanism is indicative of the preference for quantitative assessment and limited methods of instruction and subject matter that are conducive to this type of education.

Society's continued movement toward increased technology, mass production, and speed also demands particular types of assessments in the education field. The schools must maintain their pace with society and continue using the approved methods of research and data gathering.

Once the ideas of social efficiency permeated both society and schools, any other reform was measured against the objectivism proposed by the social efficiency movement. Its alignments with capitalism, consumerism, and effectiveness are so tightly woven that educators battle upstream to provide other opportunities for students. As a result of its alliance with science and society's reverence of science, social efficiency is many times untouched by questioning individuals, groups, or reform policies. This does not mean this movement has not been challenged and modified; yet it has fared well through opposition.

VOCATIONAL EDUCATION

As the desire grew to control society specifically through the institution of school so did the ways in which to accomplish this. Vocational education had been around since the 1870s, used primarily with students of color and lower-class students. Vocational education was used as an effective means to improve the character of individuals whom schools and society deemed as social misfits, deviants, or undesirables. This type of education explicitly trained students for different occupations and trades. The types of occupations varied between gender and class.

Ironically, studies revealed female students were served better by their training and were able to secure employment after their education. Most of the occupations young women trained for were in clerical or domestic fields. The skills and tools needed for these fields could be easily reproduced in the classroom; therefore young women's education was current with the job industry. Young men were trained with heavier machinery and equipment, making it very difficult or impossible to re-create the work environment in the classroom. The work industry was also changing rapidly with new technology, and the young men's education, training, and skills were considered nearly obsolete by the time they graduated. Nonetheless vocational centers and institutes continued to train both young men and women for the workforce.

The Industrial Revolution changed social life and education dramatically. The workplace became regulated by time on task and time efficiency. The educational space underwent similar changes in structure, but also in curriculum. Manual arts training was offered simultaneously with regular academic subjects (as a complement, not a substitute) in the late nineteenth century. John D. Runkle first established this type of formal manual arts training; yet he focused on the arts and crafts of different materials, not necessarily on production of artifacts. Soon manual arts training was introduced in public junior high schools and high schools serving mainly two purposes, instilling a work ethic and developing character and values, as well as training youth for the workforce. There was both a moral and a practical agenda for this curriculum. Calvin Woodward, Booker T. Washington, Elbert Hubbard, and others soon joined in the movement for manual training and vocational education for secondary schools and postsecondary education. The position Woodward took was slightly different, one actually reenergized in the 1990s by Joe L. Kincheloe, in defining vocational education as an educational reform, as an educational improvement over the traditional curriculum. The pedagogical vision Woodward put forth advocated for the full integration of the practical and academic, not a parallel existence or entity. Manual arts training would offer a well-rounded education, proposing the development of the intellect through the specificity of practice and craftsmanship. Complex theoretical concepts would be discussed and explained through actual real-life issues, problems, phenomena, or artifacts. This education prepares the student to recognize and use information everywhere, not only in the workforce or school setting. By 1995 Kincheloe developed these ideas further, stating:

> This curriculum theory of academic and vocational education brings together five features in an attempt to address the rupture between

learning what and learning how: academic learning, vocational learning, critical social concerns, worksite placement, and postformal thinking. . . . Dedicated to the critical goals of social and economic justice, good work, and the analysis of power relations, the integrated curriculum utilizes experiential knowledge gained from worksite placement of students to help produce workers and citizens of all varieties who are capable of sophisticated analysis. . . . Project-directed methods pursued in a specific context help academic teachers transcend the decontextualized purposelessness that afflicts the high school. (352, 353–354)

Through this education, teachers are free to create new instructional methods that are conducive to engaging the student in learning from present, lived experience instead of preparing for some future life. There is also greater opportunity for collaboration between teachers and for students to experience the level of connection and usability of the subject matter they are expected to learn.

Vocational education traditionally has been regarded as a remedy for misbehavior and poverty. As the population of immigrants increased, vocational education was used to help assimilate newcomers to the dominant culture of the nation. Samuel Cornish and Samuel Chapman Armstrong were extremely involved in creating manual arts colleges and institutes for African Americans and Native Americans. Booker T. Washington, a student of Armstrong, was famous for the educational enterprise he established in training young men and women of color in the trades. Washington opened the Tuskegee Institute in 1881, bringing to fruition his particular interpretation of vocational education, which did not emphasize the Christian missionary philosophy of helping and acculturating the culturally deficient. He hired African American faculty (George Washington Carver, who revolutionized southern agriculture, was a faculty member at Tuskegee until his death) and stressed the importance of skill training in order to create "an independent class of black artisans" (Kliebard 1999, 16). Washington strongly advocated for the type of education and opportunities that would make African American youth and adults economically self-sufficient. Many misunderstood his educational ideas as supporting racist philosophies that professed blacks and other minorities were incapable of partaking in any other than manual work. Du Bois similarly argued for self-sufficiency, but through an intellectual education. These two major figures, Washington and Du Bois, have been positioned at odds in respect to their philosophies; in actuality they had similar objectives that they achieved through different means. Vocational education was accessible to youth from different classes whereas an intellectual edu-

cation in the traditional sense of formal schooling was not. As Kincheloe advocates, vocational education can, if done through a politically
conscious philosophy, be as intellectual as any traditional education
and better because of its contextual application of the theoretical.

Traditional vocational education offers carpentry and wood-
working, mechanics, foundry work, drafting and architecture, medical
training, industrial arts, agriculture, culinary arts, sewing and fashion,
cosmetology, applied math and sciences, business education, technology education, and many other courses and career options. Many larger
schools today offer traditional academic and college preparatory tracks,
yet the vocational and academic tracks remain separate and not integrated. In the late nineteenth century and into the twentieth century
many technical schools and institutes admitted white males only; later,
women and students of color were admitted. Other schools offered separate education on the basis of race and gender. This type of education
was seen as a way to fit youth into their life's work, into a future occupation. Workers and apprenticeships were in high demand and schools
needed to supply these individuals. The government became intricately
involved in supporting vocational education by supplying financial
assistance and support with the establishment of the Federal Board for
Vocational Education.

The social efficiency movement and the scientific management
of curriculum fit incredibly well with vocational education and the need
to mimic the labor force and the work environment. The curriculum was
carefully outlined for each of the four years of high school. David Sned-
den was a strong proponent of both social efficiency and vocational
education. His involvement and popularity furthered Bobbitt's work
and solidified vocational education on the curricular map of the nation.

The racist and sexist practices in the construction of the vocational curriculum cannot be overlooked, nor can the immense impact
this type of education has had on the lives of youth and on secondary
education. A vocational curriculum holds great promise if taken
through the theoretical offerings of Joe L. Kincheloe for the twenty-first
century.

SOCIAL MELIORISM AND CURRICULUM

The social meliorists considered the curriculum a means or vehicle for
social reconstruction and improvement. Among the proponents of this
movement were George S. Counts and Harold O. Rugg who were
extremely vocal in raising awareness of social inequity and capitalism.

John Dewey was also discontented with society's fanatical following of prosperity and progress at the expense of many in society. At the heart of this movement was a concerted critique of the American schooling system. Many educators did not agree with the current mode of operation where the school was effective for students who were considered elite by cognitive ability or social class. In 1926 Counts published *The Senior High School Curriculum,* discussing secondary school curriculum in fifteen cities (Kliebard 1995). He found great changes in curriculum but little evidence of how schools were servicing the needs of American society. Traditional subject matter was renamed in light of the recommendations of the Cardinal Principles published in 1918. Counts believed schools were acting in antidemocratic ways in their faithfulness to particular subjects and students. Democracy was jeopardized when education was only for a few and not for all. He also investigated school boards and found that the entities controlling the schools for the most part came from economically stable and wealthy social classes, which in his view would favor particular dominant practices in the schools. "Counts's work in the 1920s called attention to what he saw as an American school system oriented not to a new and better social order but to preserving and stratifying existing social conditions" (Kliebard 1995, 160). Shortly thereafter the Great Depression hit and the social inequities Counts spoke and wrote about became increasingly evident. Many educators were persuaded by Counts's ideas and searched for ways to prepare youth in coping with society's social and economic problems. They were seeking ways in which youth could be proactive in their leadership for a better tomorrow.

The social reconstruction movement was the predecessor to critical pedagogy and to some extent the reconceptualization of curriculum. Social reconstructionists also saw schools as agents of social change. Yet the change they advocated was one of social welfare that would improve living for all of society, particularly those who were economically disadvantaged or were otherwise disadvantaged by race, ethnicity, or gender. These educators openly criticized capitalism and the public's romanticization of the progress it would bring. Counts advocated for a radical social policy that held the schools as centers for change. The curriculum would need to be infused with social and cultural analysis so that students could be made aware of the operations of social institutions and would therefore be prepared to negotiate not only their own positions, but the positions of others as well. The Commission on the Social Studies in the Schools of the American Historical Association quickly embraced Counts's ideas. "Teachers were charged with overcoming their traditional silence in political matters and encouraged to strike out boldly in the interest of a new society" (Kliebard 1995, 169). Teachers were put in an interesting position, no longer able to claim neutrality in the classroom. Educators had to expose students to the workings of American society; the belief that students were capable of processing this information was revolutionary. For the first time, knowledge was seen as a socially constructed phenomenon influenced by politics, economics, race, class, ethnicity, and ideology. Students were validated as thinking individuals capable of exercising positive influences in society. To a large extent up to this point children and youth were regarded as not fully human, or as naturally deviant, and that was the main motivation of the social efficiency movement to use schools to control youth. Some sections of the child study movement and progressive movement compensated for these viewpoints with the direct opposite, treating children and youth as capable of directing their own educational journeys without much guidance. The respect for children, their natural tendencies, and interests was almost immobilizing to the educational field. Social reconstructionism created a new perspective about the need for educators to be intricately involved in the learning of their students, as well as students being responsible for their ideas and opportunities.

Counts and other allied educators met great resistance in the actual schools from administrators. Some changes to schooling were made, but largely the ideas of the social reconstructionists were regarded as slightly communist. Even though the ideas and practices were not communist, and the representative educators did not self-identify as communists, the ideas were intended to change the social environment for all its members—not just a few who had access to certain resources. There still are many individuals completely invested in the status quo; therefore any suggestion of it changing threatens the familiarity and security of those committed to keeping things the way they are. These persons stand to lose privilege and access if things change.

Teachers and some administrators also expected more grassroots efforts to inform them and help them change schools and learning. (As is the case today, many resented the proliferation of books and articles without actual practical guidance.) One practical effect and influence of this movement was the schools' adoption of Harold Rugg's social studies textbooks. The textbooks discuss the many problems facing America throughout its history. Extensive research was done in many schools to decipher students' responsiveness and ability to process analytical problems. Considering the economic hardships of the times the textbooks sold incredibly well. Through his textbooks Rugg attempted to debunk stereotypes of others and for the junior high school series addressed the question of what is an American (Kliebard 1995, 175). In other volumes Rugg addressed the disproportion between the rich and poor in different places throughout the United States, the role of women in society, the arts, and a general introduction and in-depth study of the social sciences. His textbooks remained popular until the 1940s when much criticism about the anti-American stance of the series affected the schools' use of these books. (At this time the United States was going into World War II and anything that was deemed to criticize the nation was de-emphasized or silenced.)

Overall, the social reconstructionists made a significant impact on schools and the education field, most specifically in the curriculum of junior high and high schools. The effects of this movement are still felt in present times and were expounded upon in the 1980s through the beginning of the twenty-first century.

CURRICULUM DIFFERENTIATION

Curriculum differentiation evolved throughout the 1960s and 1970s. The acquisition of civil rights for all captured the nation and was central to education as well. As the Black Power movement and feminist movement got under way in the United States, numerous political leaders and activists called for radical reforms in education. The system that was to act as a ladder for economic success for all was only serving the upper- and middle-class white students. Lyndon Johnson, then president, made education a priority. Johnson regarded education with great equalizing potential. He commanded that Congress make funds available to back his initiatives. Great unrest was seen outside the schools and universities as parents, students, and communities protested for better education and access to a variety of courses. There were many schools that were still not integrated. But many parents questioned whether integration would really serve black, Hispanic, Native American, or other minority children. Integration seemed a superficial attempt to resolve the visual image of U.S. schools, not an attempt to redefine the curriculum to suit its students.

Two other movements at this time battled for curricular attention: the humanistic education movement and the neoefficiency movement. Proponents of the humanistic education movement sought to empower youth through education and believed that schools could be agents of change (as George Counts said decades before). They argued that students and parents should have greater choices in the curriculum. Racial minority students needed access to the college-bound track.

Up to this point students had been denied and talked out of these choices. The institutionalized racism in the schools was a problem and a difficult one to remedy since these practices were deemed neutral and a part of tradition. Many agreed with the basic premises argued for by the Black Power movement:

> (1) the primary function of the schools is to meet the "the needs" of young people; (2) the keys to meeting these "needs" are relevant courses and curriculum materials; (3) different students need different types of curricular materials and courses; (4) learning about oneself and one's local community is a prerequisite to learning about the wider world; and (5) promoting positive self-images and self-esteem is a central goal of education. (Angus and Mirel 1999, 128)

These beliefs were not radical and had been heard in curriculum history before. The major difference was the need to address racial identity, culture, and history, which the American schooling system had skirted for centuries. This curriculum differentiation sought transformation in the knowledge that was taught and made accessible to youth in America. These political and educational movements saw the inherent transformative potential in curriculum.

The second movement, neoefficiency, advocated the traditions of Franklin Bobbitt: time on task, accountability, and objective- and performance-based instruction. The philosophical framework for this movement revived the privileged quantitative science methods of seeking truth and control. Neoefficiency was not concerned with self-empowerment or self-esteem, but rather control and mastery of subject matter, in addition to ascertaining that teachers were competent in what they did. Neoefficiency advocates preferred a standard curriculum for all, and differentiation was created in preparation for different careers, particularly math and science (after Sputnik curriculum became a site for competitive performance).

During the 1970s, 1980s, and 1990s, curricular differentiation would become the central topic. Differentiation in some schools lost focus, and courses with little educational relevance became part of the curriculum. Educational achievement slipped and parents and communities once again protested about the quality of education. The reaction was to end curriculum differentiation in the hopes of making high school education more rigorous and competitive. By the 1980s Ronald Reagan, then president, saw the nation literally at risk as a result of school performance. The National Commission on Excellence in Education issued *A Nation at Risk* where it outlined the "five new basics: (a) 4 years of English; (b) 3 years of mathematics; (c) 3 years of science; (d) 3 years of social studies; and (e) one-half year of computer science and 2 years of foreign language (for the college bound)" (Angus and Mirel 1999, 167). This is reminiscent of the work of the Committee of Ten completed almost a hundred years earlier. Angus and Mirel also note that the commissioned report does not mention the Committee of Ten. For centuries educators have instituted ways in which high school education meant preparation for college regardless of whether the student decided he or she wanted to go to college. Many critique this configuration and its track system as reproducing racial and class inequalities. This gave way to another philosophy, cultural reproduction, where the curriculum and schools acted as agents of cultural reproduction, minimizing difference and promoting/creating cultural, racial, and socioeconomic inequities for all but primarily for women and minorities. The struggle continues as the left, right, independent, or in-between on the political spectrum debate over the nation's schools and curriculum. Other issues such as national security, business changes, urbanization, gentrification, immigration, and the economy also affect curriculum and schools.

POSTMODERN CURRICULUM

In the late twentieth century, postmodernism significantly influenced academic culture and some sectors of teacher education programs, subsequently affecting curriculum development for secondary education. During the 1970s, curriculum was reconceptualized and gave way to new ways of thinking about the nature of knowledge, how knowledge was constructed, and how it was learned. This reconceptualization invited a closer look at how learners learned and their particular relationship to learning; this analysis and reflection changed curriculum reform and the role of the university in preparing future educators. Learning and curriculum became avenues for greater insight into the self and society. This new philosophy of curriculum opened doors for many voices and studies that enhanced our understanding of what could be defined as curriculum, as well as the impact it could have. Postmodernism further solidified the shift in theoretical frameworks for education.

Postmodernism offers a paradigm shift away from a predetermined approach to education, learning, evaluation, and lesson planning. Postmodernism has never truly been part of the mainstream, but its effect has been substantial with particular educators, administrators, and curriculum developers. Postmodernism as a philosophy requires variety and difference, an inquiry-based model that is context-specific as it recognizes race, class, gender, language, ethnicity, culture, religion, and sexual orientation (to name a few) in the production of knowledge that is of most worth and who is capable of acquiring that information. This curricular orientation stands in opposition to the Tyler rationale and other quantitative approaches to education. As a way of conceptualizing learning experiences, postmodern educators consider the student as a central participant in the educational process. The student is not considered to be an empty vessel needing to be filled or a deviant in need of disciplinary control. On the contrary, students are seen as active learners and are required to understand their process of learning, what they are learning, and how they can apply what is learned. Learning is intricately related to living and curriculum is rich with possibilities. The inquiry process is equally important to the synthesis of knowledge at the end of the search or study. The postmodern curriculum uses various lenses of analysis to present and interpret knowledge; it borrows from history, sociology, philosophy, culture, politics, ethics, and aesthetics in order to deepen and expand the ways in which each phenomenon or objective is known, learned, understood, and applied. The postmodern educator is not satisfied to lecture on fragmented facts or sound bites of information, nor is he or she able to assess student knowledge through a standardized test alone. A postmodern curriculum requires a comprehensive investigation of knowledge, most often designed as an integrated curriculum or at the very least an interdisciplinary curriculum. Curriculum integration affords teachers the ability to connect different subject matter in order to maximize students' learning. Oftentimes through this curricular approach, teachers work in teams or with another teacher to coordinate classes and integrate their lessons. This provides teachers great opportunities to team-teach or work with colleagues in ways not possible through other philosophies of curriculum. Student engagement and learning increase with this type of collaboration. The teacher is given autonomy over the curriculum design instead of a deskilling, scripted curriculum or curriculum guide. The teacher also understands *neutrality* and *objectivity* to be, in fact, subjective processes in a realm as dynamic as education; decisions made are qualified and distinct in origin. Postmodernism may seem overwhelming for some new teachers because of its freedom and range of possibility. Many see these options as exciting ways in which to develop their teaching identity and to impact the lives of others.

Educational theorists have further developed postmodern ideas around cognitive development. Kincheloe and Steinberg (1993) introduce postformal thinking as a way to challenge and extend Piaget's formal operational stage. The tenets of postformal thinking are seeing relationships between ostensibly different things . . . [called] metaphoric cognition; connecting logic and emotion by stretching the boundaries of imagination; seeing facts as part of a larger process of connecting the holographic mind to holographic reality; perceiving different frames of reference in order to develop the cognitive power of empathy; attending to the particular place and context of the educative event; understanding the interaction of the particular and the general; transcending simplistic notions of cause-effect to create nonlinear holism; seeing the world as a text to be interpreted rather than explained; and finally, uncovering various levels of connection between the mind and the ecosystem to reveal larger patterns of life-forces for meaningful connection between causally unconnected events. (Slattery 1995, 26–27)

Postformalism promises to challenge the status quo of lesson planning and curriculum design. When knowledge is seen as connected and complicated, unable to be broken into pieces without keeping the whole in perspective, it becomes extremely difficult to compartmentalize and teach information in measurable and discrete pieces. Students are often alienated from the learning process and teachers from the instructional process when a litany of facts is barely strung together in any cohesive manner. A crucial part of postmodernism and subsequently postformalism is continuous reflection on one's practice and learning. Teachers are required to reflect about and evaluate their own practice, modifying as needed to best suit the needs of each student.

A critical analysis of language and meaning is also an imperative skill to develop through postformalism, a much needed tool in developing multiple literacies for the twenty-first century. Deconstructing language offers insight into the hidden curriculum and hidden agendas in the texts studied in school. In part this deconstruction offers a way to empower both teachers and students by stressing the importance of the knower (learner) in the knowing (learning) process, as well as the many ways in which meaning can be arrived at. Master narratives ("great books," classic works seen as staples in curriculum for each subject matter), for example the disciplines within the humanistic curriculum, can be exclusionary for many students. Through a postmodern curriculum the same things may be studied, but what changes dramatically is how. The basic premise is that anybody can learn. The master narratives are studied, researched, and deconstructed historically and sociopolitically, meaning the works are placed in the context of time, culture, and power (significance). This context provides valuable perspective in understanding the many ways in which the text can be interpreted. All interpretations are valid and students also learn the privileged interpretation, the mainstream preferred meaning, in order to gain the cultural capital necessary to exhibit what they know when necessary. Aronowitz and Giroux (1991) state:

> What is at stake in the struggle over curriculum and textual authority is the struggle to control the very grounds on which knowledge is produced and legitimated. This is both a political and pedagogical issue. It is political in that curriculum, along with its representative courses, texts, and social relations, is never value-free or objective. Curriculum, by its very nature, is a social and historical construction that links knowledge and power in very specific ways. . . . Curriculum does not merely offer courses and skills; it functions to name and privilege particular histories and experiences. (96)

Postmodern curriculum goes beyond the standards placed on each grade. The expectations are larger since this way of learning and curriculum design requires the full engagement of both learner and educator. Knowledge is learned not as a separate entity but as a piece in a much larger puzzle. Many critical pedagogy teachers, multicultural educators, progressive teachers, and feminist teachers follow a postmodern curriculum philosophy.

THE HIGH SCHOOL CURRICULUM

The traditional comprehensive high school curriculum mainly consists of completing a certain number of credits from each major discipline and electives. The general breakdown is four courses in English; three in math, science, and social studies/history/economics; one to two courses in art; and the rest electives. These electives may be reduced by requirements in health education, physical education, foreign languages, speech, or technology. If the school is of a religious denomination, theology is also a requirement. For vocational schools the curricular structure changes to accommodate multiple trades and career tracks. These general requirements are heavily influenced by what colleges and universities delineate as admissions criteria. Some high schools will differentiate in curriculum and design college-bound and noncollege-bound tracks. (This essentially differs from the Committee of Ten who determined these requirements should be for all students regardless of what they do after graduation, but tracking is a consistent practice throughout this nation's high schools.) Many schools also provide advanced placement courses for college credit. The following is a list of accepted courses and areas of study under each general discipline:

English: Grammar and Composition, Literature (American, British, Ancient, Modern, Biblical), Poetry, Creative Writing, Analysis of Literature, Oral Communications, Journalism, Drama, Debate

Mathematics: Consumer Math, Career Math, Algebra, Geometry, Trigonometry, Calculus, Drafting, Computer Aided Design (CAD), Accounting, Economics, General Math, Probability, Statistics, Business Math, Advanced Mathematics

Science: Earth Science, Physical Science, Biology, Chemistry, Life Science, Physical Mechanics, General Technology and Mechanics, Anatomy, Physiology, Ecology, Nutrition, Psychology, Human Growth and Development, Maternal and Child Care, Human Behavior and Criminology, General Science, Physics

Social Studies: History (other than U.S. History, such as European, Economic, Ancient), Western Civilization, Military History of the World, History of the Western World, Old and New Testament Survey, Religion, Geography, World Geography, Sociology, Economics, Management, Marketing, Law, Macro Economics and Micro Economics, U.S. History, America before 1877, America since 1877, History of the United States (Political, Economic, Military, Technological, Government, Religious), State Studies (a basic course in their state's history, growth, geography, products, climate, law, and relationship to other states), Contemporary American History, World History, World Cultures, Global Studies, Civics, and American Government

Arts: Visual Arts (General Art, 2D, 3D, Graphic Design, Drawing, Portfolio, Advanced Placement Art, Ceramics, Photography, Sculpture, Woodwork, Electronic Media), Performing Arts (Drama, Speech, Costume and Set Design, Improvisation), Art Appreciation, Music Appreciation, Music (Choir, Band, Orchestras, Musical Ensembles, Music Theory)

Health: Anatomy, Physiology, Disease Processes, Pathology, Interpersonal Relationships, Addictions, Nutrition, Growth and Development, Home Economics, First Aid, Aging, Safety Certificates (such as Hunter Safety and CPR)

Technology: Basic Computer Skills, Keyboarding, Applications/ Software, Web Design, Multimedia, Business Education

Physical Education: General Physical Education, Aerobics,
Weightlifting, Sports Medicine, Team Sports, Physical Train-
ing, Certificate Courses (such as Red Cross Life Saving and
CPR)

Foreign Language: Spanish, French, German, Russian

Electives: Other courses available, including practical arts, work-
study, independent study

These are general examples of what is offered around the country. Each school may offer less or more depending on its population,
mission, and type. College preparatory schools, magnet schools, charter
schools, and private, alternative, or vocational schools offer completely
different programs. Students often are bused in given each school's specialty. Curricular diversity is threatened by the overemphasis on standardized tests. Teachers, parents, administrators, students, and communities continue to be strong advocates for curricular differentiation
in order to best suit the needs of the students and to address inequities
across the nation's educational preparation.

Two other curricular differentiations of importance are the international baccalaureate curriculum and the advanced placement curriculum. These two programs offer an equivalent to college-level courses
at the high school level and sometimes even earlier. The international
baccalaureate curriculum is created by the International Baccalaureate
Organization (IBO), founded in 1968 as a nonprofit education foundation based in Geneva, Switzerland. This organization's objective is to create a universal curricular program that facilitates university admissions.
IBO offers three programs: the Diploma Programme for students in the
final two years of school before university, the Middle Years Programme
for students 11–16, and the Primary Years Programme for ages 3–12
(www.ibo.org/ibo/index.cfm). The IBO program at the high school level
offers international standards of excellence and requires students to be
intimately involved in learning and researching the subject matter. Curriculum is presented in interdisciplinary formats with a focus on both
breadth and depth of knowledge investigation and construction. Critical
thinking is essential; therefore "students are evaluated on both the content and process of academic achievement. Exams are based on broad,
general understanding of concepts and fundamental themes. Course
assessments emphasize essay and oral formats; multiple-choice format
[is] used little. IB scores are based upon a combination of internal grading of required assessments by classroom teachers and external grades
determined by 3,500 qualified examiners worldwide" (http://eclipse.cps.

k12.va.us/departments/inter_b/advanced.html). The IB program affords students some college credit although this is not guaranteed.

The other rigorous curricular program is the advanced placement curriculum, which gives students the chance to undertake first-year college-level work in high school and to gain valuable skills and study habits for college. The College Board is the organization that administers advanced placement exams. The scores on these tests determine whether high school students will be granted college credit once they are admitted to the college or university of their choice. The College Board states:

- ◆ The AP Program offers 34 courses in 19 subject areas.
- ◆ Nearly 60 percent of U.S. high schools participate in the AP Program. In those schools, 937,951 students took AP Exams in 2002.
- ◆ In 2002, 1,585,516 AP Exams were administered worldwide.
- ◆ More than 60,000 teachers worldwide attended AP workshops and institutes for professional development [in 2002].
- ◆ Over 90 percent of the nation's colleges and universities have an AP policy granting incoming students credit, placement, or both, for qualifying AP Exam grades. (www.collegeboard.com)

As a result of the programs' offerings, many schools, students, and parents seek the AP program as an alternative to the public school curriculum and a means of acquiring educational excellence. The curriculum courses are taught in isolation from one another, as separate entities similar to the regular public school curriculum. The program is completely content driven as is necessary for success on the final examinations. These conditions are said to replicate freshman-level courses in universities and colleges where students must recall a range of information in a relatively short time. The assessments are multiple-choice and essay exams, which are evaluated by qualified national examiners. Given these exams and their potential to transfer credit to university and college transcripts, teachers must follow the curriculum very carefully and ensure that most of the material is covered during the semester or year. Teachers are given some guidance through professional development, in particular of the amount of information that will be covered in the national exams.

Out of similar philosophies in providing more opportunities for excellence, some universities offer academic outreach programs as early as middle school to increase the probability of academic access and success. In these programs students with usually low grade point averages or at risk of dropping out are challenged by advanced material. If they are in middle school, they are given high school credit; if they are in high school, they are given college credit. The objective of these programs is to engage the student as early as possible in the internal and external rewards of learning and the possibilities for future development and success. Some high schools have also instituted the advisory program common to middle schools in an attempt to provide greater mentorship and guidance for students.

High schools are also well-known for their extracurricular activities such as sports, band, journalism, yearbook, and academic clubs. For many students these are the activities that make significant contributions in their lives. These opportunities are usually free from traditional, academic evaluation, even though highly competitive at times. They occur outside regular school hours. The extracurricular opportunities offer, at times, a space in which to implement what students learn during regular school hours. Their content, scope, and intent may be more meaningful than scripted or guided curricula. Students learn team membership; develop important relationships with adult mentors, coaches, and directors; develop leadership, commitment, self-discovery and reflection, community responsibility, and public activism. Unfortunately these programs are the first to be cut if there are funding problems or if academic test scores fall under the average necessary for the district or state.

Some literature reflects a strong criticism of the high school curriculum and objects to its standardization. Teachers, administrators, and parents see fewer courses and pedagogical strategies offered to their students. Many schools are also creating single-sex courses given the amount of literature that exists, particularly about young women achieving higher academic goals when they are in single-sex schools. The National Forum to Accelerate Middle-Grades Reform advocates this and pilots their program in public schools around the nation. They report significant academic achievement gains for both sexes. The school remains the same in structure, but some courses, usually math and science, are single-sex in order to ensure student success. High school in particular is an extremely important passage for adolescents. Their successes or failures may influence life decisions and internalizations about their capacity as learners, as intelligent individuals. Seldom does the mainstream or general American public regard the institution of schooling as highly problematic. There has been a significant history of looking at students as deficient or of instructional model shopping where the school goes from one instructional program to the next seeking "the answer." Often schools quiet adolescents' curiosity and energy instead of nurturing or promoting them. Only students who can successfully conform will succeed in today's schools. There have been moments in our history when schools are said to have been in crisis, but we as a nation are yet to prepare our youth for leadership, success, sustenance, and maintenance of the global environment. We continue to cut off historical instruction from our social studies curriculum and diminish the communal consciousness of our country and its responsibility for the larger world society. There are also strong critics of our educational system who highlight the system's ethnocentrism, intolerance for difference, and inequity. These voices must be central to the reform conversations in order to provide realistic alternatives for today's youth.

THE MIDDLE SCHOOL CURRICULUM

The middle school in particular has undergone significant reform since the junior high/mini–high school days. In the 1970s as a result of *Turning Points* (the Carnegie document), the time between elementary school and high school was conceptualized in a radically different way. The middle school was born and it brought forth the integrated curriculum. The majority of middle schools are a separate building housing sixth, seventh, and eighth grades, other times just seventh and eighth, but sometimes they can span from fifth grade to as late as ninth. There are several things that set middle schools apart from junior high schools, such as block scheduling, advisory groups, integrated curriculum, and teacher preparation specific to middle school. The major objective of middle schools, according to the National Middle School Association, is to provide a transition from elementary school to high school in which students can have a greater sense of connection with adults and experience knowledge as connected and dynamic. Transitions are often difficult and educators saw a need to give particular attention to early adolescents in order to best suit their emotional, physical, and cognitive development. The transition was not only happening in the school structure but also with individual students as they grew and developed.

Curriculum reform at the middle school level is perhaps the most exciting: the institutionalization of creating and experiencing curriculum as connected phenomena relevant to life. The integration of curriculum exists on a continuum from multidisciplinary to interdisciplinary to full curriculum integration. The former two are the ones schools most often implement primarily because they are easier to get off the ground without having to reconstitute school structure drastically. Multidisciplinary curriculum involves connecting an idea, concept, or skill to each particular discipline such as math, science, language arts, social studies, art, and so on. In multidisciplinary curriculum the structure, time, and content sequence of the disciplines stay mostly intact. The idea, concept, or skill is studied in each discipline simultaneously to demonstrate the connections between the different areas. All of the discipline or grade teachers plan the content, evaluation, and duration of the curriculum together. Sometimes in multidisciplinary curriculum there will be a culminating project that all students must do together. This curriculum model offers the least amount of integration. It also runs the risk of having the least meaningful connections. The point is not integration for the sake of it, but to make learning a meaningful experience for students. Sometimes when done appropriately this is the easiest place to start in terms of integration.

Interdisciplinary curriculum is more involved in its connection between disciplines and the students' lives. Teachers' planning time is usually scheduled into the day or week. Teachers across the disciplines deliberate over what topics or issues they want to create curriculum around. These teachers constitute a team and each team designs and implements a unit of instruction. The entire year or grading period is filled with one or more units of study. These units closely align various classes, blurring the disciplinary boundaries to maximize learning. These units are thematic in nature, helping students to comprehend the larger issues tying math to science to language arts, and so on. The interdisciplinary curriculum engages the interconnections between subject matter, redefining and expanding each discipline. This leads to great possibilities for discovery and inquiry for students and teachers alike.

Full curriculum integration completely blurs disciplinary boundaries as it redefines subject matter through inquiry-based learning. Curriculum integration seeks depth of knowledge comprehension and application. It attempts to involve the complexity of issues rather than discrete fragments. It looks at the whole *and* its parts, not just the parts. Beane (1998), in particular, along with Totten and Pederson (1997), advocates designing curriculum around social issues for the middle school student. Curriculum then becomes relevant and engaging to students and teachers alike. Beane envisions a collaborative approach between teachers and students in developing these integrated units around social issues. He believes and has documented in his books that students have genuine complex inquiries about the world and their lives. Why not capitalize on the inherent motivation? Beane's model includes an interconnected design of content and skills (personal, social, and technical), personal and social concerns, and concepts (democracy, dignity, and diversity). Many middle school educators and advocates see the numerous advantages of redefining curriculum to maximize a student's sense of social meaning and purpose. This type of curriculum integration is the most time-consuming and challenging since it demands a rethinking of disciplinary boundaries for the sake of inquiry, research, and transformative understanding. This type of curriculum integration is the least common with some schools, yet potentially the most beneficial.

DEFINING CURRICULUM

Curriculum has ranged in subject matter and purpose, from aiding youth in becoming proper gentlemen and ladies with distinct gender roles and class expectations to a track system designed for various goals. There are different curriculum cultures we will discuss that frame teaching and learning as well as goals. Bolotin Joseph et al. (2000) discuss six curricular cultures:

- Training for work and survival—to gain the basic skills, habits, and attitudes necessary to function in the workplace and to adapt to living within society
- Connecting to the canon—to acquire core cultural knowledge, traditions, and values from the dominant culture's exemplary moral, intellectual, spiritual, and artistic resources as guidelines for living
- Developing self and spirit—to learn according to self-directed interests in order to nurture individual potential, creativity, and knowledge of the emotional and spiritual self
- Constructing understanding—to develop fluid, active, autonomous thinkers who know that they themselves can construct knowledge through their study of the environment and collaborative learning with others
- Deliberating democracy—to learn and to actually experience the deliberative skills, knowledge, beliefs, and values necessary for participating in and sustaining a democratic society
- Confronting the dominant order—to examine and challenge oppressive social, political, and economic structures that limit self and others and to develop beliefs and skills that support activism for the reconstruction of society (12–13)

Schools and educators may argue that to some degree all of these cultures are present in their schools and classrooms. Theoretically and ideally this may be possible. Yet in today's schools the most prevalent cultures are training for work and survival, connecting to the canon, and constructing understanding. The other three may be by-products, but are not always required or aspired to. Throughout history, training for work and survival has been prioritized in education, as schools acted as large systems of assimilation and acculturation for both immigrants and natives in this country. The desire to use schools as this type of mechanism has not dissipated; nonetheless it has grown into a more complex process. The cultures outlined above present the philosophical and practical orientation for a corresponding curriculum.

Training for work and survival as a curricular culture prepares students in a variety of ways for the economic world. Job skills, not just trade skills, are emphasized. The advanced placement academic courses train students for work just as much as the vocational classes. Essentially students are prepared for different types of employment, but the end goal is to be employed, successful, and provide a monetary and service contribution to society. Education has always been regarded as an economic ladder and as a means for progress and betterment. It should come as no surprise that this culture is the core of American education. It feeds and promotes our national culture, in addition to contributing to liberal democratic ideals of economic access for anyone willing to work hard enough. Success in this culture is quantified by material wealth and acquisitions, not necessarily by what one really knows. Curriculum in this culture is constructed by giving the student all necessary knowledge and asking him or her to articulate that knowledge as it was given. Rote memorization, recall, objective tests, and specific skill tasks are usual methods of instruction and evaluation. The curriculum in general is standardized. The industry and institutions of higher education exert a strong influence on this curricular culture. There is great potential here for curriculum integration, internships, real-life connections, and reform of work environments. As in all curriculum, its vision and implementation can vary greatly. Many high schools and middle schools use the training for work and survival as the main curriculum, with deviations based on trends or changes in society and education.

Connecting to the canon is usually woven with the training for work and survival curriculum content. In preparing students for the world of work they must share a common culture and knowledge. This is where the canon of each discipline is utilized in order to create a uniform set of skills, content, and standards. This curriculum culture extends beyond content to creating a core set of values and belief systems, and therefore promoting a particular national and cultural memory and identity. Bolotin Joseph et al. (2000) contend, "Access to this education permits the acquisition of cultural capital. Through mastery of appropriate cultural knowledge, students can leave school and go out into the world and relate to others who also know 'the right stuff'" (55). This curriculum solidifies essential information in each discipline. Yet the essential knowledge is selective. In making decisions about curriculum, educators choose some authors and theories over others. These selections at times can privilege certain ways of knowing, creating a hierarchy of worth. This essentialism may also promote monoculturalism, which can be problematic in such a diverse society. The problems increase exponentially as students who do not fit the criteria and standards or relate to this curriculum are alienated from the learning process, and avenues for success are stunted if not denied. Masses of students today believe they are not cut out for school and the curriculum continues to fail them. More attention needs to be given to curriculum as a source for transformation.

The fourth curriculum culture mentioned above, constructing understanding, is pivotal in maximizing the potential learning at the crossroads of the first two curricular cultures. Constructing understanding as a curriculum culture relies on constructivist theory. This has become extremely popular in contemporary times as it highlights knowledge as a construction and the responsibility of the student in the learning process. The curriculum priorities shift to student engagement, inquiry-based learning, and complex ideas. This is the least restrictive of the cultures. In combination with the two other cultures discussed above the quality of learning for the student in high school can be extremely enriching and meaningful. A knowledge base is built that can transcend context. Sometimes the combination of all cultures does not meet the high expectations; it all depends on the individual district, school, and teacher.

The remaining cultures of curriculum hold great promise in rethinking curricular possibilities. Developing self and spirit truly challenges educators and students to shift paradigms of thinking and action. Developing a social and reflective consciousness of one's place in society as well as one's relationships to others requires the development of empathy and rigorous questioning of competition, capitalism, and inequity. Students and educators therefore must be involved in cooperative learning situations and difficult discussions on the ecological connections between self and environment. Education in this curricular culture is more holistic and lends itself to repairing sexist, racist, classist, and heterosexist practices in school and society.

Deliberating democracy follows suit from the culture described above as it further studies democracy theoretically and pragmatically. Students and educators are seen as producers of knowledge and willing participants in restructuring systems of authority and power within the school and classroom. Students actively participate in school and curriculum decisions. All individuals are regarded as important members of the learning community. Confronting the dominant order stresses the development of critical analysis, inquiry and research, and reading against the grain. Students are prepared to question current practices and social norms as they seek more appropriate and humane solutions to social problems. Both educators and students are active seekers of multiple perspectives and new possibilities for living. This curricular structure challenges the way power is wielded and works to reconstruct society for all its members regardless of who they are or what position they hold. All of these curriculum cultures provide great spaces for the pursuit of knowledge that deal with personal, political, practical, and intellectual issues. Students and educators thrive in these cultures as they find that who they are is not constantly silenced for the sake of a packaged curriculum. Anything and everything is considered for curricular potential, particularly the issues at the forefront of current events and student lives. Curriculum is indisputably seen as a racial, gender, cultural, historical, and autobiographical text.

Curriculum is a dynamic entity. As such, educators can utilize it to create more productive and significant learning experiences. Curriculum can be the space where students learn about who they are and the world they live in through both historical and contemporary accounts. Critical pedagogy (usually associated with the last curricular culture, confronting the dominant order) is a theoretical framework that regards curriculum as a site of true possibility for self and social transformation. This particular discipline within education understands curriculum through the lenses of race, class, gender, sexual orientation, language, ethnicity, culture, and so on. These lenses help contextualize how information is understood and applied, as well as what questions may be necessary to consider (e.g., what or who is excluded? who benefits? whose interests are served?). Understanding curriculum through these lenses allows students and teachers to discern knowledge as it relates to who they are and can be, and what has been constructed about who they are or their abilities. Curriculum content is not neutral and if the teacher recognizes the myriad ways to analyze curriculum, she or he can make curricular decisions in order to enhance, repair, complicate, problematize, and challenge the existing curriculum. This curriculum negotiation is at the heart of critical pedagogy and developing critical thinking skills in students (Villaverde 2003 in press). Curriculum and pedagogy are considered sites of struggle explicit with tensions over knowledge, intelligence, and identity. How curriculum is defined simultaneously defines how one is to know it, teach it, and succeed in it. Through critical pedagogy the purposes for education are thoroughly examined for democratic applications.

Adopting, understanding, and exercising this perspective will undoubtedly bring much questioning and perhaps uncertainty, yet this is the objective, to embrace and pursue inquiry in deepening how one negotiates information. At the heart of this curricular inquiry is the investigation of that which is perceived as different, unimportant, or inferior. Critical pedagogy is ultimately concerned with inequity, social injustice, disadvantage, and access to any cultural capital, that is, knowledge that would otherwise facilitate a wiser negotiation of self in society. It seems utterly important for adolescents to experience curriculum through this pedagogical/theoretical framework. Their questions are taken seriously, as points of departure for curricular inquiry, and used as a bridge between lived experience and school knowledge. This curriculum design can also serve to repair discriminatory practices in society. Risner (2003) explains, "Discrimination, in a consumer capitalist culture, directed toward those who are different or perceived to be different, develops because the ethical vision of the culture socializes citizens to view difference as a fearful threat, a menace people are obliged to compete with, to commodify, to divide and conquer" (211). Risner is specifically discussing difference as one of sexual orientation and the subsequent homophobia and heterosexism that exist in society. Schools, in particular middle schools and high schools, are places where young minds develop or stunt interpersonal and intrapersonal skills. In addition, schools are microcosms of society and students learn quickly what is deemed acceptable by the mainstream. In such high-stakes environments, the pressure to conform may seem insurmountable unless the teacher takes advantage of these incredible pedagogical moments. Curriculum can then be redefined to explore and teach how dominant culture displaces other ways of knowing and living. Exposure and true comprehension of whatever or whoever is considered "other" may blur and revoke the negative connotations of difference. This in itself is a transformative educational practice. Other types of education have alienated and marginalized most students who do not fit the norm; others undergo great sacrifices to fit in. Schooling should not have to be about the struggle to maintain the self, but a process through which learning is internalized and expanded beyond the classroom.

Curriculum can be a site in which to explore identity issues and social phenomena. Any student, whether Latino, black, Native American, white, Asian, lesbian, gay, transgendered, heterosexual, disabled, bilingual, non-Christian, or otherwise self-identified, should not be subject to any discrimination or stigmatization because of their difference or perceived difference. Any obstacles, "though certainly tangible and substantial, should not diminish or trivialize our deepest commitments and sincerest concerns for developing humanizing pedagogies that prioritize the safety and well-being of all students" (Risner 2003, 214). Any student, regardless of sexual orientation, race, religion, class, gender, ability, language, or ethnicity, deserves an opportunity to feel excited about learning and be allowed to pursue their intellectual curiosities in the classroom through creative curriculum design. Students as well as teachers need to understand their ideas and actions actually matter, "and therefore, have the potential for making a more just and liberating world in the here and now" (Risner 2003, 215).

Curriculum can be and has been an incredibly lively constant throughout educational history. To maximize curricular opportunities teachers need to question their beliefs in general about youth, education, and difference, in addition to researching what they think they know and what they do not, even if they do not care to. Precisely at this intersection or juncture are the transformative possibilities yet to be explored and ever so potentially useful for students. The socially conscious teacher is the agent of positive change within the field of critical pedagogy. Despite efforts to continuously standardize knowledge, it can never be entirely controlled. The pedagogical space in the classroom can be very elastic. Educators at all levels, especially in times of extreme standardization and commercialization, need to be more creative, imaginative, and inventive in how they design and implement learning experiences to truly reengage students in the educational process. The curriculum field offers a range of trends and movements to inform teachers in their curricular choices. This chapter introduces the middle school or high school teacher to the multiple conversations on the nature of curriculum and the larger societal-invested interests. Looking through both curriculum history and the history of secondary education to discover present and future possibilities is a powerful tool not only for youth, but for educators as well. These histories intertwine as time progresses and reforms are implemented.

In conclusion, let's review the answers to the questions posed at the beginning of this chapter: What is curriculum? What knowledge is of most worth and to whom? What is the importance of curriculum? These questions have been at the heart of the debates and reforms outlined above. Curriculum can be the scripted lesson plans teachers, districts, and companies develop. At times it is simply and solely the textbook.

Through critical lenses one can see curriculum encompassing all that is learning in the school environment and beyond. This way of defining curriculum can be quite intangible, but necessary to investigate since students are exposed to various levels of the hidden curriculum, from the minute they walk into pre-kindergarten to high school graduation. Schools not only teach subject matter, but ways of life, understanding, values, beliefs, good from bad, and ultimately future possibilities. Therefore how teachers and schools define curriculum, what they deem as knowledge, has great importance to individuals, families, institutions, and the nation. This is no light matter; curriculum has a plethora of implications. If this were not the case the history would not be so rich, and people would not be so compelled to constantly make it better.

REFERENCES

Angus, D. L., and J. E. Mirel. 1999. *The Failed Promise of the American High School, 1890–1995.* New York: Teachers College Press.

Aronowitz, Stanley, and Henry A. Giroux. 1991. *Postmodern Education: Politics, Culture, and Social Criticism.* Minneapolis: University of Minnesota Press.

Beane, J. 1998. *Curriculum Integration: Designing the Core of Democratic Education.* New York: Teachers College Press.

Bolotin Joseph, Pamela, S. Luster Bravmann, M. A. Windschitl, and N. Stewart Green. 2000. *Cultures of Curriculum.* New York: Lawrence Erlbaum Associates.

Chesapeake Public Schools. //eclipse.cps.k12.va.us/departments/inter_b/ advanced.html. Accessed April 2003.

College Board. www.collegeboard.com. Accessed April 2003.

Dewey, John. 1901. *The School and Society.* Chicago: University of Chicago Press.

IB Diploma Programme General Information and Curriculum. www.ibo.org/ ibo/index.cfm. Accessed April 2003.

Kincheloe, Joe L. 1995. "Schools Where Ronnie and Brandon Would Have Excelled: A Curriculum Theory of Academic and Vocational Integration." In William F. Pinar, ed. 1999. *Contemporary Curriculum Discourses: Twenty Years of JCT.* New York: Peter Lang.

Kincheloe, Joe L., and Shirley R. Steinberg. 1993. "A Tentative Description of Postformal Thinking: The Critical Confrontation with Cognitive Theory." *Harvard Educational Review* 63, no. 3: 296–320.

Kliebard, Herbart M. 1999. *Schooled to Work: Vocationalism and the American Curriculum, 1876–1946.* New York: Teachers College Press.

Kliebard, Herbert M. 1995. *The Struggle for the American Curriculum: 1893–1958.* 2nd ed. New York: Routledge.

Pinar, William F., William M. Reynolds, Patrick Slattery, and Peter M. Taubman. 1995. *Understanding Curriculum: An Introduction to the Study of Historical and Contemporary Curriculum Discourses.* New York: Peter Lang.

Reese, W. J. 1995. *The Origins of the American High School.* New Haven: Yale University Press.

Risner, Doug. 2003. "What Matthew Shepard Would Tell Us: Gay and Lesbian Issues in Education." In S. Shapiro and S. Harden, eds. *The Institution of Education,* 4th ed. Boston: Pearson Custom Publishing.

Totten, S., and J. E. Pederson. 1997. *Social Issues and Service at the Middle Level.* Boston: Allyn and Bacon.

Tyler, Ralph W. 1949. *Basic Principles of Curriculum and Instruction.* Chicago: University of Chicago Press.

Villaverde, Leila E. 2003, in press. "Developing Curriculum, Critical Thinking, and Pedagogy," *Critical Thinking and Learning: An Encyclopedia.* New York: Greenwood Press.

Chapter Four

● Urban, Suburban, and Rural Secondary Schools

Secondary schools are as varied as the ideas that constitute secondary education. In this chapter region and type of school are the main distinctions presented in order to further understand how curriculum, instruction, learning, structure, and resources vary. In no way is this chapter an exhaustive survey of all secondary education institutions in the United States, but a general outline and discussion of the different categories schools fall under, the places they exist, the governing structure, population, philosophies, and curriculum offered.

URBAN SCHOOLS

Urban schools are schools found in large to moderate-sized cities. They may be neighborhood schools, vocational schools, technical academies, special magnet schools, or charter schools. Also in the city, many private schools cater to those who can afford them. Some public schools may be plagued with issues of overcrowding, low funds or resources, and district mandates. Other schools are quite small in population and have ample resources available. The variety of urban schools is often as great as the people in them. It is important not to generalize or stereotype the urban school solely as a problem-ridden inner-city school. Some inner-city schools have great academic and specialty programs available for their students. Certain districts face greater challenges in achievement, attendance, and specialization. The district management tends to be more political the larger the city and district size. Urban schools are usually public institutions structured in one of the following ways: pre-K through eighth grade, pre-K through fifth grade, sixth through ninth grade, sixth through eighth grade, ninth through twelfth grade, or tenth through twelfth grade. Very few public schools are pre-K through twelfth grade; this configuration is more common to religious private schools. French (1967) states, "Our pluralistic society in the United States provides for three types of secondary schools—the public high schools, which enroll approximately 89 percent of all secondary students; the church-related secondary schools, often called parochial high schools, academies, or institutes; and so-called private or independent schools, which may or may not have some vestige of denominational affiliation or tradition" (284).

A lot of the larger public school districts have information about all of their schools on the Internet. Among the types of schools, one may find small schools with fewer than 500 total students, year-round schools, magnet schools, charter schools, academic preparatory centers, vocational schools, and institutes of various kinds. The various schools appear to provide substantial opportunities for students living in these districts. It is important to remember most of these schools are neighborhood schools guided by zoning restrictions. Exceptions to these guidelines are schools offering specialty programs where students must apply and meet specified criteria to be admitted. Transportation may or not be available. School governance for public urban and some private schools typically consists of at least three different bodies: the state school board, the district school board, and the local school council. The state school board governs and oversees policy, regulations, plans, initiatives, teacher certification requirements, funding initiatives, the evaluations of school programs, professional development, and adequate services for schools. These boards usually consist of six to ten members with a chairperson, director, or president. Most of the members are either community leaders or educational leaders appointed or elected to the position for a particular term. In order to be considered, one must be a citizen of the United States, hold at least one-year residency in the district, be registered to vote, and not be an elected official (although this particular criterion may change from state to state or district). Both states and districts have boards of education. The district office may have a superintendent, president, director, or, more commonly with larger districts, chief executive officers. The bureaucracy of business models heavily influences the larger city districts. These models create a large web of bifurcations in the system, which may then lead to great political tensions.

A local school council is another popular governing mechanism for some schools. It is a site-based management team whose primary responsibility is to select the school's principal, renew the principal's contract, approve the school improvement plans or initiatives, and approve the school budget for the school year. The council is made up of the principal, teachers, parents, community members, and one student for a total of twelve members at most. The student has very limited voting options. These bodies may have great control over the education in these schools but lack necessary expertise.

SUBURBAN SCHOOLS

Suburban schools are those schools sitting outside city limits. These schools may also be neighborhood schools and governed similarly to urban schools. The myth is that suburban schools are free from overcrowding, violence, lack of resources, and standardization. However, the large school shootings have been in suburban and rural schools. Lots of families move to the suburbs in search for a better quality of life, and no community is immune to hardships that affect schools. Just like urban schools there are a variety of schools in the suburbs that are successful and others that are struggling. Poverty levels may be higher in the city than in the suburbs, but again this varies tremendously state by state. As suburbs grow, class stratification increases and schools in the lower-income areas may suffer from problems similar to those in some city schools. Tracking is a common practice, as is the comprehensive high school, which offers a wide variety of courses and educational programs. Traditionally suburban schools had more extracurricular activities and programs available to its students. This has changed somewhat with the increase in magnet and charter schools within the city that in part are meant to attract students from the suburbs. In the suburbs there may be a lot of private church-related schools or private independent schools. Middle-class, suburban schools share similar achievement gap problems, although suburban schools are usually overlooked in their struggles. Suburban schools are also adding new programs, including career-based programs and academies.

RURAL SCHOOLS

Rural schools are perhaps the least discussed in educational debates. One-room schoolhouses still exist in some remote rural areas. These rural areas are largely farm communities where the culture and population may be very different from urban and suburban schools. It is sometimes difficult to define a rural school. Three classification systems have been developed since the 1960s: the metro status codes, then in the 1970s the Beale codes, and in the 1980s the locale codes. The latter two are the ones that will be included here since the Department of Agriculture's Economic Research Service (ERS) reports them to be more accurate. The metro status codes determine whether a school is in or near a metropolitan statistical area and whether it is a city or not. But these codes do not specify whether these areas are rural or not; therefore the results are unreliable. The Beale codes are calculated by examining the size of a county and its proximity to a metropolitan area. The last codes, the locale codes, determine both the proximity to metropolitan areas and population size and density (http://nces.ed.gov). The states that are rated with the highest number (by Beale and locale codes) of rural schools were California, Colorado, Illinois, Kansas, Michigan, Minnesota, Montana, Nebraska, New Jersey, New York, North Dakota, Ohio, Pennsylvania, South Dakota, and Texas. Also considered rural schools are schools on Indian reservations. The amount of schools that are classified as rural is quite high. The average school size is anywhere from 200 to 500 students, and there are approximately 16,000 rural schools within a metropolitan statistical area and approximately 8,000 outside these areas. These schools are challenged by the limited number of personnel and resources, particularly content specialists and technology. Some universities have created programs specific to rural high school students to take active part in college courses over the summer. These students are selected by high grade-point averages, motivation, and commitment. More attention, funds, and resources need to be made available to these communities, educators, and students. The federal government made some funds available through the Rural Education Achievement Program, allowing smaller rural schools to have access to these grants and personnel to aid in the application process. Unfortunately President Bush's new economic plan cut this funding, which left many puzzled. But Congress is extremely supportive of rural schools and improving conditions for these schools; therefore they may likely revisit this issue in order to reinstate funding.

In the educational literature more focus has been placed on the relationship between rural schools and communities.

- A healthy relationship between rural communities and their schools is crucial to school effectiveness and the communities' quality of life.
- Although it is impossible for rural communities to alter global changes that put them at risk, they can have broad-based local discussions; develop agreed-upon policies; and pursue educational, civic, and economic activities that enhance their sustainability and growth.

↝ Rural students must be prepared to work, learn, and live well, not only as participants in the global economy but also as citizens in their own communities.

↝ Rural schools, as central institutions in rural life, must assume a role in community economic development. (Collins 2001, 15–16)

Rural schools are held accountable to the same standards and policies as urban and suburban schools without true consideration of the drastic differences in geography, context, values, and resources. Urban educational models do not function as well in the rural setting. Different things are prioritized in rural schools, such as personal relationships, small-scale organization, high quality of life, democratic ideals and practices, small class size, personalized instruction, cooperative learning, opportunities for student participation in school activities, and parental involvement (Collins 2001). Rural schools can maximize their own community resources by reconceptualizing the school and its educational model. Several educators and researchers have suggested different models: the school as a community center, a lifelong learning center and vehicle for delivering numerous services; the community as curriculum, emphasizing the community in all of its complexities as part of students' learning activities in the classroom; the school as a developer of entrepreneurial skills; and the role of new technologies in building and preserving the community while linking the students to the rest of the world (Collins 2001, 18; Nachtigal 1994; Hobbs 1987; Sher 1977; Odasz 1999).

Essentially the physical distance of the rural school from the urban center can compound the lack of resources and accessibility to the information and skills students need. However, many rural schools are privileged in their access to other resources, primarily the environment, which can be an excellent bridge between school knowledge and life knowledge. Curriculum is integrated to take advantage of what nature provides, particularly in science, reading, social studies, and the arts. These conditions also provide the foundation for an ecological consciousness and a closer relationship with and understanding of the surroundings. Place-based curriculum projects are also very common in rural schools, similar to the service-learning curriculum often implemented in urban schools. The use of technology is also helping students receive the same services and resources as the urban and suburban schools. Often times because rural schools are more isolated the push and demand for technology are greater. In comparison, it is not surprising to find a higher rate of rural students using the Internet and computer skills than other students. The need seems more immediate. Rural schools are inviting more and more business partnerships into the schools to increase the resources and preparation for their students.

MILITARY SCHOOLS

Military schools are private institutions offering junior high, high school, and two-year college preparation. Some schools are all-male and others are coeducational, some are boarding schools and others day schools. The academic standards remain the same as in public schools with the exception of fewer electives and specified discipline area courses. The military training is undoubtedly at the center of the curriculum for these schools, yet they have comprehensive art programs and other extracurricular programs. Students are called cadets and are all prepared for college. These schools provide small class sizes and individual attention for all students. Military schools are found all over the nation.

COLLEGE PREPARATORY SCHOOLS

College preparatory schools devote themselves to the undivided preparation of students for prestigious colleges and universities. These schools are usually private and conduct International Baccalaureate programs or other Ivy League preparation programs. These are coeducational and usually found in large cities all over the nation. The school board governs them. The competition is steep at college prep schools, subsequently their course offerings are extensive and considered extremely rigorous. Advanced placement courses and honors-level work are required in addition to acceptable extracurricular activities that exhibit qualities desired by universities.

TECHNICAL SCHOOLS AND INSTITUTES

These schools are primarily vocational educational centers focusing entirely on preparing youth for the workforce or offering traditional academic courses alongside the vocational curriculum. Technical schools are usually found in larger cities or rural areas. They used to be single-sex schools but are now coeducational. Many schools may also offer split shifts so that students go to a regular high school for part of the day and spend the other part at the trade or technical school. Technical or vocational schools offer a variety of courses, such as cosmetology, industrial arts, fashion illustration and design, culinary arts, hospitality management, business education, technology education, computer science, carpentry and woodwork, mechanics, child care, medical technician and assistant training, and many more opportunities that may translate into a specific profession or employment with greater ease. Many schools offer certificate programs as well.

CHARTER SCHOOLS

Charter schools are usually public schools that serve as alternatives to the conventional school. These schools function primarily outside of district bureaucracy, as they set up their own rules and guidelines. Charter schools may be on three- to five-year contracts. The charter-granting body requires schools to meet performance outcomes, specifically increased student achievement. Charter schools outline the school's mission, program, goals, students served, methods of assessment, and ways to measure success. At the end of the contract, the body granting the charter evaluates the school and renews the contract or closes the school. The schools are accountable to their school board or sponsor. Weil (2000) defines charters as public schools under contract.

> These contracts, or charters, are granted from a public agency to a
> group of parents, teachers, school administrators, nonprofit agencies,
> organizations, or businesses that wish to create an alternative to exist-
> ing public schools in order to provide choice within the public school
> system. Charter schools receive public money and cannot legally dis-
> criminate or exclude students. They are also publicly accountable; they
> are not private schools. (6)

Therefore charter schools must abide by the standards and means of measurement adopted by the district and state. These schools must also show marked improvement as a result of their instruction or curriculum. Charter schools develop their own curriculum, mission statements, and standards that the board and educators agree on, yet they cannot lose sight of the district and state standards since these can be used against them in denying a continuation of their contract. Charter schools give educators and parents or community members the opportunity to create the kind of schools they envision for their students or children. The governance for charter schools in theory is said to be more democratic where parents, teachers, administrators, and students have a collective and shared decisionmaking process.

According to Bastian (1996) there are three types of charter schools.

> First are charter schools that are created out of existing public schools by teachers, parents, and community members and that take on a new mission, or charter, and create a new kind of school. Such charter schools operate under the umbrella of an existing public school district and generally within existing regulations and union contracts. They are often called charter schools, although they may not have a separate legal "charter" or special contract.
>
> A second kind of charter school would be new schools that are started from scratch within the public school system and run under a special "charter" or contract with either a local district or state. They tend to operate independently while still being part of the public school system, and may be exempted from some state and local regulations.
>
> A third kind of charter, related to the second, is a newly created, independent school run by a private entity or business. (45)

Charter schools are thematic or specific in the focus of the curriculum. The schools may serve a particular part of the population or offer a distinct focus in their curriculum and instruction. Schools are smaller in population, allowing for smaller classes and greater interaction between student and teacher. These schools also offer greater variety for educators and less standardized restrictions. The community and parents also have greater access and involvement. The first charter school opened in Minnesota in 1991 and they spread nationwide. As with all movements there are some critics who fear this will increase inequity and stratification of access. Others view charter schools as the first step to the privatization of public schooling and they strongly object.

Some very interesting curricular options are happening through charter schools at the high school level. These options range from completely online courses, to service-learning opportunities, to dual enrollment with local community colleges and universities, to traditional high school programs. Charter high schools offered online are usually for residents of a particular district and require specific equipment in order to enroll. This type of charter school caters to students who may have transportation difficulties, disabled students, students for whom the traditional high school setting is counterproductive, homeschoolers, and any other student who has had trouble in regular high schools. All courses are offered online tuition-free; in fact these are considered cyber charter schools. Most schools coordinate cyber meeting times in order to discuss subject matter and assignments, and they may use traditional distance learning strategies where both students and teachers can see each other through Web cameras.

There also exist charter schools that rely almost completely on service-learning opportunities, internships, off-site work, and seminar-style meeting times. These schools provide the best of integrating hands-on and real-life experiences into the school curriculum. With the small number of students enrolled at charter schools, coordinating these partnerships is a lot easier. The success of these programs heavily depends on the commitment and effort of educators and students. Students understand the need to be involved with and connect to the community firsthand. This form of charter schools works very well with students for whom the traditional high school was hampering their learning instead of nurturing it.

Many charter schools are creating fascinating curriculum around technology and media. Students are taught not only to understand the technology, but also to create and design it. Business partnerships and collaborations with local institutions of higher education provide the benefits of resources and support otherwise unavailable. Students gain sophisticated knowledge in manipulating media and media literacy. These programs offer curriculum options usually unavailable to high school students. Diversifying curriculum in this way allows students to maintain a connection to learning and ensures the probability of continued schooling. Most of the charter high schools also help students with college admissions and graduation.

Other charter schools have taken these concerns for college enrollment a step further by offering dual enrollment in college and high school. In collaboration with local community colleges and universities, high school students enroll in college courses for both high school credit and college credit. Their tuition is half paid by the charter schools and there are scholarships available as well. Some districts will even cover book fees. These charter schools want to ensure success for students at the college level while they still have the support services of the high school. The schools also want to make sure students are adequately challenged by their educational experiences, and the dual enrollment is one way to achieve this.

All of these different forms of charter schools at the high school level speak to the immense imagination, creativity, and commitment of educators and concerned citizens all over the nation in making public education a significant and fulfilling experience for the nation's youth. On the average these schools have been in operation for five to seven years, proving their consistent success. These educators also understand the importance of student learning and the diversity through which it needs to occur.

MAGNET SCHOOLS

During the 1960s, 1970s, and 1980s, "alternative," "open," or "free" schools offered high-quality education to students in need.

> In the United States during the 1960s, some options to public schools sprang up as a protest against racially segregated schools. They emphasized the basic subjects of reading, writing, and arithmetic, but they also included the history of African Americans, what the civil rights movement was all about, and how schools could be tied to community needs. Some of these, called street academies, led to more permanent structures. Harlem Prep, for example, first funded by foundations, businesses, and industry, became one of the public schools of New York City. (www.magnet.edu)

This movement grew and was said to act as "magnets" for students. Public schools created magnet schools all over the nation to provide a variety of educational opportunities for the diverse student body. Magnet schools are education centers that offer a special curriculum with a unifying theme or different organizational structure (primarily block scheduling) created to attract students from different racial backgrounds. Magnet schools were conceptualized to address racial segregation in school enrollment and to provide access to curriculum otherwise not offered in traditional schools to all students. Magnet schools offer an in-depth study of the arts, science, math, technology, career orientations, and so on. The federal government provides funds for these programs, sometimes spending much more on magnet school programs than on the traditional schools (www.magnet.edu). Any student can apply, and students are chosen by a lottery system, not by merit. Most magnet schools are not held accountable to district or state standards and are not pressured to show improvement or fulfillment of their objectives.

These are governed in similar ways to traditional public schools. These schools are considered schools of choice under the larger school districts. Magnet schools have become increasingly popular as parents and students seek better educational opportunities. Many times these magnet programs will be housed within traditional schools.

SMALL SCHOOLS

These schools are created as alternatives to the large comprehensive public high school. The main difference is the size and reduced number of students who attend these schools. The intent of small schools is to create a more productive and intimate learning environment in order to best suit the needs of students who have had problems with the traditional high school. This restructuring is also extremely conducive to improved collaboration among parents, community, and schools. Each small school is unique to the community that it serves; however, there are some common features that often characterize good small schools.

- A maximum population of 250–300 students in a heterogeneous mix that represents the local school community
- A nonexclusive admissions policy
- A consistent educational experience for students over an extended period of time (more than one year)
- A coherent focus and philosophy of education, and a curriculum that is integrated around that focus
- A cohesive group of teachers who collaborate and discuss the needs of their students
- A sense of shared leadership and investment among those in the small school
- Involvement of families in the school community

Each small school may be configured differently. Small schools may be:

- Free-standing small schools: Small schools with their own facilities and administration
- Schools-within-schools: One or more small schools that develop within a larger, "host" school
- Multiplex: One building specifically intended to house several small schools
- Scatterplex: Two or more small schools at different sites that share a principal
- Charter schools: Independent, often small, public schools, designed and operated by educators, parents, community

leaders, educational entrepreneurs, and others (www.
smallschoolsworkshop.org)

Small schools are considered a method of restructuring the school and
curriculum in order to provide a higher quality of educational experiences. These schools have a smaller number of students, yet this may
not necessarily mean a smaller class size. Professionals argue, however,
that

> some of the benefits of small class size (more personalized instruction
> and more manageable classroom atmosphere) can be achieved in a
> small school regardless of class size. A small school offers an environ-
> ment in which students are more visible. In other words, students can be
> better known by their teachers, allowing teachers to more easily identify
> individual talents and unique needs of each student and therefore offer a
> more personalized educational experience. A small school staff size
> allows more opportunity for teachers to know each other well, more eas-
> ily share information about their students, collaborate to solve problems,
> and generally support one another. (www.smallschoolsworkshop.org)

There is an increasing number of studies and research being done on
small schools. Both the federal government and private corporations
(like the Bill and Melinda Gates Foundation, offering $31 million) are
providing grant monies for programs and individuals wanting to take
advantage of this educational initiative.

INDEPENDENT BLACK SCHOOLS

These are independent African-centered high schools created in
response to the substandard education given to African American students in this country. Segregation and cognitive theories of cultural defi-
ciency further compounded inferior educational experiences. After
1954, desegregation was slow to take effect, but even when it did, integration did not exactly ensure a higher quality of education. In many
cases desegregation increased difficult situations and racial tensions for
students and families. Independent black schools grew out of the need
to provide quality educational programs for African American children.
Rivers and Lomotey (1998) list two elements that are common for these
schools, "the sincere belief that all children can and will learn, and the
belief that cultural knowledge is important" (346). Educators set high
expectations and standards for all students.

> IBI educators emphasize manual work and stress the importance of being able to perform both manual and mental work. Self-expression is encouraged and students are constantly challenged to think analytically, critically, and independently. They are also charged with working creatively and productively for their personal survival as well as for the survival of the African community/nation. (Rivers and Lomotey 1998, 346)

The curriculum is holistic and student-centered with the intent to make learning relevant to the student year-round and not just during Black History Month. The community is central in the school and increasing student self-esteem is a concern. Educators use a variety of strategies (cooperative learning, curriculum integration and differentiation, and individual instruction) to ensure students feel as though they are part of a connected social and cultural community. The Seven Principles of Blackness (Nguzo Saba in Kiswahili) are used throughout the curriculum and as the stated value system and moral foundation for independent black schools. These principles are unity (Umoja), self-determination (Kujichagulia), collective work and responsibility (Ujima), cooperative economics (Ujamaa), purpose (Nia), creativity (Kuumba), and faith (Imani). Educators are to foster a sense of family in their classrooms and parents are intricately involved in the schools. Academically, students are very successful even on traditional standardized tests. The change in curriculum and philosophy meets the needs of students and teachers to create successful and productive learning environments. The curriculum and school structure validate and provide extensive studies in African American history and African American contributions to the United States. Learning is therefore contextualized and discovered in ways that connect the knower to the known without excluding or negating other ways of knowing.

COMMUNITY-BASED ORGANIZATION SCHOOLS

These are public schools that are operated and governed by community-based organizations (CBO), which offer diploma-granting academic programs. These schools use experiential learning through community service in combination with positive adult relationships. These schools offer alternative options for students who struggled in traditional schools. CBO schools serve fifteen- to twenty-one-year-olds. The philosophical framework behind these schools is based on positive youth development principles providing a caring and supportive environment that engages the students in broader educational experiences and services. The educational programs focus on five areas: high and comprehensive standards, relevant and diverse learning opportunities, personalized and flexible learning environments, support and services for effective learning, and opportunities to make a contribution. More information on these schools can be found through the Academy for Educational Development (AED) Center for Youth Development and Policy Research.

DEMOCRATIC SCHOOLS

Democratic schools are mainly traditional public schools, yet through the work of teachers, students, parents, and administrators are differentiated by their curriculum. These schools are harder to detect since they are not a separate legislated body receiving special funds. These schools and classrooms are the grassroots efforts of committed people. These schools and classrooms believe in integrated curriculum, thematic units, community involvement, problem-centered inquiry-based curriculum, and critical analysis of what is being learned, excluded, and why. These schools take risks in redefining positions of authority, access, equality, and student voice in order to exercise more authentically democratic principles. Democratic schools are intended to exercise and extend the meaning of democracy for the present and future. School governance, committees, and councils involve administrators and teachers, students, their parents, and community members. In the classroom teachers and students engage in curriculum design and implementation. It is a collaborative approach. Tracking, biased testing, and other inequitable practices are eliminated and contested. The schools engage in transforming the undemocratic practices and conditions that produce inequity and lack of access to quality education for all. Curriculum and school organization address these issues directly. There are fewer schools that actively take on this fight, but Apple and Beane discuss exemplary schools in their book *Democratic Schools.*

COALITION CAMPUS SCHOOL PROJECT

This is a small school program created as an effort to move toward systemwide reform in 1992 by the New York City Board of Education and the Center for Collaborative Education. This project was initiated in New York City as a way to improve and redefine the comprehensive high school. Two large high schools were involved, Julia Richman High

School in Manhattan and James Monroe High School in the Bronx. These schools were considered neighborhood schools that served about 3,000 students each with graduation rates lower than 40 percent. The objective was to create smaller communities of learning. These small schools used looping techniques (teachers remain with the same class for two consecutive grades), block scheduling, comprehensive assessments, teacher teams, common planning time, involvement of school staff and parents, and cooperative learning. The curriculum is mainly college preparation framed by five "habits of mind," such as weighing evidence, addressing multiple perspectives, making connections, speculating on alternatives, and assessing the value of ideas (Darling-Hammond, Ancess, and Wichterle Ort 2002). Each new small school received a title according to its thematic mission, for example, Coalition School for Social Change, Landmark High School, Legacy School for Integrated Studies, Manhattan International High School, Manhattan Village Academy, and Vanguard High School. These small schools had higher attendance rates and fewer problems with misbehavior. Each school also used advisory groups, tutorial sessions, separate reading classes, and more frequent parent conferences to suit the students' needs. It took these schools several years to resolve initial student and staff issues, but the outcomes were worth the pains of growth. Student test scores increased and remained on the average at 80 percent.

SINGLE-SEX SCHOOLS

These junior high schools or high schools are either all-female or all-male schools. They may be public or private church-related schools serving either population. Many studies support assumptions of increased academic achievement, particularly for girls, but consistently for boys as well. Other studies discuss the findings to be inconclusive and point out that Title IX, as a federal statute, prohibits sex discrimination in federally funded educational programs. The issue of single-sex education is heavily debated throughout the nation. Most of the single-sex schools are religious or church-affiliated and therefore private, quickly changing the nature of the discussion. Yet in many other cases, public school administrators and teachers are deciding to create single-sex classrooms for specific subject matter. Traditionally it has been done for sex education and by default in home economics courses or woodshop. But these educators are making conscious decisions to split science and math courses at the middle, junior high, and high school levels. Many of these schools report an increased positive performance in academic achievement for both female and male students. These are attempts to remedy self-esteem issues (mostly for girls), low interest in science and math, peer sexual harassment, gender inequities in the classroom, and dropout rates (Salomone 1999).

Historically the United States has a long tradition of single-sex education; all-female and all-male elite academies were established shortly after the arrival of European settlers in the Northeast of the nation. These institutions were heavily involved in continuing the aristocracy and the curriculum was explicit and strict to achieve these goals. The academies needed to produce respectable, moral citizens who would fulfill their roles as ladies and gentlemen. The education of young women was second to that of young men. The establishment of academies for young women was a reaction to the exclusive all-male institutions in the 1700s and 1800s.

Today there are twelve public single-sex schools reported (all-girl and all-boy) in the United States, five of which are members of the National Coalition of Girls' Schools: Jefferson Leadership Academy (Long Beach, California), Philadelphia High School for Girls, Western High School (Baltimore), The Young Women's Leadership School (New York City), and The Young Women's Leadership Charter School (Chicago) (www.ncgs.org). As part of President Bush's No Child Left Behind policy to reform America's school system, the Education Department will be pushing for the creation of single-sex public schools. Many scholars and educators advocate strongly for either side, and legally there are many other issues to contend with in deciding the fate of single-sex schools in the United States.

Gender equity is a major issue on either side of the single-sex school discussion. Many worry that boys and their education are overlooked. The probability is quite high that both boys and girls are disadvantaged by current educational practices and as a result of the social conditions of schools and classrooms. The development of self-esteem, self-worth, confidence, and awareness is essential for both genders. To reform power inequities in society both females and males must learn about the miseducation of patriarchy. Stereotypical gender constructions provide a disservice to both females and males in every aspect of their life. Authors like David Sadker, Myra Sadker, and William Pollock contribute a great deal to the public's understanding of educational gender inequities for both boys and girls.

The Brighter Choice Charter School model provides a charter school for each gender in one facility that shares one administration, faculty, and staff. This is one way to provide cross gender socialization and retain single-sex academic structures. This particular approach attempts to provide equitable experiences for both male and female students (www.brighterchoice.org). Even though Brighter Choice Charter School is an elementary school, its structure and philosophy provide a potential method for secondary school reorganization.

Single-sex schools may become more popular through charters in the public school system; subsequently communities, parents, teachers, students, and administrators will have access to more educational choice and opportunities to make significant impacts on youth lives.

CHURCH-RELATED SCHOOLS

Church-related, parochial, and theological schools are usually independent or private schools. Some are closely tied to particular institutions of faith and others are not. Generally these types of schools provide an overt value and belief system for their students. The curriculum may be infused with theology or other faith-based education. Some of the schools accomplish great academic achievement through their mission, commitments, and discipline. These schools may also provide single-sex educational facilities, which may increase achievement as well. The governance for these schools consists of the usual school officials and a parent council or government. Overseeing both of these bodies is the ranking religious official of the related parochial entity.

HOME SCHOOLING

Home schooling provides individualized instruction in the home by parents or caretakers for their children. Many states require that adults serving in these capacities have appropriate and current teacher certifications. There are many resources that outline the course of study by grade and subject through the twelfth grade.

There has been a considerable rise in home schooling since the 1970s and 1980s. More and more parents consider it a viable option in taking control over their children's education. This choice used to be more common for families with ultrareligious belief systems, but this does not seem to be the leading cause anymore. Greg Toppo (2001) reports 850,000 children and youth were schooled at home in 1999, with most homes having two parents and two or more children. Parents are truly seeking a better quality of education. Toppo also notes that most homeschoolers recognize the importance of plugging into a network of other kids and families, and they use field trips and the Internet to make connections with other students.

The [1999 national] survey found that about 18 percent of homeschoolers were enrolled in schools part time, with about 11 percent saying they used books or materials from public schools. About 8 percent said they used public school curriculums, and about 6 percent participated in extracurricular activities. (www.abcnews.com)

In the home schooling movement, as in any school movement, there are many philosophies and methods of instruction. The following list provides a brief overview of each method or philosophy within the home schooling field:

Charlotte Mason Method—Charlotte Mason (1842–1923) was an innovative British educator who developed a unique approach to education. There are Charlotte Mason books and one of her mottos is "Education is an Atmosphere, a Discipline, a Life." Mason's strategies in her educational practice included narration and copywork, nature notebooks, fine arts, languages (English, Latin, French, and German), a literature-based curriculum instead of textbooks, and real-life applications.

Classical Education Method—Dorothy Sayers's well-known essay "The Lost Tools of Learning" is the basis of the new classical Christian education movement. This method attempts to tailor the subject matter to a student's cognitive development, promote critical thinking skills, and provide a moral foundation as well. Students analyze and use the trivium (the three laws of learning: grammar—grades 1–6, dialectic—grades 7–9, rhetoric—grades 10–12) and its components in order to maximize ideas for the practical application of classical education.

Eclectic Home Schooling Method—An eclectic homeschooler is one who looks at the different approaches and methods of home schooling and takes from each, forming his or her own unique philosophy. Most families following this path enjoy the incredible creativity and flexibility eclecticism affords. Families will search for resources and approaches that best suit the students, contexts, and subject matter to be learned.

Montessori Method—According to Dr. Maria Montessori (1870–1952), learning is a natural, self-directed process that follows certain fundamental laws of nature. The Montessori class environment is centered around cultural, artistic, and scientific activities. The student is not usually forced to learn, but rather considered and observed to assess his or her interests and the lessons are tailored to suit. The teacher is to model appropriate behavior and act primarily as a guide.

Traditional or School-at-Home Method—Traditional home schools would be set up public school–style with a complete curriculum, traditional grading system, and record keeping.

Unit Studies Approach—The unit studies approach integrates all school subjects together into one theme or topic. The units are structured as multidisciplinary, interdisciplinary, or fully integrated. Each unit integrates different subject matter or disciplines through an idea, theme, or skill that significantly weaves knowledge and experiences together.

Unschooling, or Natural Learning, Method—Unschooling, or natural learning, is a philosophy of child-led learning. In unschooling there is no set curriculum, but rather an exploration of knowledge as it is experienced or sought out. This method does not replicate the school (with power hierarchies between teacher, student, and knowledge) at home; parents or caretakers do not act as the expert or teacher. Both parents and youth are fellow learners and lived experience is the teacher and curriculum. Unschooling is not a technique that can be understood through a step-by-step process. Unschooling is described more as an attitude, a way of life. The focus is more on who is learning as opposed to what is learned. Therefore these learning conditions are not conducive to standardized curriculum. Learning is seen as an ongoing process, happening anywhere and everywhere as a natural process. Students are made responsible for their learning since they are constructing the curriculum as they go. It is an inquiry-based system of learning. For high school students this proves incredibly useful and engaging as it allows students to pursue their interests in an individualized open structure with limitless resources.

Waldorf Education Method—Waldorf education is based on the spiritual-scientific research of the Austrian scientist and thinker Rudolf Steiner (1861–1925). According to his philosophy, man is a threefold being of spirit, soul, and body whose capacities unfold in three developmental stages. This type of home schooling balances artistic, academic, and practical work in order to suit the whole child and provide a holistic education. The objective is to teach to the student's developmental level, to never lose sight of the learner. There is also great emphasis on the arts, as Steiner believed the arts are essential to acquiring and living a complete life. Academics are always in balance with the arts. As students figure their way through this type of learning they are supported through their discoveries and difficulties. A sense of community and learning for the self is highly prioritized. Home schooling is not the only place for this philosophy; there are many schools and small colleges around the nation following the Waldorf philosophy. (//homeschooling.about.com)

FULL-SERVICE SCHOOLS

Full-service schools are based on a holistic approach to education. The idea originated in the 1980s and Florida was the first state to provide "full service schools that integrate education, medical, social and/or human services that are beneficial to meeting the needs of children and youth and their families on school grounds" (www.saee.bc.ca/art2000_2_2.html). The majority of these schools exist in highly impacted areas where these combined services are most needed. Many studies discuss the benefits of these schools for students who are deemed "at-risk." The following are examples of provided services: stay-in-school initiatives, school meals, parenting classes, adult education, English as a second language classes, citizenship, conflict resolution, training for parent volunteers, preschool and child care services, extended school day, drop-in homework center, open computer labs, libraries and gyms, summer school, employment center for parents and youth, arts enrichment, health services for students and families, thrift shops, youth community volunteer programs, home visits, parent support coordinator, antidrug and antigang programs, storefront schools for street youth, reading and literacy programs, cultural pride programs, counseling services, tutoring services, links to postsecondary, and youth apprenticeship programs. Services vary by school depending on the needs of the students and community. Schools over a period of time have increased the services they provide for a community. Full-service schools are also growing more common in rural areas. Schools continue to be a staple in our society, and as a result of the inaccessibility of services for families, schools have provided needed assistance.

For these schools to succeed, given their complex structure, leadership is extremely important. Leadership for full-service schools may be provided by the principal and his or her staff or a project coordinator who may oversee the joint action plans and services. Community involvement is key in order for the larger needs to be met appropriately.

YEAR-ROUND SCHOOLS

Year-round schools provide educational services all year round. Twelve-month schedules are regarded as a solution to overcrowding in a growing number of districts because they allow schools to serve additional students in shortened, overlapping terms.

The following are descriptions of the many ways year-round schools are scheduled:

- ◆ Block 45/15: All students are placed on a single track and attend the same nine-week instructional blocks and three-week vacation blocks.
- ◆ Flexible 45/15: Individualized instruction is used so that students may jump tracks for special reasons on five nine-week learning blocks and three-week vacation blocks.
- ◆ Staggered block, flexible 90/20: Students rotate through three sixty-day instruction blocks and three twenty-day vacation periods, with one of four groups always on vacation.
- ◆ Concept 8: Eight six-week terms with students selecting or being assigned six of the eight terms.
- ◆ Concept 16: Sixteen three-week terms (students select twelve of the sixteen terms).
- ◆ Multiple access: A partially individualized 45/15 plan in which students can enter or leave at any three-week interval, with the curriculum in three-week or nine-week units.
- ◆ Quarter plan: Four twelve-week terms with students selecting or being assigned three of the four terms.
- ◆ Quinmester: Five nine-week quinmesters with students selecting or being assigned four of the five quins.
- ◆ Extended school year: More than 180-day calendar with staggered blocks.
- ◆ Summer term: A conventional nine-month calendar but full summer terms that offer continuous learning integrated with the nine-month curriculum rather than short, six-week, discontinuous summer school courses.
- ◆ Flexible all year: School is open 240 days with students selecting 180 days. The curriculum consists of small, self-paced packages

to allow for uninterrupted learning blocks and differentiated vacation periods of one to several weeks at a time. (Wiles and Bondi 2002, 312)

Schools can service more students this way and can expand the programs and academic tracks available to students. Inger (1994) adds, "In a year-round school, students attend school the same number of days as students on the traditional nine-month calendar. However, year-round education students have several short vacations rather than one 3-month summer break. By switching to a year-round calendar, districts can fit more students into existing school buildings, saving millions of dollars in construction costs."

Yet very little support exists for year-round schooling at the secondary level. Opponents contend the school year is shortened and therefore critical changes to curriculum content must be made to accommodate the new schedule. Students are often disappointed when important events (such as college recruiting, study sessions for standardized tests and AP exams, and so on) occur in the school when they are on vacation. Some students cannot take advantage of summer employment or internships. Many students also find it difficult to find out about school events when they are away from school. Many scholars and educators argue that the year-round schools are found in the city where conditions are already pressing learning environments while in the suburbs schools are built and not condensed. In Los Angeles's Unified district, eighteen of forty-nine high schools are year-round, and district officials say the remaining thirty-one will follow by 2006. Similarly, seventeen of seventy-two middle schools are year-round, but officials expect the number to more than double in the next five years (Helfand 2000). There are a few year-round schools in New York, Chicago, Philadelphia, Miami, and Houston, but Los Angeles exceeds their combined numbers. Educators are concerned that the year-round schedule further disadvantages students, hampers their learning, and shortchanges their opportunities, particularly through a multitrack schedule.

Some year-round schools do not stagger their student population and schedules; instead students take shorter vacations throughout the year in place of a longer summer vacation. Therefore, the whole school is on vacation simultaneously, as in traditional schools, during summer and holiday seasons. In the staggered schedule, while some students are on vacations, others are attending class. This configuration excludes part of the student population all the time, almost by default, from events. The harshest criticism is directed toward the staggered schedule in the Los Angeles Unified district because of the concentration of poor and minority students in the area. The proposed relief in overcrowding through this schedule never came through. Most schools increased their population significantly through the staggered track schedule since they could service more students. In reality, overcrowding worsened, curriculum was modified to include less, days were made longer, and students learned less and had access to fewer opportunities.

Educators are constantly asked to change classrooms between terms and during the day. This commonly is the condition through which art and music teachers must operate, out of a cart. In this type of school the majority of teachers, regardless of subject matter, must operate this way. The different tracks produce similar inequities as do traditional schools, yet many critics say these inequities are exacerbated through the year-round schedule. There are many problems with the staggered-track schedule and seemingly fewer with single-track year-round schools. These types of solutions to overcrowding obviously need to be carefully thought out and weighed with other options. Year-round schools are still not the most popular around the nation for many of the reasons described above.

VIRTUAL SCHOOLS

A "virtual school" is "an educational organization offering courses designed for K–12 learners through distance learning methods that include Web-based delivery" (www.dlrn.org/virtual.html). Technology has made the possibility of completing a high school degree from the comfort of home a reality. There are full-fledged tuition-based schools available online, as well as just coursework, and GED opportunities. Some schools are free if you are a resident of the state in which they are based. Distance education has been made available for the older adolescent or adult. These schools may be governed or sponsored by a company or a school district and school board. Some of the schools are fully accredited. Universities and colleges offer some independent study courses for high school students through continuing education programs. The increase in virtual schools or cyber schools also speaks to the attempt to cater to the diversity of the student body in the United States. Parents and communities grow increasingly disheartened by the state of public education and the struggle of youth within these institutions. As a result these new sites for learning afforded by advances in technology may be the only viable way for students to complete their high school education.

OTHER SCHOOLS, EXTRACURRICULAR
ACTIVITIES, AND SCHOOL ATHLETICS

Important to realize is that this chapter provides a general description of different schools, yet there are many more under other particular specialties (religious, organizational, cultural) that provide opportunities for students, parents, and communities. The extracurricular activities offered by many schools often create separate curriculum for students. These educational and social experiences cannot be overlooked given the incredible impact they have on students, parents, and schools.

The engagement in extracurricular activities is said to reduce high school dropout rates, especially for at-risk students. In a longitudinal study, Mahoney and Cairns (1997) followed about 400 students from middle school and high school. Engagement was measured by the extent of extracurricular participation in athletics, student government, student clubs, music or drama, journalism, and school assistantships. The number of middle school and high school dropouts significantly declined for students with higher levels of extracurricular involvement. Many experts also favor extracurricular activities as positive influences in engaging students in the learning experience as well as providing closer ties to their school.

School athletics provide another venue through which students can excel and connect to the school environment. There is an additional hidden curriculum in school athletics that adds to the school image and may increase school resources. This is another site for creating different schooling and learning experiences for all involved. School athletics are said to be particularly helpful in the development of self-esteem, leadership, and team-building skills for female students through healthy and active participation in sports and fitness. The same argument has been made for male students. Engaging both the body and mind of the student increases the ways in which knowledge is understood and applied. Unfortunately unless a student shows athletic ability or interest, these opportunities are not made available. The pressure to meet standardized test scores also jeopardizes the existence of athletic programs during the school day, limiting the opportunities for physical activity even more for the majority of students. Health education and physical fitness need to be incorporated for all students at the secondary school level in order to increase the probability of securing a healthy lifestyle in the future.

Overall there are many educational opportunities for adolescents to learn in thriving and nurturing environments, yet parents and students need to research these options and make the decisions that are best suited for them. This is, of course, easier said than done for some families who do not have access to research them or do not have the means to secure the transportation or tuition necessary to take advantage of them. More efforts need to be made to provide literally all students, and particularly those in most need, with the educational opportunities available to the few. If this does not occur we continue to perpetuate a society divided by class stratification and prejudice, feeding the ground for more disparity than success. The U.S. commitment to education must overextend itself in ways that history has not exhibited. If the United States indeed wants to improve its educational landscape, schools and professionals must be free to create a variety of learning situations without the threat of decreasing funds or support if the results are not quantifiably measurable. Better standards do not mean more standards, but rather fewer, more select standards that are attainable and open to negotiation by the educators, students, and parents who have a vested interest in educational success. The examples provided in this chapter are the results of great struggle to provide a higher-quality education for youth. Many more opportunities still wait to be crafted by courageous educators, community leaders, parents, students, academic scholars, and organizations.

REFERENCES

Apple, Michael, and James Beane, eds. 1995. *Democratic Schools*. Association for Supervision and Curriculum Development.

Bastian, Ann. 1996. "Charter Schools: Potentials and Pitfalls." *Selling Out Our Schools: Vouchers, Markets, and the Future of Public Education*. Milwaukee: Rethinking Schools.

Collins, Timothy. 2001. "Rural Schools and Communities: Perspectives on Interdependence." *The Eric Review* 8, no. 2: 15–24.

Darling-Hammond, Linda, Jacqueline Ancess, and Susanna Wichterle Ort. 2002. "Reinventing High School: Outcomes of the Coalition Campus Schools Project." *American Educational Research Journal* 39, no. 3: 639–673.

French, W. M. 1967. *American Secondary Education*. 2nd ed. New York: The Odyssey Press.

Helfand, Duke. 2000. "Year-Round Discontent at Hollywood High." *Times Education*. //members.aol.com/donohoyrs/latimes.htm?mtbrand=AOL_US. Accessed November 20.

Hobbs, D. 1987. "Learning to Find the Niches: Rural Education and Vitalizing Rural Communities." Paper prepared for the National Rural Education

Research Forum, Lake Placid, NY, October 16–17. ERIC Document #ED301365.

Homeschooling. http://homeschooling.about.com. Accessed April 2003.

Index of Newsletter Articles. www.saee.bc.ca/art2000_2_2.html. Accessed February 2003.

Inger, Morton. 1994. "Year-Round Education: A Strategy for Overcrowded Schools." *ERIC Digests*. ED378267.

Magnet Schools of America. www.magnet.edu. Accessed March 2003.

Mahoney, J. L., and R. B. Cairns. 1997. "Do Extracurricular Activities Protect against Early School Dropout?" *Developmental Psychology* 33, no. 2: 242–253.

Nachtigal, P. M. 1994. "Rural Schools, Rural Communities: An Alternative View of the Future." Keynote address. In *Issues Affecting Rural Communities*. Proceedings of an International Conference held by the Rural Education Research and Development Centre (Townsville, Queensland, Australia, July 10–15). ERIC Document #ED390602.

National Center for Education Statistics. http://nces.ed.gov. Accessed January 2003.

The National Coalition of Girls' Schools. www.ncgs.org. Accessed April 2003.

National Middle School Association. www.nmsa.org. Accessed June 2003.

Odasz, F. 1999. "Culture Club: Building Learning Communities; A Youth-Driven, Cross-Cultural, Skills, and Storytelling Exchange." Lone Eagle Consulting. http://lone-eagles.com/articles/cultureclub.htmn.

Pollock, William. 1999. *Real Boys: Rescuing Our Sons from the Myths of Boyhood*. New York: Henry Holt.

Rivers, Shariba, and Kofi Lomotey. 1998. "Models of Excellence: Independent African-Centered Schools." In William W. Pinar, ed. *Curriculum: Toward New Identities*. New York: Garland Publishing.

Sadker, Myra, and David Sadker. 1995. *Failing at Fairness: How America's Schools Cheat Girls*. New York: Simon and Schuster.

Salomone, Rosemary. 1999. "Single-Sex Schooling: Law, Policy, and Research." In Diane Ravitch, ed. *Brookings Papers on Education Policy*. Washington, DC: Brookings Institution.

Sher, J. P. 1977. "Pluralism in the Country-side: A Brief Profile of Rural America and Its Schools." In J. P. Sher, ed. *Education in Rural America: A Reassessment of the Conventional Wisdom*, pp. 43–77. Boulder, CO: Westview Press.

Small Schools Workshop. www.smallschoolsworkshop.org. Accessed April 2003.

Toppo, Greg. 2001. "Study: 850,000 Kids Schooled at Home—Parents Better Educated, but Not Richer Than Most Americans." www.abcnews.com. Accessed April 2003.

Virtual School List Survey. www.dlrn.org/virtual.html. Accessed March 2003.

Weil, Danny. 2000. *Charter Schools: A Reference Handbook*. Santa Barbara, CA: ABC-CLIO.

Wiles, Jon, and Joseph Bondi. 2002. *Curriculum Development: A Guide to Practice*. Upper Saddle River, NJ: Merril Prentice-Hall.

Chapter Five

✑ The Standardization of Secondary Education

Standardization is heralded for its promises of equality and democracy. Throughout history educators and school systems have sought standardization of curricula and schooling practices in order to bring equity to all students and to universalize curriculum throughout the nation's high schools. In 1933 the Cooperative Study of Secondary School Standards was launched and later renamed the National Study of School Evaluation. The concern over standards began early in the twentieth century and grew stronger over time. Institutions of higher learning also depended on this standardization for admissions into college. The standardization of life and schools gained incredible popularity with the social efficiency movement in the early part of the twentieth century as well. Its popularity waned through different curriculum movements, but its presence is consistent through time, inadvertently speaking to its power over social life and individual capacity. Standardization is an attempt to make curriculum and schooling similar across schools, districts, states, and the nation. If all who attend schools are being taught similar things, educational testing corporations can create national tools through which to evaluate what students know when. Discipline standards also help educators evaluate student performance. High standards may facilitate better instruction and educational experiences. The American public finds comfort in standards, in having some marker to strive for or measure against. Standards in general can serve multiple purposes. Many progressive educators have issued their own set of high standards attempting to guide schools and education into the type of possibilities it should ensure for its members. Standards in general continue to generate a heated discussion in any area of education.

In all cases standards intend to measure competency and excellence. Usually standards-based reforms involve standards, assessment, and accountability. In the early twenty-first century, there is a concerted push for standards-based school reform on a national scale. District education boards, particularly in large cities, and President George W. Bush's administration want higher standards, more high-stakes tests, and incentives for teachers and schools who meet these. Standards, tests, and accountability measures are getting the interest of powerful corporations across the nation, which will continue to have an incredible amount of influence on the quality of education and the public's access to it. The standardization business is not benign. When business, money, and image coincide in a time of uncertain national cohesion and security, schools become prime agents for the reproduction of the desired future citizen. History repeats itself. Many progressive and social reconstructivist educators discussed this in the 1920s, 1930s, and 1940s, as well as in the 1980s and 1990s. As a nation we deny schools are businesses, yet do almost nothing when we see businesses taking over the nation's public schools and advocating for the privatization of these schools. Equity, diversity, and democracy are at stake, not just subject-matter competency skills. In this chapter the effect of standardization is explored and questioned.

STANDARDS

Standards are said to provide agreed-upon district, state, or national indicators for competence in different disciplines. These indicators, or standards, define what students should know and do in each grade and discipline. At the start of the twenty-first century it seems more pressing than ever to secure a means through which youth can be prepared for what awaits them. Lachat (2000) states, "Defining clear standards for student learning is thus an important first step in the process of educating children to be effective thinkers, problem-solvers, and communicators so they can reap the rewards of full participation in a technology-driven information age" (4).

There is a developing focus on global consciousness, yet this consciousness seems to benefit market values more than humanitarian efforts. Once again schools are seen as part of the training ground for the economic and technological system worldwide. Standards promoting technical skills, mastery, and memorization are not enough to carry the society successfully into this new century. Undoubtedly, high standards need to be in place in the educational system, but in order to prepare all students to truly coexist in a global environment, these standards must embrace the complexity needed to deal and wrestle with educational purpose, analysis, and quality. Kincheloe (2000) advocates:

> Any standards of worth not only must reflect the complexity of studying the world around us but must also be developed in concordance

with an exciting vision of education that respects the untapped capacities of human beings and the role that education can play in producing a just, inclusive, democratic, and imaginative future. (11)

Standards appear to be neutral but are laden with particular political, social, and economic agendas. Educators need to support standards, but must also be extremely vigilant and analytical of the standards they are aligning their instruction and pedagogy to. The U.S. public as well must be increasingly involved in how today's youth are educated and the effects this will have on tomorrow.

The history of standards begins with Benjamin Bloom's taxonomy in 1956. This taxonomy proposed a guide toward achieving high-order thinking skills. "The philosophies of Bloom were a driving force in the first uprising of standards-based reform, then called 'Outcome Based Reform' (OBE). Critics of OBE were dismayed by the non-definitive word 'outcome,' and it was soon changed to the current term, 'Standards-Based Reform'" (www.stanford.edu/~hakuta/CalTex_SBR/historysbr. html). Through the 1980s with the release of *A Nation at Risk,* more discussion developed around how to structure American education, primarily to compete worldwide.

There are three standards-based reform movements of the twentieth century that some historians discuss: authentic learning experiences (closely relating life and school knowledge), standards movement (defining clear standards for content and performance), and a call to educate all students (and helping them achieve at a high level). All three overlap in contemporary times: "These three trends, among others, have made an impact on what students are being taught in schools today. Curriculum developers and teachers have been hard pressed to keep up with the rapid changes in philosophy and goals" (www.hope. edu/academic/education/wessman/Secondary_Block_Revised/ standards/).

Decades later during the Clinton administration, *Goals 2000* was signed into law and exhibited another attempt to reorganize educational objectives and compete on a global scale in prioritizing math and science. The following captures the objectives of this national standards-based reform:

> At the heart of the Goals 2000 Act is a grants program designed to help states and communities develop and implement their own education reforms focused on raising student achievement. States participating in Goals 2000 are asked to raise expectations for students by setting challenging academic standards. Each state is to develop comprehensive

strategies for helping all students reach those standards—by upgrading assessments and curriculum to reflect the standards, improving the quality of teaching, expanding the use of technology, strengthening accountability for teaching and learning, promoting more flexibility and choice within the public school system, and building strong partnerships among schools and families, employers, and others in the community. Finally, each state is asked to develop its improvement strategies with broad-based, grassroots involvement.

States that participate in Goals 2000 receive seed money to help launch and sustain their ongoing education reform efforts. States are also given unprecedented flexibility through Goals 2000. No new regulations have been issued to implement the program, and states and local school districts can use Goals 2000 funds for a wide range of activities that fit within their own approaches to helping students reach higher standards. In addition, Goals 2000 expands flexibility in other federal education programs by providing the U.S. Secretary of Education and some states with the authority to waive many federal rules and regulations if they interfere with local or state education reform strategies.

Goals 2000 is a direct outgrowth of the state-led education reform movement of the 1980s. By the mid- to late-1980s a number of states had put in place a series of steps to improve education. Frequently, the state education reforms included increasing high school graduation requirements, particularly in math and science, instituting statewide testing programs, offering more Advanced Placement courses, promoting the use of technology in the classroom, and instituting new teacher evaluation programs. (www.ed.gov/G2K/GoalsRpt/intro.html)

Goals 2000 did not have a tremendous impact on actual instruction. Yet Bush's No Child Left Behind is creating a significant amount of discussion and trepidation on what it demands. Through this policy, standards are directly linked to high-stakes testing in particular grades on particular subjects, incentives for meeting the desired scores, and resources for special programs. The unfortunate outcome is the modification of instruction to the extent where educators find themselves teaching to the test. The danger of standardization is the transformation of learning to only experiencing what is on the test. This type of education deskills youth for today and tomorrow as opposed to increasing their abilities to succeed. The desired standard to educate all students seems contradictory through these means.

The Regents of the University of California's Lawrence Hall of Science provide the following considerations in administering a standards-based system:

Which standards should be used? National, state, or district?
What mix of knowledge and reasoning skills should standards
be based on?
Which knowledge? State capitals? Phases of the Moon? The peri-
odic table?
Who chooses the standards?
For which students? all students, or only the best?
What role should standards play? Should they be voluntary or
required? For schools? districts? states?
Do all students have an equal opportunity to learn?
Are there good standardized tests aligned to standards?
(www.lhsparent.org/standardreform.html)

These are a few questions to facilitate a closer assessment of the use of
standards in secondary education.

ASSESSMENTS

After the content standards are created, methods of assessment must be
aligned with them. Standardized tests have become the most popular
method of assessment. These tests are high-stakes, usually resulting in
retention, remedial work, or summer school for students who do not
meet the desired scores. These tests may be either end-of-grade tests for
each grade or for selected grades from second grade through eighth.
Recent reports state President Bush's policy is beginning testing as early
as in Head Start programs (www.childrensdefense.org; www.edweek.
org). It is important for educators to familiarize themselves with the
tests so that they effectively prepare their students to succeed. Yet many
educators have not been adequately prepared to teach test content,
subsequently disadvantaging their students. Many educators and
organizations loudly contest the exclusive use of high-stakes testing in
evaluating student knowledge. Student performance in the classroom is
said to be a much better indicator of what a student knows. Standardized tests as norm-reference tests offer "objectivity" and "reliability" in
easily quantifiable results. Again, educators and organizations protest
such objectifications of learning and students. Successful results on the
tests are also variable on many factors (teachers, training, resources,
and curriculum).

Cloud Duttweiler and McEvoy report, "Tests have become a universal measure of success in public schools. Principals and teachers
have received bonuses or been fired, students have been promoted or

retained in their current grade, and high school students have graduated or been denied a diploma based on test results" (http://virtual.clemson.edu/groups/clarkstudy/report1.htm). Assessment instruments are either formative or summative in nature. Formative assessments are used mainly to improve learning, such as a pretest. The results of formative tests allow the teacher to modify instruction based on student needs. Summative assessments evaluate whether students have met the prescribed standards for the grade or subject matter. The majority of standardized tests are summative in nature, proctored at the end of an academic year. If standardized tests were used as formative evaluations, it is foreseeable that many students would receive a higher-quality education because students would not be penalized for what they do not know. The use of current standardized tests as summative evaluations creates enormous problems and life alterations. These types of assessments restrict instruction considerably. Teachers find themselves teaching to the test and pedagogy is severely modified and restricted. Sanders and Horn (1995) add:

> No responsible person claims that any form of assessment can appraise the totality of a student's school experience or even the entirety of the learning that is a part of that experience. However, it is possible to develop indicators to measure learning along important dimensions, closely related to the curriculum, both in standardized assessment instruments and in alternative forms of assessment. (http://epaa.asu.edu/epaa/v3n6.html)

Alternative assessments to standardized tests allow teachers to individualize evaluation for each project or assignment or student. Yet the educational system is less likely to entrust the judgment of teachers than to standardize best practice. The assumption is that there is *a* right way to instruct. Standardized tests provide one effective way to simultaneously standardize teaching. By aligning instruction and assessment the formula for universalization of knowledge and success is created and practiced. The public comes to rely on the results from such standardization. There are many schools today that publish their test scores in the local paper to inform the public of its students' standing.

Popham (1999) states:

> A standardized test is any examination that's administered and scored in a predetermined, standard manner. There are two major kinds of standardized tests: aptitude tests and achievement tests.

Standardized *aptitude* tests predict how well students are likely to perform in some subsequent educational setting. The most common examples are the SAT-I and the ACT both of which attempt to forecast how well high school students will perform in college.

But standardized *achievement*-test scores are what citizens and school board members rely on when they evaluate a school's effectiveness. Nationally, five such tests are in use: California Achievement Tests, Comprehensive Tests of Basic Skills, Iowa Tests of Basic Skills, Metropolitan Achievement Tests, and Stanford Achievement Tests. (www.ascd.org/readingroom/edlead/9903/extpopham.html)

The erroneous assumption is that schools, students, and teachers can be evaluated by these measures alone. A teacher's effectiveness is demonstrated by his or her students' high or low test scores; a school's quality and resources are determined by the high or low scores of students as well. There seems to be an inordinate amount of weight and responsibility placed on students' scores. This message is loud and clear for many students given the commonplace discussion of the need to meet desired scores. Learning is then no longer the objective of the school or classroom, but rather a sort of rat race, of who can accomplish what when. The nation's schools are heavily swayed by some politicians and educators to understand the present use of these standardized tests as a good thing. Many parents, students, teachers, administrators, and communities in general are quite frustrated by the pressures to perform. Parents with enough resources will seek other options to educate their children. Even parents without resources are making serious sacrifices to provide better learning conditions for their children. The privatization of schools and the voucher system is not the answer, but many families are opting for these means as the lesser of two evils.

In and of themselves standardized tests are not necessarily obstructive to the learning process, yet their use as the sole means of measuring academic performance is. Effective schooling programs have found that the best way to assess student learning and program quality is through a variety of assessment tools.

PERFORMANCE AND PORTFOLIO ASSESSMENTS

Performance assessment looks at actual student work produced over time, and—potentially, at least—at the processes by which the students produce such work, both individually and collaboratively. "Portfolio assessment" is similar. The term seems to imply that students' work will be collected in an actual portfolio, though in fact other containers may be more practical and, furthermore, the essence of portfolio assessment lies not in the container but in the concept. Like performance assessment, portfolio assessment focuses on students' products and processes of learning, but also on their growth in other areas, such as their interest in reading and writing, their concept of themselves as readers and writers, and their ability to evaluate their own work and set goals for themselves as learners. (http://homepage.tinet.ie/~seaghan/articles/10.htm)

Both performance and portfolio assessments provide the possibility of more accurate representations of student learning and ways of knowing. In addition, through these different performance-based assessments students are required to be active participants in their own evaluation of their progress. The assessments are certainly of a more qualitative nature and not easily quantified or objectified by a machine. But both performance and portfolio assessments can be evaluated through a variety of rubrics. These rubrics can also be excellent moments of learning and reflection. Most rubrics are constructed by the teacher, yet many teachers are requiring students to make up their own as well. A rubric is a set of criteria that guide the evaluation, allowing both student and teacher to focus on the specific points of evaluation. These types of assessment are part of what is termed "authentic assessment," indicating these evaluation strategies are closer to capturing students' actual performance and academic achievement. There are many ways in which teachers and students can document student work. In addition to collecting student work, teachers may photograph, tape-record, or video-record conversations, oral reports, presentations, group work, and classroom behavior for further representative documentation. Often times these documents are accompanied by observational notes. All of these are extremely useful for teacher-parent conferences, teacher-student conferences, and for teachers' summative evaluations of student work. Performance-based assessments portray a more comprehensive explanation of how a student is doing and what he or she has learned. Teachers may also learn a great deal about their own performance through these assessments. Standardized forms of assessments simply cannot cover or lend the depth of analysis that authentic assessments can. Ascher (1990) paraphrases Archbald and Newmann in 1988 to say, "Like life, where most of the important problems faced are open-ended and complex, performance-based assessments require each student to demonstrate mastery in a personal and more integrated way."

Students should be completely involved in the construction of the portfolios so they feel a sense of ownership of and in their learning. The increased student involvement also facilitates a more accurate reading of what students know and report to know or have questions about. Educators must set a required number of pieces to be included in the portfolio. The selection process is just as important as the final product. Students ultimately should select the pieces, with guidance from the teacher when necessary. This process is often used with much success during student teaching at the undergraduate level. Students need to make appropriate decisions as to what will represent not only what they have learned, but their progress as well. Rough drafts and unfinished works are acceptable portfolio entries. The ultimate goal is to develop self-directed and independent learners in control and with a deep understanding of their educational experiences.

These alternative assessments focus on productive insights into both strengths and weaknesses; students are not penalized for their weaknesses, rather they are assisted in improving. Educators periodically hold conferences with students about their work to modify learning plans and objectives. There are many alternatives to standardized learning and evaluation; the above are just two commonly preferred options.

ACCOUNTABILITY

Accountability is another delicate subject in the discussion of standardization. The Annenberg Institute for School Reform at Brown University has defined accountability in the following ways:

1. Agreed-upon high standards that offer direction to curriculum and instruction provide benchmarks by which to measure student progress and make explicit the goal of reducing disparities among groups of students.
2. A variety of rigorous assessment instruments (from standardized tests to portfolios of student work and anecdotal evidence) that enable school communities to document individual student progress as well as achievement across classes and schools.
3. Distributed responsibility for high-quality education among all stakeholders (not only teachers, administrators, and school boards but also parents, community members, policy makers, businesses, and universities).

4. Access to conditions and resources such as strong leadership, skillful instruction, adequate finances, time for collaboration and reflection, and openness to community involvement.
5. A system for the continuous and reflective use of data which allows school communities to examine their practices, formulate questions, reflect on intended outcomes, and take action to improve learning within a school culture that values continuous improvement. (www.edwebproject.org/edref.accountability. html)

These definitions or elements necessary in accountability measures present a comprehensive approach to assessment. However, accountability measures in most public schools are based on success or failure on standardized tests. In North Carolina, Ohio, and several other states, teachers who gain certification from the National Board for Professional Teaching Standards are rewarded bonuses. And in 1998, a group of business leaders in New York announced it would offer $30 million in financial prizes to teachers and administrators who successfully raised the academic performance of their students (www.edwebproject.org/edref. accountability.html). This bonus system raises extreme concerns over what some teachers and administrators are doing to secure the desired test scores. The use of incentives to alter curricular content and the overall purpose of education skews the intent of using summative assessments in K–12 instruction. Accountability is necessary and appropriate if it is going to maximize learning and quality, not subvert or undermine it. There is also concern over the practices exercised when schools are "failing." Some states reconstitute the school, essentially firing all personnel and requiring anyone who wants to continue working in that school to reapply. In addition to personnel being fired, the school seeks a university partner in order to solve instructional problems and raise test scores. Other states employ teacher peer reviews and professional development to help teachers who are deemed incompetent. Many other states are firing teachers without further recourse. Teacher unions are quite critical of these practices and have actively opposed particular cases. Tenure also prohibits a school system from firing a teacher who is tenured without a justified reason, which usually requires extreme amounts of documentation. To define "good" and "bad" teaching, or the more popular term "best practices," is a difficult task given the varying philosophies, preferences, and needs of teachers, students, administrators, businesses, university teacher preparation programs, and school systems.

University teacher preparation programs are also held account-able for better preparing teachers. The National Council for Accredita-tion of Teacher Education (NCATE) and state accrediting institutions have aligned in many states to require universities and colleges to redesign their assessment procedures for prospective teachers. Many times these assessment requirements are based on standards, objec-tives, skills, and dispositions. Some of these are difficult to assess and measure. In addition, universities and colleges are required to supply student products as evidence of the standards. Like some of the national assessment initiatives, the requirements and artifacts become quite cumbersome for both university faculty and students.

The form of accountability pervasive through the above examples is based on monitoring performance. Policymakers create general stan-dards that university programs and schools must define through objec-tives and performances. Accrediting institutions and districts then hold students and schools accountable for these standards. As a result of the material and financial rewards, the accountability system in the schools mimics that of the business industry. The problem comes when the prod-uct of schools, that being students, cannot (and should not) be as easily manipulated or manufactured as raw materials in business. Regardless of the false parallel between businesses and schools, policymakers and some administrators continue to push for greater high-stakes account-ability. Standards and performance outcomes are also used to determine the effectiveness of programs and entire schools, and as a result the stakes involved in securing positive results are incredibly high. To continue the narrow focus on standardized test scores as well as only using standard-ized tests for assessment creates more problems than it solves. The nega-tive impact on students' sense of self-worth and teachers' sense of com-petence is significant. The economic, social, and psychological effects of reducing instruction and learning to standardized formats are disastrous for the future of the nation in the twenty-first century.

IMPLICATIONS

The implications of standardized practices are multilayered and com-plex. On the one hand standards for education are necessary as guide-lines for quality learning experiences. On the other hand the abuse of standards prevents teachers from educating and students from learning in successful ways. Kincheloe (2001) makes an elaborate point worth quoting at length here:

Technical standards that focus simply on performance on standardized tests remove the all-important meaning-making process from the everyday life of the classroom. Meaning in this context has already been determined by the curriculum makers and is simply imposed on students as a "done deal"—there is no room for negotiation about the interpretation of information. In this manner, the kinetic energy is drained from school knowledge and rendered dull and inert; it becomes "dead matter" to be inserted into the passive mind of the learner.

In this "cleansing" of knowledge, the complexities and ambiguities that give it meaning and use-value are washed away. Educational reforms and standards-based reconfigurations often focus on the most efficient way to insert the sterilized data and measure students' retention of it. In an exciting world struggling with problems of globalization and information production, such data is virtually irrelevant, if learners are not aware of who produced it, the circumstances under which it was produced, and for whose interests it was produced. Students also need an appreciation of alternative forms of knowledge about the same subjects and the ways such information might relate to and be used in the world. (4)

In conclusion the matter of standardization is not easily discarded as a good or bad norm of today's schools. There are much larger implications to the use and overuse of standards in ways that flatten and deskill instead of enliven and challenge future adult members of a democratic society. I reiterate: the issue is not whether or not to have standards. The issue is how to maintain a level of quality with reasonable standards and multiple methods of assessment that support and push teachers and students into new and triumphant learning situations. Important creations and advancements to our society and livelihood were not born out of a lack of imagination or creativity, nor from individuals in classrooms that restricted these essential components of transformation and growth.

Teachers, students, administrators, and communities must feel confident in reclaiming their influence in schools all over the nation and reconsidering the fit between business leaders in the market system and the educational world. There is one feature of standards that Elliot Eisner highlights, which is particularly useful in rethinking the use of standards in secondary education:

A ... problematic feature of the aspiration to adopt a common set of standards for all is a failure to recognize differences among the students with whom we work. I am well aware of the fact that deleterious self-fulfilling prophecies can be generated when the judgments educators make about individuals are based on a limited appreciation of the potentialities of the students. This is a danger that requires our constant vigilance. However, the reality of differences—in region, in aptitude, in interests, and in goals—suggests that it is reasonable that there be differences in programs. (Eisner 1998, 180)

With standardized tests learning is severely compromised and reduced to rote memorization and recall. These tests leave little room for critical thinking, problem solving, knowledge application, and inquiry-based learning. These excluded skills and ways of thinking allow students, as whole individuals, to be engaged in the learning process and life. If these are continuously disregarded, society runs the risk of being overcompartmentalized, losing the ability to process complex levels of information.

Standards and therefore the process of institutionalizing them should not curtail the discussion of educational possibility. The way that standards are constructed, the language used, and their application are extremely important to notice and rethink. The aims of education are not to domesticate youth but to prepare them and help them develop in positive ways. Students need richer experiences in and out of the classroom, and need to be challenged to use high-order thinking to both pose and resolve inquiries. Educators and policymakers hope standardization helps them achieve a higher-quality education. Constant pressures to meet the high-stakes standards may be a case of misused means toward much desired ends.

REFERENCES

Archbald, D. A., and F. M. Newmann. 1988. *Beyond Standardized Testing: Assessing Authentic Academic Achievement in the Secondary School.* Reston, VA: National Association of Secondary School Principals.

Ascher, Carol. 1990. "Can Performance-Based Assessments Improve Urban Schooling?" *ERIC Digest* Number 56, *ERIC Clearinghouse on Urban Education,* New York, #ED327612. www.ericfacility.net/ericdigests/ed327612.html.

Children's Defense Fund. "Comprehensive Bill to Truly Leave No Child Behind Unveiled." www.childrensdefense.org. Accessed June 2003.

Clemson University. http://virtual.clemson.edu/groups/clarkstudy/report1.htm. Accessed January 2003.

Cloud Duttweiler, Patricia, and Undine McEvoy. "Standards-Based Reform: What Is Missing?" http://virtual.clemson.edu/groups/clarkstudy/report1.htm. Accessed January 2003.

Davis, Michelle R. 2003. "Administration Addresses Concerns about Head Start Testing Plan. *Education Week on the Web.* January 22, 2003. www.edweek.org.

EdWeb: Exploring Technology and School Reform. www.edwebproject.org/edref.accountability.html. Accessed February 2003.

Eisner, Elliot W. 1998. *The Kind of Schools We Need: Personal Essays.* Portsmouth, NH: Heinemann.

Facts on Standardized Tests and Assessment Alternatives. http://homepage.tinet.ie/~seaghan/articles/10.htm. Accessed April 2003.

Goals 2000: Increasing Student Achievement through State and Local Initiatives—April 1996. www.ed.gov/G2K/GoalsRpt/intro.html. Accessed April 2003.

Kincheloe, Joe L. 2001. "Introduction: Hope in the Shadows—Reconstructing the Debate over Educational Standards." In Joe L. Kincheloe and Danny Weil, eds. *Standards and Schooling in the United States: An Encyclopedia,* pp. 1–103. Santa Barbara, CA: ABC-CLIO.

Kincheloe, Joe L., and Danny Weil, eds. 2001. *Standards and Schooling in the United States: An Encyclopedia.* Santa Barbara, CA: ABC-CLIO.

Lachat, Mary Ann. 2000. *Standards, Equity, and Cultural Diversity.* Providence, RI: Brown University.

Popham, W. James. 1999. "Using Standards and Assessment: Why Standardized Tests Don't Measure Educational Quality." *Educational Leadership* 56, no. 6 (March). www.ascd.org/readingroom/edlead/9903/extpopham.html.

The Regents of the University of California Lawrence Hall of Science. 2002. Standards-Based Reform. Parental portal. www.lhsparent.org/standardreform.html. Accessed January 2003.

Sanders, William L., and Sandra P. Horn. 1995. "Educational Assessment Reassessed: The Usefulness of Standardized and Alternative Measures of Student Achievement as Indicators for the Assessment of Educational Outcomes." *Education Policy Analysis Archives* 3, no. 6 (March). http://epaa.asu.edu/epaa/v3n6.html.

Secondary Block Homepage. www.hope.edu/academic/education/wessman/Secondary_Block_Revised/standards/. Accessed December 2002.

Stanford University. www.stanford.edu/~hakuta/CalTex_SBR/historysbr.html. Accessed January 2003.

Chapter Six

●◆ The Commercialization of Secondary Education

The commercialization of schools is a current hot topic in education and probably the most influential to the future of public and private education. There are significant groups supporting business alliances and many more opposing the commercialization of learning and students. Schools, particularly public education, were developed for public good, for members of the society to be educated in free and accessible ways. We know this grand idea never came to complete fruition, but in the early part of the twenty-first century, public education is in great jeopardy. Schools in the United States and Canada are suffering from budget cuts and increased demands for testing, teacher training, and curriculum change. School conditions continue to worsen and some schools have turned to businesses to provide the funds government will not. In exchange the school experience is altered tremendously. Schools become structurally commercial with advertisements, dispensing of products, and changes to dietary choice. Changes to technology and curriculum are also prevalent in schools that seek partnerships with businesses. In this chapter we will take a look at the arguments posed and the implications for secondary education. Of particular interest are the various federal and local programs like vouchers, Channel One, ZapMe!, Edison Schools, and Disney's Celebration School that have significantly altered the ways we approach, perceive, and define education, in addition to what is made possible in the institution of education.

COMMERCIALIZATION

What is commercialization of and in the schools? What does it look like and what does it change? According to the Ontario Secondary School Teachers' Federation (OSSTF) Public Education Works, commercialization "refers to increasing corporate involvement in schools, curricula, and other areas of education" (www.media-awareness.ca/eng/med/class/edissue/cebuine2.htm). Corporations gain great financial benefits for their involvement with schools. OSSTF offers several ways in which to assess or recognize commercialization in schools:

- Businesses and schools arranging partnerships whereby the corporation offers financial assistance to schools (equipment or expertise)
- Advertisers sending materials to teachers for classroom use (i.e., a scientific method poster encourages students to use a slotted spoon to compare the thickness of Prego spaghetti sauce to that of its leading contender, Ragu)
- Boards of education offering monopoly contracts to food and/or beverage companies that allow for the sale of their products in the schools
- Cable TV networks offering free curriculum programming to schools in return for the inclusion of commercial ads
- Corporations sponsoring school teams, clubs, or field trips, in return for some form of publicity for the company within the school
- Fast food vendors taking over cafeterias
- Boards of education selling advertising space on buses, etc.
- Corporations offering their assistance to schools to help them function in a more businesslike manner

These are only a few illustrations of the many ways in which corporations find a place in the schools and curriculum. Advocates and opponents also raise important issues; some examples are listed below.

Advocates believe that commercial involvement in schools will:

- Help financially strapped schools and boards of education by providing learning materials that otherwise would be unaffordable
- Help to provide state-of-the-art equipment—for computer or other technological subject areas—which students could not otherwise access
- Acquaint students with the world of business

Opponents believe that commercial involvement in the schools:

- Gives students the impression that the products advertised are implicitly endorsed by the teacher and the school system, and that the ads are therefore "true"

- Establishes monopoly access to a captive consumer audience through business/school partnerships or by allowing a single product into schools with an implicit academic endorsement
- Allows politicians to underfund the school system and to not provide students with the necessities for a good and equitable education
- Discriminates against students in poorer areas that do not attract the interest of corporations seeking out more affluent consumers
- Operates against the democratic intent of publicly funded school systems to encourage free and critical thinking and freedom of choice
- Subverts the curriculum for marketing purposes, while overshadowing the influence of teachers and parents (www. media-awareness.ca/eng/med/class/edissue/cebuine2.htm)

Both advocates and opponents present thought-provoking arguments in this debate. The reader must carefully look at the advantages and question their expense. Having appropriate materials for instruction and learning is necessary, but the negotiations sealed in order to secure these materials should not shortchange other aspects of learning. Students should critically understand and learn about these business transactions. The curriculum must include understanding what limitations are placed when deals of this nature are made. Acquainting students with business must then be a comprehensive project, not a selective exposure to a business's involvement in the community or its willingness to give back. A critical media and business literacy education is essential for schools who have corporate sponsors. If schools are to promote the democratic intent of the educational system in the United States, students need access to all the steps in the process of developing a product, targeting an audience, using marketing strategies, and securing product consumption. Students need to be savvy and informed consumers if schools are going to be outwardly part of the consumer culture. Some may argue schools without uniforms may already participate in this consumer culture by allowing students to compete with fashion and materials. For school districts and individual schools to endorse the overt modification of curriculum and particular products related and unrelated to learning garners ethical and pedagogical questioning.

The scope of schooling and learning seems to be at stake in a time when youth need crucial direction for their future. The educational world tends to seek immediate solutions without a deep contemplation of future implications. If students have such great spending power, how will they understand how to manage their finances through good and bad economies? How will students manage others' finances? How are students prepared to sustain and lead this country through the rest of the century and beyond?

Proponents for and opponents of school partnerships agree schools provide captive audiences. This opportunity is at times used to sell products, lifestyle, and ideas to a target audience. Corporations see this as a means to create lifelong clients. The corporations and businesses are interested in how these school ventures will increase profit margins. Shaker (2000) discusses why classrooms are such prime places:

- The classroom is the most effective environment in which to change behavior and attitudes of present and future workers and consumers. The legitimizing classroom environment provides added weight to corporate products, messages and curricular supplements, because school is an environment "that kids love and adults trust."
- The teacher, a trusted authority figure, acts as an effective corporate spokesperson.
- Corporations who are seen to be "helping" underfunded schools receive positive public relations in the community.
- Parents are likely to buy the same educational products for home use that are used in their child's classroom. This provides corporations with "two markets for the price of one."
- Schools tend to be a less "cluttered" environment in which to market to kids because exclusive contracts allow for product monopolies.
- Tax receipts maximize benefits to corporations practicing "strategic philanthropy" in education. (www.osstf.on.ca/www/abosstf/ampa01/commercialization/commercinschools.html)

The interests of companies remain intact; however, schools' objectives and culture are altered significantly. The impact of this commercialization extends into family life and society. The commercialization of schools gained popularity in the 1990s. With vouchers, charter schools, and President George W. Bush's No Child Left Behind policy, commercialization proves to prolong these educational initiatives as permanent school reform. There is a range of businesses that have aligned themselves with public schools, such as Pepsi, Coca-Cola, Pizza Hut, Disney, McDonald's, Microsoft, Primedia (Channel One), Procter &

Gamble, and many others. A typical example, GymBoards, created by American Passage Media Corporation, puts billboards in high school locker rooms with panels advertising products for hair removal or tampons with panels displaying health-related or social issues (multinationalmonitor.org). Even "educational" businesses, which supply textbooks and instructional resources, monopolize instruction, curriculum guides and scripts, and standardized tests. These "educational" businesses in particular specialize in curriculum standardization. The influx of big business originates from all sectors of the economic community. The general public may be surprised by the alliances that exist when big business and education come together. On President Bush's first day in the White House the president of McGraw-Hill was invited to join him with other "educational leaders" (mainly other CEOs) (Metcalf 2002). Bush wants to make education a priority in his administration and has brought his business connections onboard to facilitate his high-stakes vision.

The effect of commercialization on schools and students varies from school to school. Curriculum intervention and branded equipment are two examples of how businesses sponsor or contribute to schools. These distinctions are important since they vary in potential benefits and hazards. Regardless of the degree of commercialization, schools can still take the opportunity to build curriculum on such alliances in order to increase the learning as opposed to accepting its dilution. Education is mediated at all levels and contexts. Educators should be able to capitalize on the wealth of curriculum afforded in the above-stated market transactions.

The Center for Research and Evaluation at the University of Maine's College of Education conducted a study on the commercialization of schools. The study looks at categories of commercial activities in school, advantages and disadvantages of commercial partnerships, and suggested critical questions for stakeholders to aid in assessing corporate proposals (www.ume.maine.edu). This study also highlights the incredible spending power of children and youth in the United States. Companies understand this now more than ever and therefore will seek venues to increase their exposure to the new target audience. A coalition of groups opposing commercialization, the Stop Commercial Exploitation of Children (SCEC), contends, "Children influence $500 billion in spending per year. As a result, they are bombarded with commercials for products, including violent toys and junk food" (www.commercialexploitation.com). The Commercialism in Education Research Unit at Arizona State University has done extensive research on the commercialization of schools as well. The unit presents various studies, from the branding of schools to the effects on students' health. Molnar (2002) states:

> Of the trends reported the rapid increase in the number of schools signing exclusive agreements with soft drink bottlers is among the more troubling from a public health perspective. . . . In any school the health and nutrition curriculum children are taught advocates a well balanced diet that is low in fat, sugar, and salt. When a school enters into an exclusive agreement with a bottler it, in effect, undermines its own curriculum and puts the school in the position of tacitly promoting unhealthful behavior. Soft drink consumption has increased dramatically over the last decade. Since soft drink consumption is closely associated with childhood obesity, and is a risk factor for diabetes, enlightened child-oriented policy would remove soft drinks from schools altogether instead of seeking to profit from their consumption. (www.asu.edu/educ/epsl/ceru.htm)

When the ramifications of corporate partnerships extend beyond curricular restrictions to affect children's health, school leadership must intervene. Access to soft drinks and fast food should be monitored and restricted given dietary guidelines. Principals and administrators should be able to place parameters on corporate contributions and partnership in order to safeguard the holistic physical, psychosocial, and intellectual well-being of students. Unfortunately, many times there are contract clauses to prevent this monitoring and regulation. Butler-Wall (1997) stresses the importance of carefully looking at how physical, psychosocial, and intellectual development is seriously hampered by the commercialization of schools. She also warns against endangering democracy as a result of "whole corporate takeovers." Wohl (2001) contends:

> Making sure that commercial interests are not allowed to take precedence over schools' responsibilities to their students will require a combined effort from everyone concerned: teachers and administrators, who must be alert to the danger of opening students to coercion—and provide the first line of defense against this danger; businesses, who need to continue their commitment to public education but with fewer strings and without overwhelming cash-needy schools; policymakers at both the state and federal level, who must do far more to provide all public schools with the kind of funding they need; and, perhaps most important, citizens at the local level—parents and other members of

the community—who create a climate of opinion that determines to a large extent what goes on in the schools and whose votes on school-bond and tax issues often make the difference between a school district that has enough money for its needs and one that is pinched. If these groups pull together, we can provide schools with more equal bargaining power, and we can achieve an appropriate balance between kids as students and kids as consumers. But limiting corporate involvement in the schools will also demand a renewed commitment, on the part of all citizens, to our public schools—as public institutions that exist for the common good and that are therefore worthy of sufficient support from public dollars. (www.aft.org/american_educator/fall2001/marketplace.html)

Obviously, stricter legislation needs to be established in order to protect the interests of schools and students. The United States General Accounting Office issued a report in September 2000 stating:

Nineteen states currently have statutes or regulations that address school-related commercial activities, but in fourteen of these states, statutes and regulations are not comprehensive and permit or restrict only specific types of activities. For example, of the states we visited, California laws restrict many commercial activities, Michigan laws do not address commercial activities, and New Mexico laws allow advertising in and on school buses. As a result of this piecemeal approach to regulation, in most states, local school boards have the authority to make policy decisions about commercial activities or to delegate these decisions to district officials. In the districts we visited, local school board policies differed in terms of the number and types of activities they addressed, but most delegated responsibility to superintendents and principals, who often make decisions on a case-by-case basis. (5, 13–14)

The report gives precise information state by state of policies and regulations, as well as the type of commercial activities found in schools. Leadership is crucial for the future of secondary education in dealing with the popularity of corporate partnerships. Commercialization affects all aspects of an individual's life in and out of school. In secondary education, teachers and administrators can be ultimately proactive in creating educational experiences and lessons that expose, discuss, and redefine student economic and social consciousness and participation.

CHANNEL ONE AND ZAPME!

Channel One and ZapMe! are two other commercial initiatives in schools all over the nation. Channel One, started by Chris Whittle in the late 1980s and owned by Primedia, offers middle schools and high schools free televisions, video recorders, and satellite dishes in exchange for watching the network's twelve-minute broadcast with two additional minutes of commercials. The schools must agree to 80 percent of their students watching the broadcast, 90 percent of the time during the school year. Channel One Network claims "a learning community of 12,000 American middle, junior and high schools representing over 8 million students and 400,000 educators" (www.channelone.com). Great opposition from conservatives and progressives has been a constant since the channel's inception. The educational content of the broadcast is highly debated as well. Many argue that the news broadcasts are watered down and glossed over with MTV gimmicks to attract the audience. Underlying this method of presenting news coverage to youth is the assumption that young women and men cannot process complex information, so it must be made superficial and into sound bites.

The commercials tend to cater once again to the potential buying power of teenagers today. Manning (1999) alerts the public to the works of Channel One, particularly to Renee Hobbs, the director of the Media Literacy Project at Babson College in Wellesley, Massachusetts, also a paid consultant to Channel One:

> A founder of the U.S. media literacy movement and perhaps its most well-known and articulate promoter, Hobbs was once a Channel One critic. Her opinion changed, she says, while observing the program being used in the Billerica, MA, public schools. "It was clear to me that the show served an educational purpose and could help teachers," Hobbs says. "Even the advertisements can be used for lessons."
>
> Hobbs has developed a set of media literacy lesson plans to accompany Channel One broadcasts that will be distributed free to tenth-grade Channel One users beginning in February 2000. The lesson plans use basic media literacy techniques such as categorizing different types of news programs (hard news, soft news, etc.) and decoding the meaning of advertisements—though no Channel One news segments or ads will be used as examples. (www.RethinkingSchools.org/Archives/14_02/chan142.htm)

Many argue the consumerism in Channel One is so pervasive one is hard-pressed to find substantial educational content. This is another situation where schools accept the equipment with the added expense of initiating a lengthy hidden curriculum. Channel One in particular prides itself on providing global coverage to a teenage audience. They believe in providing a space for the teenage perspective on news of all kinds. The Web component of Channel One has a layout and informational structure resembling the home pages of Netscape or MSN. It has the usual national news, entertainment news, current issues, sports, polls, surveys, promotions, and the like. The website knows its teenage audience and caters entirely to them. The website potentially extends the corporate learning beyond school walls. It is lifelong consumer learning at its technological peak. The website has links to a variety of other sites that teenagers might be interested in or have questions about. The academic content is only one part of the website, which includes further information relevant to current events, homework help, dealing with stress, preparing for college, a student exchange, and ways to improve grades. The website presents itself as a comprehensive site for all of youth's needs.

Another recent program, ZapMe! created by Lance Mortensen, was initiated in 1996, giving free computers and Internet access to schools nationwide. It was able to wire 2,300 schools in 45 states, providing approximately 2 million students with Internet access (Schiffman 2000, www.forbes.com/2000/11/28/1127zapme.html). The service and equipment came in exchange for placing advertisements in school classrooms, as banners on websites, and for tracking student demographics and surfing preferences. ZapMe! met great resistance from the public and educators. Ralph Nader publicly criticized and organized against the company. Many educators, parents, students, and community members raised serious questions about the educational merit of such initiatives. As a result of the critiques and campaigns against the company, ZapMe! was unable to fulfill its commitment and asked schools to pay for its Internet service and equipment. This put already underfunded schools in further economic stress. ZapMe! attempted to switch its clientele to businesses instead of schools to secure funding. The company faced tumultuous times and serious financial problems as a result of the negative criticism and objections.

THE EDISON PROJECT

The Edison Project was founded in 1992. This project is said to be the nation's leading private manager of public schools, with control of approximately 150 schools. Edison opened its first four schools in August

1995. This organization prides itself on having done extensive research all over the world, documenting exemplary schools and using these as models for Edison schools. The Edison Project also uses verified scientific research to support its own research. This is the only company in the for-profit education realm that is publicly owned. Microsoft and J.P. Morgan Chase are among the major shareholders of the Edison Project.

The Edison schools are structured so that small schools can exist within schools. These subgroups are named academies, such as a

> Junior Academy (grades 6–8), a Senior Academy (grades 9 and 10), and a Collegiate Academy (grades 11 and 12). Within academies students are organized into multigrade houses of 100–180 students each. The students in each house are taught by a team of four to six teachers who stay with the same house of students for the duration of their academy experience. (www.edisonproject.com)

These schools' schedules provide longer days and more school days so that a variety of classes, including the arts, humanities, and others, are offered. (These classes are usually seen as expendable by most public school systems pressured by standardized test scores.) The Edison Project's philosophy focuses on ten fundamentals behind school design:

- School organized for every student's success
- A better use of time
- A rich and challenging curriculum
- Teaching methods that motivate
- Assessments that provide accountability
- A professional environment for teachers
- Technology for an information age
- A partnership with families
- Schools tailored to the community
- The advantage of system and scale (www.edisonproject.com)

Another important part of the Edison Project is the use of technology throughout the curriculum. Students are to use and understand technology as a means or vehicle for research, analysis, writing, communicating, and, most important, preparing them for the technologically driven society. In fact every student, teacher, and staff member is connected electronically through

> The Common, Edison's intranet message, conferencing, and information system. Connecting to The Common allows members to commu-

nicate with one another and also to tap into the vast electronic resources that Edison makes available. These include a digital library of periodicals; "learning links" that connect students to selected (and carefully previewed) sites on the World Wide Web; and discussion and support groups especially for students, parents, and teachers. The Common also hosts areas unique to each individual school. (www.edisonproject.com)

This common ground also allows greater partnerships with parents. The network system does exactly what it promises: connects all of its constituents and extends learning beyond the walls of the classroom or school. These schools, as exhibited in its administration and mission, are committed to providing a different learning experience and affording parents choice over the quality of education for their children.

Despite these positive elements and conditions, the Edison schools have received negative press since the turn of the twenty-first century in New York, Kansas, Texas, and California. In these schools, attendance had gone down, many teachers left, the administration in Kansas "helped" students with standardized tests, test scores went down, and in New York parents forced Edison to relinquish control of five schools. The Edison Project has met its share of resistance in the arena against privatization. Mismanagement of funds and poor administration appear to plague many attempts at providing a different schooling experience. In addition to the Edison schools, several other corporations have developed charter schools and private schools. These management companies, Sabis Educational Systems, Advantage Schools, Beacon Education Management, and the Governor French Academy, also act as consultants for existing schools. These companies claim great improvements in academic achievement as exhibited through standardized test scores.

CELEBRATION SCHOOL

Celebration School in Celebration, Florida, is the Walt Disney school situated within the town constructed by the Disney Corporation just outside of Orlando, Florida. The school has K–12 and offers a middle school housing sixth through eighth grades with an integrated curriculum and collaborative teaching. The middle school has a block schedule in order to provide greater flexibility in instruction. Grades nine through twelve are housed in the high school where students are required to fulfill a traditional college preparatory curriculum with community service and a capstone senior project. The senior project must involve an area of study that students might pursue after graduation. These projects are evaluated by a panel of teachers, business leaders, and peer judges.

Celebration School has extraordinary resources with Auburn University, Johns Hopkins University, Stetson University, the University of Central Florida, the Celebration Company, Sun Microsystems, Apple Computer, Rauland-Borg, APUNIX, Cortelco, Lares Technology, SIRSI, McGraw-Hill, Florida Hospital Celebration Health, Jones Communication, National Business Education Alliance, and Walt Disney Imagineering as the corporate sponsors and partners. This school is the only one in its county considered a professional development school where student achievement is maximized, effective practices are developed, and clinical settings for student-teachers are provided.

The objectives of Celebration School are to prepare students to be lifelong learners, to be effective decisionmakers, and to be respectful citizens through integrated learning, multiple intelligences, multi-age groups, and cooperative learning (www.school.celebration.fl.us). The Celebration Company developed the entire town of Celebration. This town is reminiscent of a Rockwell painting with everything manicured and guided by strict community regulations. The company embedded both the school and community with "technology to enhance on-site learning and stimulate continuous learning at home through community-wide communication. The community/school Intranet fosters academic achievement and parental involvement by allowing parents and students direct connection to daily events, schoolwork and even homework assignments" (www.school.celebration.fl.us). The Walt Disney Corporation gathered a think tank to help in the creation of the school and community. In addition the school is a technology showcase for many of the corporate partners; subsequently the school is afforded many examples of the latest technology. Perhaps this school and community is the epitome of commercialism.

Walt Disney Company, in addition to creating theme parks all over the world, is now in the business of constructing towns inclusive of schools. This community is quite insular and exclusive. But further analysis of the school curriculum shows the students are surrounded by constant aspects of the commercialization that made their learning environment possible. Of concern to many critics of the commercialization of schools is the normative practice this creates. By the students' entire world being a product of commercialism, they fear that the critical skills students are supposed to acquire through their schooling will be numbed by the extreme familiarity of the commercial. The disneyfication of school and of community in this case is an alarming trend. Some may focus on the incredible resources and possibilities afforded to Celebration students and others understand the continued disparity this creates in a society attempting to provide equitable opportunities for all its youth.

VOUCHERS

"School vouchers, also known as scholarships, redirect the flow of education funding, channeling it directly to individual families rather than to school districts. This allows families to select the public or private schools of their choice and have all or part of the tuition paid" (www.schoolchoices.org/roo/vouchers.htm). Vouchers are a part of the school choice program, a government initiative to help parents choose a better education for their children. The controversy centers on taking funds from struggling schools, vouchers being utilized by parents who have resources to move their children to other schools, vouchers offering minimal tuition assistance, and vouchers facilitating the privatization of public schools. Sometimes these vouchers are used for schools that exist outside the residing school district. Schools also have the option not to accept incoming students; therefore vouchers do not guarantee admission into a better educational situation. Some advocates of vouchers see these as part of individuals' right under a democratic system to choose the type of schooling that best suits their beliefs. Opponents see it as jeopardizing democracy, public education for all, and equal access. Both agree with choice fundamentally and with the right to have it, but each side defines choice very differently. Advocates of school choice and vouchers see these initiatives as a way to exercise a democratic right to access the type of education they deem appropriate. This comes from the market-value system where the consumer choice has priority. Private enterprise and the marketplace are seen as better than public institutions. Opponents to vouchers and similar initiatives believe school choice has to do with providing better, more comprehensive educational institutions. It is founded on the right to true education for all.

Funding for vouchers can come from the government, private industry, or a combination of both. Coulson (1999) argues that the American public conflates the idea of public education and public schooling. He discusses the failures of public schooling and supports market-based school reform in the interest of public education. He states that public schools have failed to fulfill one of our most important and universally held ideals of public education—providing a decent education to all low-income children. . . . The bulk of evidence, both historical and modern, points to the superiority of markets (supplemented with a mechanism for subsidizing the education of low-income children) over state school systems in their ability to serve the poor. Throughout history, low-income parents have consistently made better educational decisions for their own children than government experts have made for them, no matter how well-intentioned those experts have been. Poor parents, indeed all parents, need to be empowered to once again take control of their children's education. (www.schoolchoices.org/roo/edweek1.htm)

Others in support of market-based reforms argue that a monopoly system operates from one ideology or school of thought and is not suitable for a pluralistic society. They highlight the possibility of suiting the public's various needs through independent schools, whether private or government subsidized. Coulson (1996) contends:

Competition and the profit motive must be reintroduced into education so that teachers and school administrators will once again have a powerful incentive to meet the needs of the children and parents they serve. It can also be expected that the elimination of existing educational monopolies will alleviate many of the ongoing battles over curriculum and religion in the schools, by allowing families to pursue an education in accordance with their own values, without the need to impose those values on others. What remains to be resolved is the question of how to integrate the reintroduction of market forces with the subsidization of families with limited financial means. Vouchers and tax-credits no doubt offer a viable approach to the problem, though the need for more work in the design and application of these plans is paramount. (http://olam.ed.asu.edu/epaa/v4n9.html)

Many recognize the continuing problems with public schooling and seek concrete answers for the nation's youth. The future of vouchers and other market-based reforms is uncertain and worth further investigation. In a time when public schooling is further restricted by the imposed standards-based testing policy, any possibility for a difference in the pedagogical lives of students may be necessary to pursue. Either side, in support of or against vouchers, offers poignant critiques of the claims of each side. This debate is a rich and complex discussion worthy of serious examination.

IMPLICATIONS

As stated previously, the commercialization of schools is a serious concern for the future of schooling in this country. Some constituents see significant benefits to commercializing schools; others see grave problems. Still others advocate a balance where schools can get the funds they need and not have to compromise the integrity of public education. The commercialization of schools is a current topic and it is crucial for the reader to stay abreast of recent developments and legislation. Bush's administration is keenly concerned with education and business partnerships. It is evident that vouchers may be a creative possibility or a detriment to the idea of public education. Many hope a market-based education and the ensuing competition will increase the quality of education. Parental involvement is also expected to increase since they would be partly consumers of this education. Others argue vouchers would only provide small tuition assistance for some private school tuition. More restrictions exist, so vouchers are offered only to families under a particular income bracket. Ultimately vouchers do not guarantee admission into better schools. Still, many are beginning to question the benefits of vouchers for any student truly in need of a better education.

In terms of commercialization, vouchers are just one piece of the puzzle. Many struggling schools welcome corporate aid in order to keep programs open for students; to secure needed materials, resources, and equipment; and as a way to increase the quality of the overall educational experience. The benefits outweigh the hazards for some, yet for those fervently against any kind of commercialization there are no benefits. Schools are said to be in crisis, students are not performing up to standards, schools have high personnel turnover, and dropout rates continue to rise.

Giroux (2002) states:

> There is, of course, more at stake in the privatization of public schooling than issues of public versus private ownership or public good versus private gain. We must weigh individual achievement against equity and the social good. We must decide how teaching and learning get defined. We must ask what identities are produced in defining students' histories, experiences, values, and desires through corporate rather than democratic ideals. . . .
>
> Within the language of privatization and market reforms, a strong emphasis exists on standards, measurements of outcomes, and holding teachers and students more accountable. Privatization is an appealing prospect for legislators who do not want to spend taxpayers' money on

schools and for those who do not want to support education through increased taxes. These appeals are reductive in nature and hollow in substance. They remove questions of equity and equality from the discourse of standards. Furthermore, they appropriate the democratic rhetoric of choice and freedom without addressing issues of power. (107, 108)

The realm of education has long been at the center of defining and actualizing American democratic possibilities. Yet when corporate interests interfere with access to a quality education, not only is democracy at stake, but the stability of the entire nation. If one of the only systems that influences all youth does not concern itself with securing the growth and development of young minds, the future (and present) of the nation is severely compromised. How is citizenship understood and exercised? How is a sense of community and responsibility developed? How does an individual come to know his or her capacities and abilities if a range of experiences are not had? How does an entire generation learn about the past? How does a society progress? Issuing universal standards for all schools and not universalizing resources and funds makes it impossible for struggling schools to be held equally accountable for information not taught or mistaught. Allowing for some schools to reinvent their curriculum and therefore their success in standardized tests through corporate business deals further increases the inequity between schools and districts, and ultimately between class structures in the nation.

Advocating privatization and commercialism in schools also places teachers in precarious positions. As big businesses offer and impose specific curriculum guides (and sometimes scripts) in the classroom, teachers are seen merely as carriers of the information, deskilled to vehicles for subject matter. Classroom teachers are deprived of exercising their professional and intellectual capacities. Bracketing teachers' identities out of the instructional path and denying their capacities for production of knowledge deadens the educational atmosphere and increases the probabilities for more and more students to be successfully alienated from the learning/schooling experience. Teacher turnover is more likely as well, since they are asked to work in limiting conditions and potentially hostile environments if they do not follow the program. Education continues to slip out of the hands of those trained and educated in the field of education. Simply because corporations see an investment in schools as an investment in potential workers and consumers, this investment does not qualify them to dictate or create curriculum.

A curriculum influenced by the commercialization of the school severely compromises learning. Consumerism is normalized and students are discouraged from questioning its effects or methods of operation. The educational experience is further complicated and short-changed as students lose prime opportunities to develop skills necessary to navigate the commercialization of our society. Unless all stakeholders in the educational process are involved in the construction (or deliberation) of curriculum and learning opportunities, vested interests may be disproportionately prioritized at the expense of appropriate and ethical pedagogy.

The implications of commercialization in schools are varied for all involved in the educational realm. There are many questions and promises about vouchers and other market-based reforms. The debate is old enough to trace discussions of initiatives that worked and others that failed. Yet the discussions are recent enough to not have longitudinal studies and results about significant long-term effects of these initiatives and the companies funding them. The intersection of big business, the president of the United States, and public education, many argue, interferes with democratic ideals. The political atmosphere is unsettled and the ultimate expenses in students' lives are still unclear, but based on the above examples, they seem to outweigh the benefits. Unfortunately the current controversies within schools will not be easily resolved by administrators, teachers, students, parents, or community members alone. Little legislation exists to protect schools from corporations seeking to extend their profit margins and target audiences. Policies need to be established and enforced while educational leaders are simultaneously made aware of the effects of commercialism, as other funding resources are made available.

REFERENCES

Butler-Wall, Brita. 1997. "Risks of Commercializing Education: Why We Need Commercial-Free Schools." Pamphlet for Citizen's Campaign for Commercial-Free Schools.

Celebration School. www.school.celebration.fl.us. Accessed April 2003.

Coulson, Andrew J. 1999. "Are Public Schools Hazardous to Public Education?" *Education Week* 18, no. 30 (April 7). www.schoolchoices.org/roo/edweek1.htm.

Coulson, Andrew J. 1996. "Markets versus Monopolies in Education: The Historical Evidence." *Educational Policy Analysis Archives* 4, no. 9 (June). http://olam.ed.asu.edu/epaa/v4n9.html.

The Edison School Project. www.edisonproject.com. Accessed April 2003.

Giroux, Henry A. 2002. "Schools for Sale: Public Education, Corporate Culture, and the Citizen-Consumer. In Alfie Kohn and Patrick Shannon, eds. *Education, Inc.: Turning Learning into a Business*. Portsmouth, NH: Heinemann.

Manning, Steven. 1999. "Channel One Enters the Media Literacy Movement." *Rethinking Schools* 14, no. 2 (Winter). www.rethinkingschools.org.

Media Awareness Network. www.media-awareness.ca/eng/med/class/edissue/cebuine2.htm. Accessed February 2003.

Metcalf, Stephen. 2002. "Reading between the Lines." In Alfie Kohn and Patrick Shannon, eds. *Education, Inc.: Turning Learning into a Business,* rev. ed. Portsmouth, NH: Heinemann.

Molnar, Alex. 2002. "Commercializing Schools: A Threat to Our Children." Conference proceedings, American Dietetic Association Food and Nutrition Conference and Exhibition. www.asu.edu/educ/epsl/ceru.htm.

Multinational Monitor. http://multinationalmonitor.org. Accessed February 2003.

Schiffman, Betsy. 2000. "ZapMe Kills Computers in the Classroom." *Forbes.* www.forbes.com/2000/11/28/1127zapme.html.

School Choices. www.schoolchoices.org/roo/vouchers.htm. Accessed March 2003.

Shaker, Erika. 2000. "Strategic Philanthropy and Other Corporate Classroom Assaults." Conference proceedings, OSSTF Summer 2000 Leadership Conference. www.osstf.on.ca/www/abosstf/ampa01/commercialization/commercinschools.html.

United States General Accounting Office. 2000. "Public Education: Commercial Activities in Schools." GAO Report. Washington, DC: United States General Accounting Office.

University of Maine. www.ume.maine.edu. Accessed January 2003.

Wohl, Alexander. 2001. "The School Marketplace: Has Commercialization Gone Too Far?" *American Educator.* (January). www.aft.org/american_educator/fall2001/marketplace.html.

Chapter Seven

•◆ Organizations, Associations, and Government Agencies

The following are organizations, associations, government agencies, and groups whose work deals with education and learning, educational reform, and specifically secondary education. I have expanded the scope to include agencies or groups that address secondary education more broadly and issues that would be better suited for educators in secondary education. I encourage the reader to visit these websites or call these organizations for further resources since the small synopses here may not do justice to the important work these organizations are doing and the resources they make available. In this chapter there are many important organizations that will augment teaching practices, learning, and professional identity. There are some organizations, associations, and centers listed here that provide a rich historical perspective on underrepresented groups in the history of secondary education. The main purpose of this chapter is to provide a comprehensive selection of tools for the individual committed to the betterment of secondary education.

Academy for Educational Development (AED)
AED Headquarters
1825 Connecticut Avenue, NW
Washington, DC 20009-5721
Telephone: (202) 884-8000

New York office:
100 Fifth Avenue
New York, NY 10011
Telephone: (212) 243-1110
www.aed.org
admindc@aed.org

Founded in 1961, AED is an independent, nonprofit organization committed to solving critical social problems in the United States and throughout the world through education, social marketing, research, training, policy analysis, and innovative program design and management. Major areas of focus include health, education, youth development, and the environment.

Achieve, Inc., Resource Center on Standards, Assessment, Accountability, and Technology
8 Story Street, First Floor
Cambridge, MA 02138
Telephone: (617) 496-6300

400 North Capitol Street, NW, Suite 351
Washington, DC 20001
Telephone: (202) 624-1460
www.achieve.org

Achieve was founded in 1996 and formed by governors and CEOs who believe in standardized tests to help states raise academic standards and to measure performance standards. Its mission is also to strengthen public confidence in our education system.

Alliance for Excellent Education
1101 Vermont Avenue, NW, Suite 411
Washington, DC 20005
Telephone: (202) 842-4888
Fax: (202) 842-1613
http://www.all4ed.org/index.html

The mission of the Alliance for Excellent Education is to make it possible for America's six million at-risk middle and high school students to achieve high standards and graduate prepared for college and success in life.

American Educational Research Association (AERA)
1230 17th Street, NW
Washington, DC 20036
Telephone: (202) 223-9485
www.aera.net

AERA is concerned with improving education by encouraging inquiry in the development of theory and practice. Within AERA there are numerous subgroups concentrating on issues specific to secondary education. This is the most prominent international professional organization, with its main goal to advance educational research and practice. Its membership crosses multiple disciplinary fields.

American Federation of Teachers, AFL-CIO

555 New Jersey Avenue, NW
Washington, DC 20001
Telephone: (202) 879-4400
http://www.aft.org/

Its mission is to improve the lives of its members and their families; to give voice to their legitimate professional, economic, and social aspirations; to strengthen the institutions in which they work; to improve the quality of the services they provide; to bring together all members to assist and support one another; and to promote democracy, human rights, and freedom in their union, in the nation, and throughout the world.

American Indian Education Foundation (AIEF)

Attn: Debbie Combs
PO Box 27491
Albuquerque, NM 87125-9847
Telephone: (800) 881-8694

Program Offices
American Indian Education Foundation
10029 SW Nimbus Avenue, Suite 200
Beaverton, OR 97708
Telephone: (866) 866-8642
info@aiefprograms.org
www.aiefprograms.org

The mission of the American Indian Education Foundation is to give American Indian students the tools and opportunities to learn. AIEF focuses on four areas: college scholarships, school supplies, incentive programs to keep students in school, and structural projects to improve facilities.

The American School Counselor Association (ASCA)

801 North Fairfax Street, Suite 310
Alexandria, VA 22314
Telephone: (703) 683-ASCA
http://www.schoolcounselor.org/

The American School Counselor Association (ASCA) is a worldwide non-profit organization based in Alexandria, Virginia. Founded in 1952, ASCA supports school counselors' efforts to help students focus on academic, personal, social, and career development so they not only achieve success in school but are prepared to lead fulfilling lives as responsible members of society. The association provides professional development, publications, other resources, research, and advocacy to more than 13,000 professional school counselors around the globe.

The Americans with Disabilities Act (ADA) National Access for Public Schools Project
374 Congress Street, Suite 301
Boston, MA 02210
Telephone: (800) 893-1225, ext. 28
kgips@adaptiveenvironments.org
www.adaptiveenvironments.org

The ADA National Access for Public Schools Project is funded by the National Institute on Disability and Rehabilitation Research of the U.S. Department of Education to help public elementary and secondary schools implement the Americans with Disabilities Act. Its services include technical assistance to school administrators, teachers, students, parents, and the public through a toll-free phone line; training programs; presentations at national and state conferences; question-and-answer sheets and other resources; and a listserv on ADA and public school issues.

Appalachia Educational Laboratory (AEL)
PO Box 1348
Charleston, WV 25325-1348
Telephone: (304) 347-0400; (800) 924-9120
www.ael.org
aelinfo@ael.org

The AEL focuses on combined research and practice to improve teaching and learning. It works with people in the university, schools, and community searching for innovative services and ideas. Its key initiatives are facilitation and evaluation services, the Kentucky writing project, promoting high academic performance for underserved students, and teaching and learning mapping strategy. Similar to the other labs, it has several signature programs and publications also available.

Aspira: An Investment in Latino Youth
1444 Eye Street, NW, Suite 800
Washington, DC 20005
Telephone: (202) 835-3600

Fax: (202) 835-3613
info@aspira.org
http://www.aspira.org

This national nonprofit organization focuses on the education and leadership development of Puerto Rican and other Latino youth. Founded in 1961, Aspira believes "Puerto Ricans and Latinos have the collective potential to move their community forward." It also participates in a youth leadership development program, focusing on schools where there is a large Latino population and empowering Latinos to be community leaders through education and community service. Each local organization has clubs that provide Latino youths with college and career counseling, advocacy, financial aid, and scholarships. The organization has branches in Connecticut, Florida, Illinois, New Jersey, New York, Pennsylvania, and Puerto Rico in addition to its national office in Washington, D.C.

Association for Supervision and Curriculum Development (ASCD)
1703 North Beauregard Street
Alexandria, VA 22311-1714
Telephone: (703) 578-9600; (800) 933-ASCD
www.ascd.org

ASCD is an international, nonprofit education association founded in 1943, concerned with teaching and learning for the success of all students. This organization provides professional development, curriculum development, and leadership support.

Association for the Advancement of Computing in Education (AACE)
PO Box 3728
Norfolk, VA 23514
Telephone: (757) 623-7588
Fax: (703) 997-8760
http://www.aace.org/

The association is dedicated to the advancement of the knowledge, theory, and quality of learning and teaching at all levels with information technology. Its purpose is accomplished through the encouragement of scholarly inquiry related to information technology in education and the dissemination of research results and their applications through conferences, publications, and organizational projects.

Bilingual Private Schools Association (BIPRISA)
904 SW 23rd Avenue

Miami, FL 33135
Telephone: (305) 643-4888
Fax: (305) 649-2767

BIPRISA is an organization dedicated to increasing community awareness of the purposes and principles of bilingual education. Its membership consists of bilingual private schools, and it is the parent organization to several private school institutions.

Black Alliance for Educational Options (BAEO)
501 C Street, NE, Suite 3
Washington, DC 20002
Telephone: (202) 544-9870
www.baeo.org/options

BAEO is a national organization actively supporting parental choice to
help families and develop more educational options for black children.
It recognizes each child's individuality and strives to suit his or her
needs. Included in the options are extended learning opportunities in
multiple subject matters. It provides various resources for parents and
students in order to make informed decisions.

California Consortium for Critical Educators
www.cce.net

A social movement established with an expanded commitment to serve
critical educators, as well as students, parents, and communities, California Consortium for Critical Educators works to advance the reconstruction of schooling and society. As such, it seeks to provide a critical
analysis of education that fully engages the cultural and material forces
within society and how these position each in particular ways. The consortium develops effective strategies for social action in order to resist
and transform the oppressive and dehumanizing conditions of social
injustice and economic inequality.

The Center for Civic Education
5146 Douglas Fir Road
Calabasas, CA 91302-1467
Telephone: (818) 591-9321
www.civiced.org
cce@civiced.org

Its main aim is to develop informed, responsible participation in civic
life by members of the society. The center specializes in civic/citizen-

ship education, law-related education, and international educational exchange programs for developing democracies. It provides curriculum, teacher training, and community-based programs.

The Center for Collaborative Education in New York City (CCE)
1573 Madison Avenue, Room 201
New York, NY 10029
Telephone: (212) 348-7821
www.cce.org

CCE was formed in 1987 by six public schools in New York City and now has forty elementary and secondary public schools as members. It is a school-based advocate for educational change, a facilitator between and within schools, and an initiator of new projects while providing technical assistance and developing research and projects to illustrate the educational practices of student-based education. CCE is part of parent-teacher coalitions to mobilize against budget cuts and other systemwide problems, such as its participation in a legal suit, the Campaign for Fiscal Equity, for equitable distribution of state funds for New York City schools.

Center for Critical Thinking
Sonoma State University
PO Box 220
Dillon Beach, CA 94929
Telephone: (707) 878-9100
Fax: (707) 878-9111
www.criticalthinking.org

The center conducts advanced research and disseminates information on critical thinking. Each year it sponsors an International Conference on Critical Thinking and Educational Reform. It has worked with the College Board, the National Education Association, the U.S. Department of Education, as well as numerous colleges, universities, and school districts to facilitate the implementation of critical thinking instruction focused on intellectual standards.

The Center for Education Reform
1001 Connecticut Avenue, NW, Suite 204
Washington, DC 20036
Telephone: (202) 822-9000; (800) 521-2118
www.edreform.com
cer@edreform.com

This is an advocacy organization founded in 1993 to provide support and guidance for teachers, parents, and the community. It has various resources, suborganizations, links, and networks for the educationally concerned.

Center for Education Research, Analysis, and Innovation (CERAI)
College of Education
Educational Leadership and Policy Studies
Box 872411
Arizona State University
Tempe, AZ 85287-2411
www.asu.edu/educ/epsl/

CERAI, now called Educational Policy Studies Laboratory, is a research and information center focusing on student performance standards, assessment, and curriculum. This is available to anyone concerned about these educational issues. Six projects exist under this larger center: Commercialism in Education Research Unit (CERU), Education Policy Analysis Archive (EPAA), Education Policy Reports Project (EPRP), Education Policy Research Unit (EPRU), Language Policy Research Unit (LPRU), and Student Achievement Guarantee in Education (SAGE).

Center for Excellence in Educational Options
Nova Southeastern University
Fischer Graduate School of Education and Human Services
1750 NE 167 Street
North Miami Beach, FL 33162-3017
www.fcae.nova.edu/options
options@fcae.nova.edu

This national center works to improve education through professional development and research in assisting all stakeholders to improve the quality of learning. This center houses several projects and outreach programs.

Center for Innovation in Education
PO Box 2070
Saratoga, CA 95070-0070
Telephone: (800) 395-6088
www.center.edu

This center is a nonprofit public policy research organization focusing on school reform based on four Cs: choice, charter schools, content, and competition. It is a leading provider of mathematics in-service materials and training. It believes all children can learn and every child matters, so its commitment is to make this happen.

Center for Research on Education, Diversity, and Excellence (CREDE)
University of California–Santa Cruz
1156 High Street
Santa Cruz, CA 95064
Telephone: (831) 459-3500
Fax: (831) 459-3502
www.crede.ucsc.edu

CREDE is a federally funded research and development program focused on improving the education of students whose ability to reach their potential is challenged by language or cultural barriers, race, geographic location, or poverty.

Center for School Change
Hubert H. Humphrey Institute of Public Affairs
University of Minnesota, Twin Cities (West Bank)
301 19th Avenue South, Room 234
Minneapolis, MN 55455
Telephone: (612) 626-1834
www.hhh.umn.edu/centers/school-change

The center works with any person interested in education to increase student achievement, raise graduation rates, improve students' attitudes toward learning, and strengthen communities by developing stronger public schools.

Center for the Advancement of Hispanic and Science and Engineering Education (CAHSEE)
George Washington University
707 22nd Street, NW, Room 105
Washington, DC 20052
Telephone: (202) 994-6529
Fax: (202) 994-2459
cahsee@seas.gwu.edu
http://www.cahsee.org

CAHSEE is an organization created by Latino engineers and scientists dedicated to the advancement of Hispanics in science and engineering careers. Its efforts are concentrated in preparing Latino youth to enter and succeed in science and engineering schools and to complete graduate degrees, and in mentoring young Latino scientists and engineers to assume leadership positions in corporate America, academia, government research labs, and government. Its goals include the development of a cohesive national network of Latino engineers and scientists working together to achieve success in the professional and civic arenas.

Center for the Study of White American Culture: A Multiracial Organization
245 West 4th Avenue
Roselle, NJ 07203
Telephone: (908) 241-5439
Fax: (908) 245-4972
contact@euroamerican.org
www.euroamerican.org

The center was founded in 1995 to address the lack of information and discussion of the role of white people and white culture in American society. In some venues this topic was given only marginal consideration. In others, discussion of whiteness seemed to be taboo and any attempts to broach the subject were met with hostility and denial. Explicitly a multiracial organization, the center predicates its work on the belief that a complete examination of white American culture must include the perspectives of both insiders and outsiders to that culture, particularly that whiteness must be named and its privilege examined.

Center for Women Policy Studies
1211 Connecticut Avenue, NW, Suite 312
Washington, DC 20036
Telephone: (202) 872-1770
Fax: (202) 296-8962
cwps@centerwomenpolicy.org
www.centerwomenpolicy.org

The center was founded in 1972 as the nation's first feminist policy research organization. It has been on the front lines of efforts to promote justice and equality for women in education, welfare reform, and policy.

Coalition of Essential Schools
1814 Franklin Street, Suite 700

Oakland, CA 94612
Telephone: (510) 433-1451
www.essentialschools.org

This is a high school–university partnership that attempts to redesign high schools for better student learning and achievement. The effort is to rethink school priorities and redesign practices and structures. Each school has the prerogative to develop its own programs to fit the needs of the school, students, teachers, and community. The coalition provides professional development opportunities as well. This work is based on the work of Theodore R. Sizer.

Consortium for Chicago School Research
1313 East 60th Street
Chicago, IL 60637
Telephone: (773) 702-3364
www.consortium-chicago.org

This is an independent federation of Chicago organizations founded in 1990 to conduct research on Chicago public schools. The consortium seeks to reframe the conventional boundaries among researchers, policymakers, and practitioners by conducting studies of high technical quality while broadly engaging the local constituency. The research is shaped by a vision of democratic policymaking, therefore including multipartisan perspectives and membership. It provides various publications for the public and schools.

The Council for Exceptional Children (CEC)
1110 North Glebe Road, Suite 300
Arlington, VA 22201
Telephone: (703) 620-3660
TTY: (703) 264-9446
Fax: (703) 264-9494
http://www.cec.sped.org/

This is the largest international professional organization dedicated to improving educational outcomes for individuals with exceptionalities, students with disabilities, and the gifted. CEC advocates for appropriate governmental policies, sets professional standards, provides continual professional development, advocates for newly and historically underserved individuals with exceptionalities, and helps professionals obtain conditions and resources necessary for effective professional practice.

Council of Chief State School Officers
1 Massachussetts Avenue, NW, Suite 700
Washington, DC 20001-1431
Telephone: (202) 408-5505
www.ccsso.org

A nationwide nonprofit organization composed of public officials who lead the state departments responsible for elementary and secondary education. By representing the chief education officers, it works on behalf of state agencies. It has several publications and press releases of interest.

Council of the Great City Schools (CGCS)
1301 Pennsylvania Avenue, NW, Suite 702
Washington, DC 20004
Telephone: (202) 393-2427
www.cgcs.org

This council brings together some of the largest urban public school systems in the country in an effort to improve education in the inner cities. It was founded in 1956 and incorporated in 1961. CGCS works to promote urban education through legislation, research, media relations, instruction, management, technology, other initiatives, and other programs.

Education Commission of the States (ECS)
700 Broadway, Suite 1200
Denver, CO 80203
Telephone: (303) 299-3600
www.ecs.org
ecs@ecs.org

The ECS is a national organization helping state leaders improve education for youth. The ECS provides policymakers with news, information, research, analysis, conferences, publications, and partnerships. Its focus is to stay on top and disseminate current and emerging trends and innovations in state education policy.

Education Development Center (EDC)
55 Chapel Street
Newton, MA 02458-1060
Telephone: (617) 969-7100
www.edc.org

EDC is committed to education that builds knowledge and skill, makes possible a deeper understanding of the world, and engages learners as active, problem-solving participants. It believes that authentic education begins with questions: a teacher wanting to know a new way to solve a mathematics problem, a doctor wondering how to ease the transition for the family of a dying patient, a teenager wanting to know why school matters in life and career, a principal searching for better ways to meet the needs of students with disabilities, a mother considering whether to breastfeed. Over the decades, the best of EDC's projects have helped people raise and explore questions of importance in their lives.

Education Leaders Council (ELC)
1001 Connecticut Avenue, NW, Suite 204
Washington, DC 20036
Telephone: (202) 822-9000
www.educationleaders.org

ELC is working to inform the public about the education debate in this country. It has published important work reviewing the history of standards, successes and failures, and resources. It is committed to the fundamental reforms parents demand. The council believes the focus of education should be on the student, not the school system.

EdVoice
Headquarters
3 Twin Dolphin Drive, Suite 200
Redwood City, CA 94065
Telephone: (650) 595-5023

Sacramento office:
926 J Street, Suite 810
Sacramento, CA 95814
Telephone: (916) 448-3868
www.edvoice.com

EdVoice is a grassroots organization advocating for education reform and support for public education across California. Its focus is to pass legislation that will reshape California's public education policy. It believes true education reform requires a seismic shift from process to outcomes, yet it will take serious resources.

Environmental Education and Communication Network
Station B, PO Box 948

Ottawa, ON, Canada K1P5P9
www.eecom.org

This is a site for international environmental education and communication professionals to improve interaction on topics of interest, receive program information, and learn of progress in the field.

Environmental Education and Training Partnership (EETAP)
College of Natural Resources
University of Wisconsin–Stevens Point
Stevens Point, WI 54481
Telephone: (715) 346-4958
http://eetap.org

EETAP provides resources for students, teachers, and professionals that support K–12 environmental education with media specialists, in-service providers, nature center staff, and curriculum developers.

FairTest
342 Broadway
Cambridge, MA 02139
Telephone: (617) 864-4810
Fax: (617) 497-2224
info@fairtest.org
www.fairtest.org

The National Center for Fair and Open Testing is an advocacy organization working to end the abuses, misuses, and flaws of standardized testing and ensure that evaluation of students and workers is fair, open, and educationally sound. The center places particular emphasis on racial, gender, and cultural barriers in standardized tests and in their use by educational facilities.

The Gay, Lesbian, and Straight Education Network (GLSEN)
121 West 27th Street, Suite 804
New York, NY 10001-6207
Telephone: (212) 727-0135
Fax: (212) 727-0254

Western office:
870 Market Street, Suite 547
San Francisco, CA 94102
Telephone: (415) 551-9788

Fax: (415) 551-9789
glsenwest@glsen.org
http://glsen.org

GLSEN is the leading national organization fighting to end antigay bias in K–12 schools. It strives to ensure that each member of every school community is valued and respected regardless of sexual orientation or gender identity/expression. It works to educate teachers, students, and the public at large about the damaging effects of homophobia and heterosexism on youth and adults alike. GLSEN welcomes as members any and all individuals, regardless of sexual orientation, gender identity/expression, or occupation, who are committed to seeing this philosophy realized in K–12 schools. Its aim is to combat harassment and discrimination leveled against students and school personnel. GLSEN believes that the key to ending antigay prejudice and hate-motivated violence is education. This organization provides curriculum materials and support as well as helps students organize projects providing support and resources to youth in even the most isolated of places. It supports students as they form and lead gay-straight alliances—helping them to change their own school environments from the inside out.

Global Youth Action Network (GYAN)
211 East 43rd Street, Suite 905
New York, NY 10017
Telephone: (212) 661-6111
www.takingitglobal.org
gyan@youthlink.org

The Global Youth Action Network is an international collaboration among youth and youth-serving organizations to share information, resources, and solutions. Its purpose is to promote greater youth engagement. The GYAN creates the opportunity for every young person to be heard, leverages their voices to impact national and global agendas, and provides tools, recognition, and financial support for youth who take positive action to improve our world—community by community.

Harmony Foundation
PO Box 50022
Unit 15-1594
Fairfield Road
Victoria, BC, Canada V8S 1G1
Telephone: (250) 380-3001

www.harmonyfdn.ca
harmony@islandnet.com

Founded in 1985 on the belief in the importance of cooperation and education as the cornerstones of a successful transition to a sustainable society, the Harmony Foundation is committed to development based on sound environmental practices and progressive social programs. Its focus is on creating innovative training programs and educational materials for educators, youth, the workplace, and communities.

Institute for Democracy in Education
College of Education
McCracken Hall
Ohio University
Athens, OH 45701-2979
Telephone: (740) 593-4531
www.ohiou.edu/ide/

In 1985 the Institute for Democracy in Education (IDE) was founded by a group of local teachers dismayed that the debate over public school reform overlooked the historic purpose of public education—the development of participatory citizens who have cultivated democratic habits of heart and mind. Promoting democratic education became the group's focus. Today IDE is a partnership for all participants in the educational process—teachers, administrators, parents, and students—who believe that restructuring for democratic education must come from those at the heart of education. IDE works to provide teachers committed to democratic education with a forum for sharing ideas, with a support network of people holding similar values, and with opportunities for professional development.

Institute for Development of Educational Activities, Inc. (IDEA)
PO Box 807
East Dundee, IL 60118
Telephone: (847) 783-6900
Fax: (847) 783-6901
http://www.idea.org/

IDEA utilizes knowledge gained over more than thirty years on how to help individuals become part of sustainable, interconnected learning communities. The transfer of research to practice is a core value of IDEA and the staff are committed to helping school districts and communities become focused on creating a better world for children, families, and the communities in which they learn and grow. IDEA learning community members include leaders from every aspect of a community, such as administrators, students, families, parents, and business partners.

Institute for Elementary and Secondary Education (IESE)
Box 1938
Brown University
Providence, RI 02912
Telephone: (401) 863-1486
www.brown.edu/departments/IESE

IESE was founded in 1983 in response to teachers' needs for ongoing professional development in areas of school reform and educational issues. The importance here is in development and maintenance of relationships with schools, the community, and organizations so that together they can develop programs to build collaborations of benefit to teaching and learning initiatives.

International Society for Technology in Education (ISTE)
www.iste.org

ISTE is dedicated to the improvement of education through computer-based technology. It is concerned with the appropriate uses of information technology to support and improve learning, teaching, and administration in K–12 education and teacher education. Its role is leadership as ISTE provides members with information, networking opportunities, and guidance.

Interstate New Teacher Assessment and Support Consortium (INTASC)
One Massachusetts Avenue, NW, Suite 700
Washington, DC 20001-1431
Telephone: (202) 336-7048
Fax: (202) 408-8072
http://www.ccsso.org/intasc.html

The consortium was established to enhance collaboration among states interested in rethinking teacher licensing and assessment for education professionals. In 1993, the consortium proposed model standards that described what beginning teachers should know and be able to do. The standards are compatible with the national teacher certification standards proposed by the National Board for Professional Teaching. INTASC is also developing subject-area standards.

Laboratory for Student Success: The Mid-Atlantic Regional Educational Laboratory at Temple University Center for Research in Human Development and Education
933 Ritter Annex, 1301 Cecil B. Moore Avenue
Philadelphia, PA 19122-6091
Telephone: (215) 204-3030; (800) 892-5550
www.temple.edu/LSS
lss@vm.temple.edu

Its mission is to bring about lasting change in learning for the mid-Atlantic region's increasingly diverse student population. Its goal is to establish research, development, and dissemination of information that connects all stakeholders in education. Its key initiatives include a field-based development and applied research initiative, a program of outreach and services to the field, and the creation of strategic alliances and learning communities. Laboratory for Student Success has seven signature programs, specializes in urban education, and provides several publications on its research.

LAMBDA Educational Research Foundation
Institute of Gay and Lesbian Studies
10654 82nd Avenue, NW (Whyte Avenue), Suite 199
Edmonton, AB, Canada T6E 2A7
Telephone: (780) 988-2194
www.ualberta.ca/~cbidwell/cmb/lambda
lambda_1@telusplanet.net

The foundation was established as a nonprofit and autonomous organization in 1994. The LAMBDA Institute of Gay and Lesbian Studies formed in 1995. The organization is composed of a volunteer group of educators from various disciplines and is for any educator, student, scholar, or organization concerned with gay and lesbian social issues, culture, stability, security, and political and social changes. Members research and develop materials on these issues for workshops, seminars, and discussions. The idea is that public education can be a key element toward creating awareness and growth toward equality.

The Latino/a Education Network Service (LENS)
Columbia University Station
PO Box 250073
New York, NY 10025
information@palante.org
http://palante.org

LENS is a nonprofit organization dedicated to social, economic, and racial justice. LENS works to raise awareness and promote activism and social justice for Latinos and Latinas, people of color, and poor communities. It also conducts workshops and consults on community projects.

Leadership for Quality Education
21 South Clark Street, Suite 3120
Chicago, IL 60603
Telephone: (312) 853-1200
www.lqe.org

This is an advocacy organization that works to address and correct any obstacles to improving the quality of education at the local school level. It brings business resources to initiatives, advances smart ideas, and supports innovation in education, as it empowers new leaders to rethink schools.

Magnet Schools of America
733 15th Street, NW, Suite 330
Washington, DC 20005
Telephone: (202) 824-0672
www.magnet.edu
director@magnet.edu

The organization seeks to promote goals of desegregation, equity, and excellence through the expansion and improvement of magnet schools. It also aims to encourage the passage of legislation at both the state and national levels that will promote the development and improvement of magnet schools, explore and establish linkages with other professional groups with similar interests, and promote networking among magnet schools.

Mid-continent Regional Educational Laboratory (McREL)
2550 South Parker Road, Suite 500
Aurora, CO 80014-1678
Telephone: (303) 337-0900
www.mcrel.org
info@mcrel.org

McREL's objective is to improve the quality of education and learning through excellence in applied research, product development, and service. It accomplishes this through constant collaboration with all involved. The key initiatives are straightforward: development, applied research, state and local services, comprehensive school reform, and partnerships. The signature programs involve mathematics, learning, literacy, and standards as they focus on curriculum and instruction.

National Art Education Association (NAEA)
1916 Association Drive
Reston, VA 20191-1590
Telephone: (703) 860-8000
www.naea-reston.org
naea@dgs.dgsys.com

NAEA focuses on arts education, both theoretical and practical issues. Two subgroups focus on middle school and high school arts education; other issue-oriented subgroups are also pertinent to secondary arts instruction. It promotes arts education through professional development, service, advancement of knowledge, and leadership.

The National Association for Bilingual Education (NABE)
1030 15th Street, NW, Suite 470
Washington, DC 20005
Telephone: (202) 898-1829
Fax: (202) 789-2866
www.nabe.org

This is a professional national organization devoted to representing both the interests of language-minority students and the bilingual education professionals who serve them. It focuses on improving instructional practice for linguistically and culturally diverse students, provides professional development for teachers, seeks federal funding, and commits to educational reform.

The National Association for Multicultural Education (NAME)
733 15th Street, NW, Suite 430
Washington, DC 20005
Telephone: (202) 628-6263
Fax: (202) 628-6264
http://www.nameorg.org/

It is the mission of NAME to bring together individuals and groups with an interest in multicultural education from all levels of education, different academic disciplines, and diverse educational institutions and occupations. NAME is an active organization with members throughout the United States and several other countries.

National Association of Secondary School Principals (NASSP)
1904 Association Drive
Reston, VA 20191-1537
Telephone: (703) 860-0200
www.principals.org

The NASSP serves all educational leaders in middle schools and high schools. It was founded in 1916 and its mission is to promote excellence in school leadership. It provides members with a variety of programs and reviews to assist them in administration, supervision, curriculum planning, and effective staff development.

The National Board for Professional Teaching Standards (NBPTS)
1525 Wilson Boulevard, Suite 500
Arlington, VA 22209
Telephone: (703) 465-2700
www.nbpts.org

The National Board for Professional Teaching Standards focuses on making teaching a profession dedicated to student learning and to upholding high standards for professional performance. The mission is to advance the quality of teaching and learning by maintaining high standards, certifying teachers, and advocating reforms.

The National Center for Education Information (NCEI)
4401 Connecticut Avenue, NW, Suite 212
Washington, DC 20008
Telephone: (202) 362-3444
Fax: (202) 362-3493
http://www.ncei.com/

This is a private research organization specializing in survey research and data analysis. NCEI is the authoritative source of information about alternative teacher preparation and certification. Founded in 1980, NCEI has conducted several national and state studies that include surveys of teachers, school administrators, school board presidents, state departments of education, local school districts, and individuals interested in becoming teachers.

National Center for Research on Evaluation, Standards, and Student Testing (CRESST/UCLA)
301 GSE&IS, Mailbox 951522
300 Charles E. Young Drive North

Los Angeles, CA 90095-1522
Telephone: (310) 206-1532
Fax: (310) 825-3883
http://www.cse.ucla.edu/

CRESST is a partnership of UCLA, the University of Colorado, Stanford University, RAND, the University of Pittsburgh, the University of Southern California, Educational Testing Service, and the University of Cambridge (UK). CRESST's mission focuses on the assessment of educational quality, addressing persistent problems in the design and use of assessment systems to serve multiple purposes.

**National Center for the Restructuring of Education,
Schools, and Teaching**
Telephone: (212) 678-3432
www.tc.columbia.edu/~ncrest/

NCREST, established at Teachers College in 1990, supports restructuring efforts by documenting successful initiatives, creating reform networks to share new research findings with practitioners, and linking policy to practice. It works to develop understandings that help schools become learner-centered, by focusing on the needs of learners in school organization, governance, and pedagogy; knowledge-based, by restructuring teacher learning and professional development; and responsible and responsive, by restructuring accountability and assessment practices.

National Center for Urban Partnerships
National Center for Educational Alliances
Gould Memorial Library
Bronx Community College
West 181 Street and University Avenue
Bronx, NY 10453
Telephone: (718) 289-5164
www.ncup.org
info@thenationalcenter.org

The center provides technical assistance to support citywide partnerships between K–16 educators and various sectors and individuals in the community. It helps organize strategic planning institutes, staff development workshops, and other necessary initiatives. The center was backed by the Ford Foundation in 1991.

National Center on Accessing the General Curriculum
39 Cross Street
Peabody, MA 01960
Telephone: (978) 531-8555
www.cast.org/ncac
cast@cast.org

In a collaborative agreement with the U.S. Department of Education's Office of Special Programs (OSEP), the Center for Applied Special Technology (CAST) has established a National Center on Accessing the General Curriculum to provide a vision of how new curriculum, teaching practices, and policies can be woven together to create practical approaches for improved access to the general curriculum by students with disabilities.

National Center on Educational Outcomes
University of Minnesota
350 Elliott Hall
75 East River Road
Minneapolis, MN 55455
Telephone: (612) 626-1530
Fax: (612) 624-0879
http://www.coled.umn.edu/nceo/

The National Center on Educational Outcomes provides national leadership in the participation of students with disabilities in national and state assessments, standards-setting efforts, and graduation requirements.

National Center on Secondary Education and Transition
Institute on Community Integration
University of Minnesota
Pattee Hall, 150 Pillsbury Drive SE
Minneapolis, MN 55455
Telephone: (612) 624-2097
http://ici.umn.edu/ncset
ncset@icimail.coled.umn.edu

This center attempts to increase the capacity of national, state, and local agencies, organizations, and institutions to improve secondary education and transition results for youth with disabilities and their families. The center connects national resources with individuals in need, conducts workshops and training, develops tools, and provides technical assistance. The center aims to assist anybody concerned with or inquiring about disability issues.

National Clearinghouse for English Language Acquisition and Language Instruction Educational Programs (NCELA)
2121 K Street NW, Suite 260
Washington, DC 20037
Telephone: (202) 467-0867; (800) 321-6223
askncbe@ncbe.gwu.edu
www.ncbe.gwu.edu

NCELA (formerly the National Clearinghouse for Bilingual Education) strives to address critical issues dealing with the education of linguistically and culturally diverse (LCD) students in the United States; serve as a broker for exemplary practices and research as they relate to the education of LCD students; become a valuable source of information for individuals working in foreign language programs, English as a Second Language programs, Head Start, Title I, Migrant Education, or Adult Education programs. The name changed as a result of President Bush's No Child Left Behind Act; the Bilingual Act ceased to exist with the policy as well.

National Coalition of Advocates for Students
100 Boylston Street, Suite 737
Boston, MA 02116
Telephone: (617) 357-8507
www.igc.org/ncas/
ncasmfe@mindspring.com

The National Coalition of Advocates for Students (NCAS) is a national, nonprofit, education advocacy organization with twenty member groups in fourteen states. NCAS works to achieve equal access to a quality public education for students who are most vulnerable to school failure. NCAS's constituencies include low-income students; members of racial, ethnic, and language-minority groups; recent immigrants; migrant farm workers; and those with disabilities. Focusing on K–12, NCAS informs and mobilizes parents, concerned educators, and communities to help resolve critical education issues. Utilizing national projects and studies, public hearings, and outreach through publications and the media, NCAS raises concerns that otherwise might not be heard.

National Coalition of Education Activists (NCEA)
PO Box 679

Rhinebeck, NY 12572
Telephone: (845) 876-4580
NCEA@aol.com
www.nceaonline.org

NCEA is a multiracial network and membership organization of parents, school staff, union and community activists, and children's advocates. It shares a commitment to social justice, the elimination of bias of all kinds, and high-quality public schools that serve all children well. It believes excellent and equitable public schools are essential to helping all students reach their potential and to building a just and democratic society. Its mission is to help activists develop their knowledge and skills, creating opportunities for mulitracial groups of parents, educators, and community activists to discuss key education issues and their practical solutions. It also links individuals with activists and groups they can work with and learn from. The coalition develops and provides materials that translate information on key issues, policy, and research into nontechnical language.

**National Council for Accreditation of
Teacher Education (NCATE)**
2010 Massachusetts, Avenue, NW, Suite 500
Washington, DC 20036-1023
Telephone: (202) 466-7496
Fax: (202) 296-6620
www.ncate.org

The council evaluates and accredits institutions for the preparation of elementary and secondary schoolteachers, school service personnel, and administrators through standards that focus on the overall quality of the professional education unit. Themes throughout the standards include the conceptual framework, diversity, intellectual vitality, technology, professional community, evaluation, and performance assessment. Performance-based standards are the new focus for the twenty-first century.

National Council for History Education
26915 Westwood Road, Suite B-2
Westlake, OH 44145
Telephone: (440) 835-1776
www.history.org/nche/
nche@nche.net

National Council for History Education is a nonprofit corporation dedicated to promoting the importance of history in schools. It also provides a network for all advocates of history education. A disciplined-based advocacy group, it brings together school and university people to tackle all the issues that concern them—from curriculum design for K–Ph.D. through state, local, and university standards and requirements, teacher education, and professional development.

National Council for the Social Studies (NCSS)
8555 16th Street, Suite 500
Silver Spring, MD 20910
Telephone: (301) 588-1800; (800) 683-0812
www.ncss.org
information@ncss.org

NCSS's sole focus is on strengthening and advocating social studies education in schools. A subgroup focuses on secondary social studies education as well as content-specific education. It provides leadership, numerous resources, conferences, awards, grants, and fellowships.

National Council of Teachers of English (NCTE)
1111 West Kenyon Road
Urbana, IL 61801-1096
Telephone: (800) 369-6283
www.ncte.org
public_info@ncte.org

NCTE is the largest subject-matter association of teachers. It is devoted to improving the teaching of English and language arts at all levels of education and provides various opportunities for professional development. It has tools and resources specific to middle and secondary schoolteachers.

National Council of Teachers of Mathematics (NCTM)
1906 Association Drive
Reston, VA 20191-1502
Telephone: (703) 620-9840
www.nctm.org
infocentral@nctm.org

NCTM was founded in 1920 and has chapters all over the United States and Canada. Its primary function is improving mathematics teaching and learning from kindergarten to high school. It makes recommendations on instruction, content, and assessment. Its mission is to take the lead in changing mathematics education for the better.

National Education Association (NEA)
1201 16th Street, NW
Washington, DC 20036
www.nea.org

Founded in 1857, the NEA is the oldest and largest organization committed to advancing the cause of public education. The NEA offers anybody interested in education a variety of resources, guidance, and support for their educational endeavors. It is actively involved in professional standards for the teaching profession and maintaining academic freedom. At the national level, the NEA coordinates innovative projects and work that ranges from restructuring how learning takes place to fighting congressional attempts to privatize public education.

National Latino Children's Institute
nlci@nlci.org
http://www.nlci.org

This organization focuses on the needs of Latino children and teenagers in the United States and advocates policies that will improve education, community involvement, and good child-parent relationships. Its website provides news, its agenda, and events and projects that the institute is involved in.

National Library of Education
400 Maryland Avenue, SW
Washington, DC 20202
Telephone: (800) 424-1616
Reference desk: (202) 205-5015
Circulation desk: (202) 205-4945
www.ed.gov/NLE
library@ed.gov

National Library of Education is the world's largest federally funded library devoted solely to education. It is the federal government's main resource center for education information.

National Middle School Association (NMSA)
4151 Executive Parkway, Suite 300
Westerville, OH 43081

Telephone: (800) 528-6672
www.nmsa.org
info@NMSA.org

Started in 1973, NMSA is the only national education association dedicated exclusively to the growth of middle-level education. It is committed to middle schools that are academically excellent, developmentally responsive, and socially equitable for every young adolescent. In addition it provides professional development, journals, books, research, and valuable information.

National Parent Teachers Association
330 North Wabash Avenue, Suite 2100
Chicago, IL 60611
Telephone: (312) 670-6782; (800) 307-4PTA
www.pta.org

National Parent Teachers Association was founded in 1896 to help promote parental involvement, student advocacy, and support in schools and education. Its main mission is to support and speak on behalf of children and youth in the schools, in the community, and before governmental bodies and other organizations and to encourage parent and public involvement in the public schools of this nation.

National Rural Education Association
820 Van Vleet Oval, Room 227
University of Oklahoma
Norman, OK 73019
Telephone: (405) 325-7959
www.nrea.net

Its origins trace back to 1907, originally named the Department of Rural Education. The National Rural Education Association is the oldest established national organization of its kind in the United States. It is interested in maintaining the vitality of rural school systems across the country.

National School Boards Association (NSBA)
1680 Duke Street
Alexandria, VA 22314
Telephone: (703) 838-6722
www.nsba.org
info@nsba.org

The NSBA is a nationwide advocacy and outreach organization for public school governance. Its mission is to foster equity and excellence in elementary and secondary education through school board leadership.

National Science Teachers Association (NSTA)
1840 Wilson Boulevard
Arlington, VA 22201-3000
Telephone: (703) 243-7100
www.nsta.org

The NSTA strives to improve science education at all levels and to make science accessible to all students while promoting excellence and innovation in science teaching and learning. It provides support and leadership, as well as bountiful resources and publications. Its website also has specifics links for middle and high school teachers.

National Women's Studies Association (NWSA)
University of Maryland
7100 Baltimore Boulevard, Suite 500
College Park, MD 20740
Telephone: (301) 403-0525
Fax: (301) 403-4137
nwsa@umail.umd.edu

Founded in 1977 to further the development of women's studies throughout the world at every educational level and in every setting. To this end, the organization is committed to being a forum fostering dialogue and collective action among women who are dedicated to feminist education and change. It also has a subgroup that focuses specifically on K–12 education. It is an interdisciplinary organization that speaks to the needs of feminists at all educational levels and works to smooth the path of women's studies students today—and in the future.

New American Schools
1560 Wilson Boulevard, Suite 901
Arlington, VA 22209
Telephone: (703) 908-9500
info@nasdc.org
www.naschools.org

New American Schools (NAS) is a nonprofit organization whose mission is to increase student achievement through comprehensive school improvement strategies. To achieve this mission, NAS works to develop and support conducive environments at the state, district, and school levels necessary for continuous school improvement. It provides consulting services and partnerships for public schools.

New Standards Project of the Center on Education and Economy
Telephone: (212) 678-3432
www.ncee.org

The center believes it is possible for almost everyone to learn far more and develop far higher skills than most of us have thought possible. The hallmark of the center's work is standards-based reform based on the belief that education and training systems work best when clear standards are set for student achievement, accurate measures of progress against those standards are devised, and the people closest to the students are given the authority for figuring out how to get the students to the standards and are then held accountable for student progress. It stresses student responsibility as a necessity for student success.

No Excuses Campaign
214 Massachusetts Avenue, NE
Washington, DC 20002-4999
Telephone: (202) 546-4400
www.noexcuses.org

This is a national effort to mobilize public pressure for better education for the nation's disadvantaged. It connects concerned citizens who are committed to high academic achievement among children of all races, ethnic groups, and family incomes. It is based on the stories and lived experiences of high-performing, high-poverty schools.

North Central Regional Laboratory (NCREL)
1900 Spring Road, Suite 300
Oak Brook, IL 60523-1480
Telephone: (630) 571-4700; (800) 356-2735
www.ncrel.org
info@ncrel.org

NCREL works to strengthen and support schools and communities so that students achieve educational excellence. Its main work is in educational policy, technical assistance, and partnerships. It has four key initiatives and four signature programs, and it specializes in technology. Curriculum and community development, evaluation, and policy are just a few of the major issues it tackles. In keeping with the rest of the laboratories, they provide several publications on these matters.

Northeast and Islands Regional Educational Laboratory at Brown University (LAB)
222 Richmond Street, Suite 300
Providence, RI 02903-4226
Telephone: (401) 274-9548; (800) 521-9550
www.lab.brown.edu
LAB@brown.edu

The LAB's mission is to improve teaching and learning, as well as strategically work for educational reform and alliances that solidify crucial legislation. Its key initiatives are urban school reform, professional development for educational leadership, school change and community involvement, secondary school restructuring, standards, assessment, and instruction. It provides various signature programs, specialty areas, and publications accessible to all concerned.

Northwest Regional Educational Laboratory (NREL)
101 SW Main Street, Suite 500
Portland, OR 97204-3297
Telephone: (503) 275-9500
www.nwrel.org
info@nwrel.org

Its main goal is to improve educational results for children, youth, and adults by providing research and development assistance to a variety of agencies and institutions. The key initiatives entail assessment and evaluation, early childhood education, rural education, school improvement, community-based learning, and mathematics and science education. Its two signature programs are trait-based assessment and instruction, and onward to excellence II. It specializes in school change processes. NREL also provides a series of publications discussing its works.

Office of Elementary and Secondary Education
400 Maryland Avenue, SW
Washington, DC 20202
Telephone: (202) 401-0113
www.ed.gov/offices/OESE
oese@ed.gov

OESE's desire is to provide useful and timely information on elementary and secondary programs and issues. Its mission is to promote academic excellence, enhance educational opportunities and equity for all of America's children and families, and improve the quality of teaching and learning by providing leadership, technical assistance, and financial support.

Office of Indian Education Programs (OIEP)
1849 C Street, NW/MS-3512 MIB
Washington, DC 20240-0001

500 Gold Avenue, SW, Seventh Floor
Albuquerque, New Mexico 87103
www.oiep.bia.edu

This is a service organization devoted to providing quality education opportunities for Native Americans. Established in the latter part of the nineteenth century, OIEP has become the only national education system for American Indian children and adults. OIEP's aim is to create a preeminent education system by fulfilling its mission of serving children and their families from birth through life, working in partnership with tribes, families, communities, and American Indian education organizations.

The Office of Special Education and Rehabilitative Services
U.S. Department of Education
400 Maryland Avenue, SW
Washington, DC 20202
Telephone: (202) 205-5465
http://www.ed.gov/offices/OSERS/index.html

The Office of Special Education and Rehabilitative Services (OSERS) is committed to improving results and outcomes for people with disabilities of all ages.

Pacific Resources for Education and Learning
Ali'I Place 25th Floor
1099 Alakea Street
Honolulu, HI 96813
Telephone: (808) 441-1300
www.prel.org
askprel@prel.org

The mission of Pacific Resources for Education and Learning is a commitment to maintaining cultural literacy and improving the quality of life by helping to strengthen educational programs and processes for all students. The key initiatives are strengthening teaching and learning, transforming schools and other learning environments, fostering partnerships and connections, and addressing literacy as a priority. The signature programs provide educators in residence, leadership teams, research and development, conferences, and Project Al Maron. Among this organization's publications is a CD-ROM that provides an interactive framework of its works.

Parents, Families, and Friends of Lesbians and Gays (PFLAG)
1726 M Street, NW, Suite 400
Washington, DC 20036
Telephone: (202) 467-8180
Fax: (202) 467-8194
www.pflag.org

Parents, Families, and Friends of Lesbians and Gays is a national nonprofit organization. It celebrates diversity and envisions a society that embraces everyone, including those of diverse sexual orientations and gender identities. Only with respect, dignity, and equality for all will we reach our full potential as human beings, individually and collectively. PFLAG welcomes the participation and support of all who share in and hope to realize this vision. PFLAG promotes the health and well-being of gay, lesbian, bisexual, and transgendered persons and their families and friends through support, to cope with an adverse society; education, to enlighten an ill-informed public; and advocacy, to end discrimination and to secure equal civil rights. Parents, Families, and Friends of Lesbians and Gays provides opportunity for dialogue about sexual orientation and gender identity, and acts to create a society that is healthy and respectful of human diversity.

Parents Raising Educational Standards in Schools (PRESS)
PO Box 26913
Milwaukee, WI 53226
Telephone: (414) 607-3950
www.execpc.com/~presswis
presswis@execpc.com

PRESS is a grassroots education group started by a few individuals and now has a significantly large membership of people from various professions passionately concerned about their children's education.

Phi Delta Kappa International
408 North Union Street
PO Box 789
Bloomington, IN 47402-0789
Telephone: (812) 339-1156; (800) 766-1156
www.pdkintl.org

Phi Delta Kappa is an international association of professional educators. Its mission is to promote quality education, with particular emphasis on publicly supported education, as essential to the development and maintenance of a democratic way of life. It provides numerous resources and links.

Public Agenda Foundation
6 East 39th Street
New York, NY 10016
Telephone: (212) 686-6610
www.publicagenda.org

Public Agenda Foundation is a public opinion research and citizen education organization to help leaders better understand the public's perspective on major policy issues and also tries to help the public understand critical policy issues so that they can make more informed choices.

REFORMA: The National Association to Promote Library and Information Services to Latinos
PO Box 832
Anaheim, CA 92815-0832
frgarcia@ucla.edu
http://clnet.ucr.edu/library/reforma/

This organization is committed to the improvement of library and information services for the approximately 35.3 million Spanish-speaking and Latino people in the United States. It is an affiliate of the ALA (American Library Association), seeking to provide Latinos all around the United States with bilingual and bicultural library staff, Spanish-language materials, and education about library services.

Rethinking Schools
1001 East Keefe Avenue
Milwaukee, WI 53212
Telephone: (414) 964-9646; (800) 669-4192
www.rethinkingschools.org

Started by a group of Milwaukee area teachers in the 1980s with a vision to improve education in their own classrooms and schools and to promote reform throughout the public school system in the United States. It began as a local effort to address issues like basal readers, standardized testing, and textbook-dominated curriculum. It has flourished into an entity of school change and courage. It offers numerous publications to challenge educational thought.

Small Schools Workshops
Lewis and Clark College
0615 SW Palatine Hill Road, MSC 93
Portland, OR 97219
Telephone: (503) 768-6020
www.lclark.edu/~ssw/
ssw@lclark.edu

Educators, organizers, and researchers collaborating with teachers, parents, and principals comprise Small Schools Workshops to create innovative new learning communities in existing public schools while discussing and exploring larger educational reform issues.

Society for the Advancement of Chicanos and Native Americans in Science (SACNAS)
PO Box 8526
Santa Cruz, CA 95061
Telephone: (831) 459-0170
Fax: (831) 459-0194
info@sacnas.org
k12program@sacnas.org
www.sacnas.org

The mission of SACNAS is to encourage Chicano/Latino and Native American students to pursue graduate education and obtain the advanced degrees necessary for research careers and science-teaching professions at all levels. The goal of the K–12 education program at SACNAS is to ensure that elementary, middle school, and high school students from traditionally underrepresented minority backgrounds receive superior educational opportunities, role models, and the encouragement needed to pursue careers in science, mathematics, engineering, and technology.

Society of the Educational Arts, Inc. (SEA)
Clemente Soto Vélez Cultural and Educational Center

107 Suffolk Street, Second Floor
New York, NY 10002
Telephone: (212) 529-1545
Fax: (212) 529-1567
sea@sea-ny.org

Condominio Dalia 15, Suite 204
Isla Verde, Puerto Rico 00979
Telephone and Fax: (787) 253-9949
seapuertorico@aol.com

3908 Blazing Star Drive
Orlando, FL 32828
Telephone and Fax: (407) 382-8552
sea-orlando@avalonpark.com

Founded in 1985 in Puerto Rico, the Society of the Educational Arts, Inc./Sociedad Educativa de las Artes, Inc. (SEA) is a not-for-profit Hispanic/bilingual arts-in-education organization dedicated to the empowerment and educational advancement of children and young adults. SEA is one of the few Hispanic/bilingual arts-in-education organizations in New York City, Puerto Rico, and Orlando. Through various programs SEA provides opportunities for children and young adults to examine, challenge, and create possible solutions for current educational, social, and community issues while fostering their talents, potential, self-esteem, and self-confidence.

The SouthEastern Regional Vision for Education (SERVE)
1100 West Market Street, Third Floor
Greensboro, NC 27403-1830
Telephone: (336) 334-3211; (800) 755-3277
www.serve.org
info@serve.org

SERVE's main goal is to improve educational opportunities for learners in the Southeast. Among their initiatives are improvements for low-performing schools, the National Center for Homeless Education, and a cross-organizational initiative on teachers and teaching. It offers six signature programs focusing on assessment, families, policy, science and mathematics, school reform, and technology. Early childhood education is its specialty area as it provides leadership and support. Its publications are available as well.

Southwest Educational Development Laboratory (SEDL)
211 East 7th Street
Austin, TX 78701-3281
Telephone: (512) 476-6861; (800) 476-6861
www.sedl.org
info@sedl.org

SEDL's mission is to locate, share, and maintain critical solutions for problems facing schools, teachers, and policymakers in the Southwest. Its major emphasis is educational equity for Latinos, African Americans, and other minorities. The key initiatives focus on collaboration, community deliberation and policymaking, instructional coherence, technology, inquiry, and improvement. It has three signature programs on early childhood, leadership for change, and policy analysis. In contrast to the other laboratories, SEDL has several specialty areas. These areas are true to its mission statement: language and cultural diversity, organizing for diversity, and adapting comprehensive school reform. In addition SEDL has developed resources for teachers, administrators, and community members on these areas and native education and language.

Teacher Education Accreditation Council (TEAC)
One Dupont Circle, Suite 320
Washington, DC 20036-0110
Telephone: (202) 466-7230
Fax: (202) 466-7238
www.teac.org

The Teacher Education Accreditation Council was developed in 1998 in response to a concern of the Council of Independent Colleges (CIC) that NCATE was the only national teacher education accreditation association. Its mission is to promote professional programs in colleges and universities.

Teaching for Change
NECA
PO Box 73038
Washington, DC 20056
Telephone: (202) 588-7204; (800) 763-9131
www.teachingforchange.org

The Network of Educators on the Americas (NECA) works with school communities to develop and promote pedagogies, resources, and cross-cultural understanding for social and economic justice in the Americas.

It organized in 1986 as a coalition of K–12 teachers across the United States and Canada to address concerns about the U.S. role in Central America and the education of Central American refugees. The United States was heavily involved in El Salvador and Nicaragua at the time, yet there were few resources about Central America for the classroom. The influx of immigrants and refugees from Central America gave further impetus to the demand for materials that reflected students' histories and experiences. In 1993 and 1994, NECA sponsored a number of seminar series, including Multiculturalism and Anti-Racism: Perspectives, History, and Strategies for Change and Uncovering Community: Strengthening Schools. It also offered miniworkshops on the background of Central American students, designed to address anti-immigrant sentiment by presenting, through history and literature, the region's history and, particularly, the U.S. foreign policy that forced many Central Americans to leave their homeland.

Ten Regional Education Laboratories
www.relnetwork.org

This is a network of ten regional laboratories working to ensure educational improvement at the local, state, and regional levels. These laboratories are the U.S. Department of Education's largest research and development investment established to help all those involved in educational endeavors. They are administered by the Office of Educational Research and Improvement. Congress initiated the Lab Program in 1985 as part of the Elementary and Secondary Education Act. In 1994 it was reauthorized. Each laboratory has specific aims and goals suited to its region and population. Its collective mission is to improve education at the national level.

Thomas B. Fordham Foundation
1627 K Street, NW, Suite 600
Washington, DC 20006
Telephone: (202) 223-5452; (888) TBF-7474
fordham@dunst.com

The foundation supports research, publications, and action projects of national significance in elementary and secondary education reform. It has assumed the work of the Educational Excellence Network and is affiliated with the Manhattan Institute for Policy Research. It also provides grants and scholarship funds. Recently it commissioned a set of papers in response to President Bush's educational policy.

U.S. Department of Education
400 Maryland Avenue, SW
Washington, DC 20202-0498
Telephone: 800-USA-LEARN
www.ed.gov

This is the federal government's Department of Education with a wealth of resources on policy, programs, budget, links, staff, and job opportunities.

WestEd
730 Harrison Street
San Francisco, CA 94107
Telephone: (415) 565-3000
www.wested.org
tross@wested.org

Its purpose, as an agency, is to ensure excellence and equity, and improve learning for children, youth, and adults. Its initiatives involve whole school reform, language and cultural diversity, and state alliance projects. The signature programs focus on math case methods, child and family studies, and collaborative assessment. The specialty area is in assessment and accountability.

STATE DEPARTMENTS OF EDUCATION

This is a list of departments of education by state and office location to facilitate any queries on licensure requirements, certification, procedures, or specific schools.

ALABAMA
Alabama State Department of Education
50 North Ripley Street
PO Box 302101
Montgomery, AL 36104
Telephone: (334) 242-9700
www.alsde.edu/html/home.asp

ALASKA
Alaska Department of Education and Early Development

Juneau office:
801 West 10th Street, Suite 200
Juneau, AK 99801-1878
Telephone: (907) 465-2800
Fax: (907) 465-3452

Anchorage office:
619 E. Ship Creek, Suite 230
Anchorage, AK 99501
Telephone: (907) 269-4500
Fax: (907) 269-4520

Fairbanks office:
542 4th Avenue, Suite 212
Fairbanks, AK 99701
Telephone: (907) 451-3198
Fax: (907) 451-3196
www.educ.state.ak.us

ARIZONA
Arizona Department of Education
1535 West Jefferson
Phoenix, AZ 85007
Telephone: 602-542-4361
http://ade.state.az.us

ARKANSAS
The Arkansas Department of Education (ADE)
#4 Capitol Mall
Little Rock, AR 72201
Telephone: (501) 682-4475
http://arkedu.state.ar.us

CALIFORNIA
California Department of Education (CDE)
PO Box 944272
Sacramento, CA 94244-2720
Telephone: (916) 319-0791
http://goldmine.cde.ca.gov

COLORADO
Colorado Department of Education (CDE)

201 East Colfax Avenue
Denver, CO 80203-1799
Telephone: (303) 866-6600
Fax: (303) 830-0793
www.cde.state.co.us

CONNECTICUT
Connecticut State Department of Education
165 Capitol Avenue
Hartford, CT 06145
Telephone: (860) 713-6548
www.state.ct.us/sde

DELAWARE
State of Delaware, Department of Education
John G. Townsend Building
401 Federal Street
PO Box 1402
Dover, DE 19903-1402
Telephone: (302) 739-4601
Fax: (302) 739-4654
www.doe.state.de.us

FLORIDA
Florida Department of Education
Turlington Building
325 West Gaines Street
Tallahassee, FL 32399-0400
Telephone: (850) 487-1785
www.firn.edu/doe/index.html

GEORGIA
Georgia Department of Education
205 Jesse Hill Jr. Drive, SE
Atlanta, GA 30334
Telephone: (404) 656-2800; (800) 311-3627
www.doe.k12.ga.us/index.asp

HAWAII
Hawaii Department of Education
PO Box 2360
Honolulu, HI 96804

Telephone: (808) 586-3230
Fax: 808-586-3234
http://doe.k12.hi.us

IDAHO
Idaho Department of Education
650 West State Street
PO Box 83720
Boise, ID 83720-0027
Telephone: (208) 332-6800
www.sde.state.id.us/Dept

ILLINOIS
Illinois State Board of Education

Springfield office:
100 North 1st Street
Springfield, IL 62777
Telephone: (217) 782-4321
TTY: (217) 782-1900
Customer Service Center: (866) 262-6663

Chicago office:
100 West Randolph, Suite 14-300
Chicago, IL 60601
Telephone: (312) 814-2220
TTY: (312) 814-5821

Mt. Vernon office:
123 South 10th Street, Suite 200
Mt. Vernon, IL 62864
Telephone: (618) 244-8383
www.isbe.state.il.us

INDIANA
Indiana Department of Education
State House, Room 229
Indianapolis, IN 46204-2798
Telephone: (317) 232-0808
Fax: (317) 233-6326
http://doe.state.in.us

IOWA
Iowa Department of Education
Grimes State Office Building
Des Moines, IA 50319-0146
Telephone: (515) 281-5294
Fax: (515) 242-5988
www.state.ia.us/educate

KANSAS
Kansas State Department of Education
120 Southeast 10th Avenue
Topeka, KS 66612-1182
Telephone: (785) 296-3201
Fax: (785) 296-7933
www.ksbe.state.ks.us/Welcome.html

KENTUCKY
Kentucky Department of Education (KDE)
500 Mero Street
Frankfort, KY 40601
Telephone: (502) 564-4770; (800) 533-5372
www.kde.state.ky.us

LOUISIANA
Louisiana Department of Education
PO Box 94064
Baton Rouge, LA 70804-9064
Telephone: (225) 342-4411
Fax: (225) 342-0193
www.doe.state.la.us/DOE/asps/home.asp

MAINE
Maine Department of Education
23 State House Station
Augusta, ME 04333-0023
Telephone: (207) 624-6600
www.state.me.us/education/homepage.htm

MARYLAND
Maryland State Department of Education
200 West Baltimore Street
Baltimore, MD 21201

Telephone: (410) 767-0100
www.msde.state.md.us

MASSACHUSETTS
Massachusetts Department of Education
350 Main Street
Malden, MA 02148-5023
Telephone: (781) 338-3000
TTY: (800) 439-0183
www.doe.mass.edu

MICHIGAN
Michigan Department of Education
608 West Allegan
Lansing, MI 48933
Telephone: (517) 373-3324
www.michigan.gov/mde

MINNESOTA
Minnesota Department of Children, Families, and Learning
1500 Highway 36 West
Roseville, MN 55113
Telephone: (651) 582-8200
http://cfl.state.mn.us

MISSISSIPPI
Mississippi Department of Education
Central High School
PO Box 771
359 North West Street
Jackson, MS 39205
Telephone: (601) 359-3513
www.mde.k12.ms.us

MISSOURI
Missouri Department of Elementary and Secondary Education
PO Box 480
Jefferson City, MO 65102
Telephone: (573) 751-4212
Fax: (573) 751-8613
http://services.dese.state.mo.us

MONTANA
Montana Office of Public Instruction
PO Box 202501
Helena, MT 59620-2501
Telephone: (406) 444-3095; (888) 231-9393
www.opi.state.mt.us/OPISiteMap.html

NEBRASKA
Nebraska Department of Education
301 Centennial Mall South
Lincoln, NE 68509
Telephone: (402) 471-2295
www.nde.state.ne.us

NEVADA
Nevada Department of Education
700 East Fifth Street
Carson City, NV 89701
Telephone: (775) 687-9200
Fax: (775) 687-9101
www.nde.state.nv.us

NEW HAMPSHIRE
New Hampshire Department of Education
101 Pleasant Street
Concord, NH 03301-3860
Telephone: (603) 271-3494
Fax: (603) 271-1953
www.ed.state.nh.us

NEW JERSEY
New Jersey Department of Education
PO Box 500
Trenton, NJ 08625
Telephone: (609) 292-4469
www.state.nj.us/education

NEW MEXICO
New Mexico Department of Education
300 Don Gaspar
Santa Fe, NM 87501
Telephone: (505) 827-6574

Fax: (505) 827-7611/6694
http://sde.state.nm.us

NEW YORK
New York State Education Department
89 Washington Avenue
Albany, NY 12234
Telephone: (518) 474-3852
www.nysed.gov

NORTH CAROLINA
North Carolina Department of Public Instruction
301 North Wilmington Street
Raleigh, NC 27601
Telephone: (919) 807-3300
www.dpi.state.nc.us

NORTH DAKOTA
North Dakota Department of Public Instruction
600 East Boulevard Avenue, Dept. 201
Floors 9, 10, and 11
Bismarck, ND 58505-0440
Phone: (701) 328-2260
Fax: (701) 328-2461
www.dpi.state.nd.us

OHIO
Ohio Department of Education
25 South Front Street
Columbus, OH 43215-4183
Telephone: (877)-644-6338
www.ode.state.oh.us

OKLAHOMA
Oklahoma State Department of Education
2500 North Lincoln Boulevard
Oklahoma City, OK 73105-4599
Telephone: (405) 521-3301
Fax: (405) 521-6205
www.sde.state.ok.us/home/defaultns.html

OREGON
Oregon Department of Education
255 Capitol Street NE
Salem, OR 97310-0203
Telephone: (503) 378-3569
TDD: (503) 378-2892
Fax: (503) 378-5156
www.ode.state.or.us

PENNSYLVANIA
Pennsylvania Department of Education
333 Market Street
Harrisburg, PA 17126
Telephone: (717) 783-6788
www.pde.state.pa.us/pde_internet/site/default.asp

RHODE ISLAND
Rhode Island Network for Educational Technology
646 Camp Avenue
North Kingstown, RI 02852
Telephone: (401) 295-9200
Fax: (401) 295-8101
www.ri.net

SOUTH CAROLINA
South Carolina State Department of Education
1429 Senate Street
Columbia, SC 29201
Telephone: (803) 734-8815
Fax: (803) 734-3389
www.sde.state.sc.us

SOUTH DAKOTA
South Dakota Department of Education and Cultural Affairs (DECA)
700 Governors Drive
Pierre, SD 57501-2291
Telephone: (605) 773-4748
Fax: (605) 773-6139
www.state.sd.us/deca

TENNESSEE
Tennessee Department of Education

Sixth Floor, Andrew Johnson Tower
710 James Robertson Parkway
Nashville, TN 37243-0375
Telephone: (615) 741-2731
www.state.tn.us/education

TEXAS
Texas Education Agency (TEA)
1701 North Congress
Austin, TX 78701
Telephone: (512) 463-9734
www.tea.state.tx.us

UTAH
Utah State Office of Education
250 East 500 South
PO Box 144200
Salt Lake City, UT 84114-4200
Telephone: (801) 538-7500
www.usoe.k12.ut.us

VERMONT
State of Vermont Department of Education
State Office Building
120 State Street
Montpelier, VT 05620-2501
Telephone: (802) 828-3111
www.state.vt.us/educ

VIRGINIA
Virginia Department of Education
PO Box 2120
Richmond, VA 23218
Telephone: (800) 292-3820
www.pen.k12.va.us

WASHINGTON
State of Washington Office of Superintendent of Public Instruction
(OSPI)
Old Capitol Building
PO Box 47200
Olympia, WA 98504-7200

Telephone: (360) 725-6000
TTY: (360) 664-3631
Fax: (360) 753-6712
www.k12.wa.us

WASHINGTON, DC
District of Columbia Public Schools (DCPS)
District of Columbia Board of Education
825 North Capitol Street, NE, Ninth Floor
Washington, DC 20002-4232
Telephone: (202) 442-4289
www.k12.dc.us/dcps/home.html

WEST VIRGINIA
West Virginia Department of Education
1900 Kanawha Boulevard East
Charleston, WV 25305-0330
Telephone: (304) 558-2118
Fax: (304) 558-0882
http://wvde.state.wv.us

WISCONSIN
Wisconsin Department of Public Instruction (DPI)
125 South Webster Street
PO Box 7841
Madison, WI 53707-7841
Telephone: (608) 266-3390; (800) 441-4563
www.dpi.state.wi.us/index.html

WYOMING
Wyoming Department of Education
2300 Capitol Avenue
Hathaway Building, Second Floor
Cheyenne, WY 82002-0050
Telephone: (307) 777-7673
www.k12.wy.us

Chapter Eight

✺ Selected Print and Nonprint Resources

The resources listed in this chapter provide a variety of works on secondary education, both historical and contemporary. These resources are divided into two major categories, print and nonprint, and within these there are other classifications to better help educators find a variety of resources for their own information and classroom practice.

PRINT RESOURCES

Organization Papers, Reports, and Publications

Bottoms, Gene. 2001. *The Lost Opportunity of the Senior Year: Making Grade 12 Count.* Update, Southern Regional Education Board.

This article presents information and data from the High Schools That Work project, including how U.S. high school students compare with their counterparts in other countries and how well prepared high school seniors are for postsecondary education.

Braddock, J. H., II. 1990. "**Tracking the Middle Grades: National Patterns of Grouping for Instruction**." *Phi Delta Kappan* 71, no. 6 (February): 445–449.

This article presents current data on using between-class grouping and regrouping in American schools serving early adolescents, based on the 1988 Johns Hopkins University middle school survey. Findings show that learning opportunities in the middle grades remain highly stratified.

Brown, Cynthia G. 2002. *Opportunities and Accountability to Leave No Child Behind in the Middle Grades.* Edna McConnell Clark Foundation.

This report analyzes the impact that the No Child Left Behind Act of 2001, which was signed into law by President George W. Bush on January 8, 2002, will have on our nation's education system. In particular, the report focuses on the opportunities and challenges that middle schools will be facing, in light of this new legislation, to improve the learning environment for their students.

Burton-Szabo, S. 1996. "**Special Classes for Gifted Students? Absolutely.**" *Gifted Child Today Magazine* 19, no. 1 (January–February): 12–15, 50.

This article makes a case for special classes for gifted students and answers objections to special classes raised by the middle school movement and the cooperative learning movement.

Butty, Jo-Anne, L. Manswell, Velma LaPoint, Veronica G. Thomas, and Deirdre Thompson. 2001. "**The Changing Face of After-School Programs: Advocating Talent Development for Urban Middle and High School Students.**" *Bulletin* 85, no. 626. National Association of Secondary School Principals.

This article focuses on school-based, after-school initiatives aimed at middle and high school students in urban schools. It discusses the benefits of after-school programs and offers guidelines for enhancing their success.

Carnegie Foundation. 1998. *Turning Points: Preparing American Youth for the Twenty-First Century.*

This landmark report recognized the need to strengthen the academic core of middle schools and establish supportive environments to value adolescents. In 1998 Carnegie turned to the Center for Collaborative Education in Boston to develop a new whole-school reform design that would be based on the research and work of the preceding nine years.

Center for Education, Research, Analysis, and Innovation. 2001. *Congress, Teachers, and the Perils of Merit Pay.*

In this paper C. Lugg analyzes the problems with economic rewards for prescribed performance as related to standardized test scores.

Chudowsky, Naomi, Nancy Kober, Keith S. Gayler, and Madlene Hamilton. 2002. *State High School Exit Exams: A Baseline Report.* Center on Education Policy.

The Center on Education Policy has begun a three-year study of state exit exams, one of the most comprehensive overviews to date. This report—the first in a series of annual reports—describes baseline findings, drawn from data collected from all of the states with current or planned exit exams, case studies conducted in five states, and a review of other major research in the field. The study examines the impacts of exit exams on students, as well as the major challenges states face in implementing such exams.

Clinkenbeard, P. R. 1991. **"Unfair Expectations: A Pilot Study of Middle School Students' Comparisons of Gifted and Regular Classes."** *Journal for the Education of the Gifted* 15, no. 1: 56–63.

Analysis of essays comparing experiences in gifted and regular classes written by sixth-grade gifted students found that many students felt teachers and peers outside the gifted class had unfair expectations of them. Other topics addressed by students include grading, group work, lack of acknowledgment for effort, treatment by peers, and teacher expectations.

Cooney, Sondra. 2000. *A Middle Grades Message: A Well-Qualified Teacher in Every Class Matters.* Southern Regional Education Board.

Are middle school teachers prepared to teach the depth of content necessary to prepare students for high school in the twenty-first century? This report addresses that question and includes a rating instrument that states and districts can use to gauge their commitment to having a well-qualified teacher in every middle grade classroom.

Dorn, Sherman. 2003. *High-Stakes Testing and the History of Graduation.* Education Policy Analysis Archives.

This article provides historical perspective on high-stakes testing and suggests that tests required for high school graduation will have mixed results for the supposed value of high school diplomas.

Epstein, J. L. 1990. **"What Matters in the Middle Grades—Grade Span or Practices?"** *Phi Delta Kappan* 71, no. 6 (February): 438–444.

A 1988 Johns Hopkins University survey gathered data on organizational variations among schools to study how grade span affects school programs, teaching practices, and student progress. This article reports selected results on the relation of grade span to school size, grade-level enrollment, school goals, report card entries, and relevant trends.

Epstein, J. L., and D. J. MacIver. 1990. *Education in the Middle Grades: Overview of National Practices and Trends.* Baltimore, MD: Center for Research on Elementary and Middle Schools, Johns Hopkins University. ERIC Document Reproduction Service (EDRS), ED330082.

In spring 1988, the Johns Hopkins Center for Research on Elementary and Middle Schools (CREMS) conducted a national survey of principals in 2,400 public middle grade schools that include seventh grade. Using the 1988 survey date, this document presents an overview of educational approaches and practices in schools that serve early adolescents.

Gallagher, J. J., M. R. Coleman, and S. Nelson. 1995. **"Perceptions of Educational Reform by Educators Representing Middle Schools, Cooperative Learning, and Gifted Education."** *Gifted Child Quarterly* 39, no. 2 (Spring): 66–76.

The perceptions of 175 gifted education teachers and 147 middle-school teachers concerning gifted education needs are compared. Gifted educators disagree with proponents of cooperative learning concerning student needs and disagree with middle-school educators on the value of ability grouping and the social consequences of being labeled gifted.

Heller, Rafael, Sarah Calderon, Elliott Medrich, Gene Bottoms, Sondra Cooney, and Caro Feagin. 2002. *Academic Achievement in the Middle Grades: What Does Research Tell Us?* SREB.

This literature review from the Southern Regional Education Board (SREB) assesses the state of middle grades education that led to reform. This review found that best practices for promoting achievement in the middle grades include providing accelerated and rich core curriculum, setting high expectations and creating a supportive climate of encouragement, grouping students to help them connect what they are learning across the curriculum, and assigning highly qualified teachers to every classroom.

Kirst, Michael, Andrea Venezia, and Anthony L. Antonio. 2003. *Betraying the College Dream: How Disconnected K–12 and Postsecondary Education Systems Undermine Student Aspirations.* Stanford University.

Within the six states studied (California, Georgia, Illinois, Maryland, Oregon, and Texas), the authors found that over 80 percent of African American and Latino students surveyed plan to obtain some form of postsecondary education. However, this study also found that the states have created multiple barriers between high school and college. Other findings highlight issues such as inequalities in college counseling, college preparation course offerings, and connections with local postsecondary institutions. In addition to the full report, there is a policy brief and executive summary available.

Kirst, Michael W. 2001. "**Overcoming the High School Senior Slump: New Education Policies.**" *Education Week Review.* IEL and NCPPHE.

The strategy for keeping high school seniors seriously engaged in academic work lies in better coordination between K–12 school systems and colleges and universities, according to this report from the Institute for Educational Leadership (IEL) and the National Center for Public Policy and Higher Education (NCPPHE). The author makes suggestions on how high schools can address the problem to make senior year a priority. The report can be ordered from IEL, 1001 Connecticut Avenue, NW, Washington, DC 20036; 202-822-8405; or e-mail: iel@iel.org.

LAB at Brown University. 2000. *Benchmarks for Success in High School Education: Putting Data to Work in School-to-Career Education Reform.*

This discusses the work of five communities who created connected learning systems that redesigned high school learning as they worked in conjunction with Jobs for the Future.

LAB at Brown University. 2000. *What It Takes: 10 Capacities for Initiating and Sustaining School Improvement.*

This is a guidebook with practical applications and research on the processes schools initiate to sustain reform.

LAB at Brown University. 1999. *Quality Bilingual Education: Defining Success.*

This paper provides a comprehensive framework for success in bilingual education. It considers a range of research and the debate on effective school practices.

Lachat, M. 2000. *Standards, Equity, and Cultural Diversity.* The Center for Resource Management.

This work raises equity questions and issues pertinent to educational standards and reform.

Lankard, Bettina A. 1990. *Employability—The Fifth Basic Skill.* ERIC Clearinghouse on Adult, Career, and Vocational Education.

This ERIC Digest (#104) discusses employability as a basic skill and introduces strategies for incorporating this skill into academic and vocational instruction.

Martinez, Monica, and Judy Bray. 2002. *All over the Map: State Policies to Improve the High School.* NAAHS.

The recently formed National Alliance on the American High School (NAAHS) has released a report examining trends and assumptions in state high school education policy. The report finds that, despite years of education reform, high schools have remained relatively unchanged. Policymakers should devote more attention to innovative secondary education approaches.

McEwin, C. K., and J. Thomason. 1991. "**Curriculum: The Next Frontier.**" *Momentum* 22, no. 2 (April): 34–37.

This article discusses the national movement to improve middle school education with respect to school reorganization, curricular issues, instructional strategies, and various ways of applying the middle school concept.

Mizell, M. Hayes. 2002. *Shooting for the Sun: The Message of Middle School Reform.* Edna McConnell Clark Foundation.

This collection of speeches and essays discusses the challenges that teachers and principals face in their work to improve student achievement in sixth, seventh, and eighth grades. The author also offers suggestions on how schools can more effectively educate our nation's youth and improve student academic performance in the middle grades.

Molnar, A. 2003. *Profiles of For-Profit Education Management Companies, 2002–2003.* CERU. Arizona State University.

This annual report found that forty-seven education management companies operate in twenty-four states and the District of Columbia, enrolling 190,000 students. The report is the most comprehensive resource for the for-profit education management industry.

National Center for Education Statistics. 2001. *High School Academic Curriculum and the Persistence Path through College.*

The findings of this study demonstrate a consistent advantage for students who complete rigorous high school curriculum—and to a lesser extent for those completing mid-level curriculum—over their peers enrolled in lower-level courses. Students who complete rigorous curriculum are more likely to stay enrolled in their first institution or, if they transferred, to stay on track to a bachelor's degree. The more challenging courses also may help students overcome socioeconomic disadvantages such as low family income and parents with no college experience.

National Coalition for the Homeless. 1999. *Making the Grade: Successes and Challenges in Providing Educational Opportunities to Homeless Children and Youth.* September.

A new report by the National Coalition for the Homeless documents the efforts of state and local educational agencies to help homeless children enroll in, attend, and succeed in school.

National Education Association. 1918. *The Cardinal Principles of Secondary Education.*

The year 1918 marked the conceptualization of the curriculum field (for some), and in that came the need to rethink secondary education. This report sets forth seven areas of life secondary education curriculum to be addressed and calls for unified studies of these subject areas.

National Education Association. 1893. *Report of the Committee of Ten on Secondary School Studies.*

This highly influential document was commissioned by the National Education Association (NEA) in an attempt to standardize the secondary curriculum given the amount of variation that had developed in the nineteenth century.

National Middle School Association. 2001. *This We Believe—And Now We Must Act.*

National Middle School Association (NMSA) is making available *This We Believe—And Now We Must Act*, a collection of twelve essays suggesting ways to implement recommendations NMSA made in its seminal document, *This We Believe: Developmentally Responsive Middle Level Schools*, to improve middle-level learning, which was released in 1995. Topics include high expectations for everyone involved in the school, varied teaching and learning approaches, flexible organizational structures, a positive school climate, a shared vision, and school, family, and community partnerships.

Ogbu, John. 1994. "**Racial Stratification and Education in the United States: Why Inequality Persists.**" *Teachers College Record* 96, no. 2: 264–298.

This article identifies three links that relate racial stratification to poor academic achievement in black students.

Pool, H., and J. A. Page, eds. 1995. *Beyond Tracking: Finding Success in Inclusive Schools.* Bloomington, IN: Phi Delta Kappa Educational Foundation. ERIC Document Reproduction Service (EDRS), ED386873.

This collection of papers addresses tracking, whether it should be abolished, the movement toward inclusiveness in schools, strategies to meet all students' needs, and the process of untracking.

Ravitch, Diane, ed. 2003. *Building a Successful High School: Brookings Paper on Education Policy 2003.* Washington, DC: Brookings Institute Press.

Two decades after the seminal report issued by the 1983 National Commission on Excellence in Education, a group of prominent scholars explored the current state of America's high schools with a focus on new research about how to reform them.

Rethinking Schools. 1999. *Selling Out Our Schools: Vouchers, Markets, and the Future of Public Education.*

This work provides a critical look at the attempts to privatize public education. Included are short commentaries from individuals across the educational field.

Rethinking Schools. 1997. *Funding for Justice: Money, Equity, and the Future of Public Education.*

This publication contains commentary from diverse perspectives on equitable public education.

Reyner, Jon. 1993. "**American Indian Language Policy and School Success,**" *Journal of Educational Issues of Language Minority Students* 12, no. 3 (Summer): 35–59.

It provides a historical perspective of the impact the implementation of the American Indian Languages Act might have on Indian education.

Reyhner, Jon. 1992. **"American Indian Cultures and School Success,"** *Journal of American Indian Education* 32 (October).

This article challenges an earlier article by Glen Latham advocating an assimilationist approach in the education of Native Americans.

Rigden, Diana W. 1991. *Business/School Partnerships: A Path to Effective School Restructuring.* Council for Aid to Education.

This provides guidelines and models for companies interested in establishing partnerships with schools that lead to restructuring outcomes. It covers goal setting, costs, management, and assessment issues.

Steinberg, Adria, and Uli Allen. 2002. *From Large to Small: Strategies for Personalizing the High School.* Jobs for the Future.

The conversion of large high schools into small, focused learning environments is gaining popularity as an education reform strategy in communities across the country. This is a result of research indicating that small high schools generally have higher achievement levels, higher graduation rates, and lower dropout rates, and that they are safer than larger high schools. Strategies that have emerged from the ongoing work of converting large high schools into small ones include communicating a clear vision and mission, building community support, and developing a process for continuous improvement.

Thinking K–16. 2001. **"Youth at the Crossroads: Facing High School and Beyond."** *Education Trust* 5 (Winter).

Prepared for the National Commission on the High School Senior Year, this report provides a detailed look at various aspects of high school education in America, including achievement trends, curriculum design, dropout rates, demographic factors, and school size. Even though greater numbers of high school students are completing the academic sequence recommended for college preparation, this progress has not been nearly as fast as the increases in the numbers of students going to college. Even when high schools eliminate formal tracking and give all students an opportunity to take college-prep courses, many students don't. Much of the report focuses on the lack of alignment between the high school curriculum and the kind of knowledge and skills required for success in both the workplace and the postsecondary system.

Tomlinson, C. 1995. **"All Kids Can Learn: Masking Diversity in Middle School."** *Clearing House* 68 (January–February): 163–166.

This article suggests that the cliché that "all kids can learn" validates educational practices that mask middle school learners' diversity. It presents case studies of two middle school learners, one student who could not read and one who was gifted. It also suggests that the hard truth is that middle schoolers differ greatly in the ways they learn and in their learning needs.

Weiss, Suzanne. 2001. **"The Progress of Education Reform: High School Curriculum."** *The Progress of Education Reform, 1999–2001* 3, no. 1.

Research shows that the kind and level of courses high school students take affect their performance on tests, their readiness for college-level work, and their persistence toward a degree. This also examines what a rigorous high school curriculum should look like.

Wolk, Ron. 2000. *Cross City Campaign Report: Changing Urban High Schools.* Report from National Working Meeting sponsored by Cross City Campaign and cosponsored by the Annenberg Institute for School Reform in Baltimore, MD.

Government Publications

National Commission on Excellence in Education. *A Nation at Risk: The Imperative for Education Reform* 1983.

A report that set into motion several waves of reform and concerns about the effectiveness of American schools and the preparation of future citizens.

No Child Left Behind Act. 2001.

This act reauthorizes the Elementary and Secondary Act with significant changes, particularly in the way of testing and curriculum standardization.

Rasmussen, L. 1988. *Migrant Students at the Secondary Level: Issues and Opportunities for Change. Eric Digest.*

This report discusses the special problems migrant students encounter due to frequent moving, lack of continuity in schooling, and obligations to contribute to the family financially at an early age. Their dropout rate is alarming and the author implores that steps be taken at the secondary school level to serve them more successfully.

U.S. Department of Education and National Clearinghouse for Comprehensive School Reform. 2002. **Summary of Regional Symposia for Comprehensive School Reform.**

The symposia were designed so that the Comprehensive School Reform (CSR) program office could solicit participants' feedback on ways to improve the CSR program guidance, which was still in draft form at the time of the symposia, and to encourage dialogue, sharing, and networking among participants. The summary, prepared by NCCSR, highlights key points of four symposia.

Books

Allard, A., and S. Wilson. 1995. *Gender Dimensions: Constructing Interpersonal Skills in the Classroom.* Armadel, NSW: Eleanor Curtain Publishing.

Written in three parts, this book highlights the main issues of sexist language and harassment, unequal access, and classroom interactions that discourage risk-taking and cooperative problem solving in the classroom. It also provides practical activities that encourage and help teachers to design their own gender inclusive activities.

Apple, M. W., and J. A. Beane, eds. 1995. *Democratic Schools.* Alexandria: Association for Supervision and Curriculum Development.

This publication both makes the case for democratic schools and discusses examples of actual schools operating in democratic ways.

Ayers, William, Michael Klonsky, and Gabriele Lyon, eds. 2000. *A Simple Justice: The Challenge of Small Schools.* New York: Teachers College Press, Columbia University.

Part of the Teaching for Social Justice Series, this book focuses on the role the small schools movement plays in democracy, social justice, and educational activism.

Baca, Leonard M., and H. Cervantes. 1998. *The Bilingual Special Education Interface,* 3rd ed. Upper Saddle River, NJ: Merrill.

The purpose of this work is to present some of the current dilemmas within bilingual special education and special education as a whole and to explore why change is necessary for language-minority students to achieve educational equity.

Bigelow, Bill, Linda Christensen, Stan Karp, Barbara Miner, and Bob Peterson, eds. 1994. *Rethinking Classrooms: Teaching for Equity and Justice.* Milwaukee: Rethinking Schools.

This collection of articles, stories, and lessons from different academic grade levels and disciplines is designed to create more justice in schools and classrooms. The overarching theory is that curriculum and practice must be grounded in the lives of children.

Brown, T. 1996. *Faithful, Firm, and True: African American Education in the South.* Macon, GA: Mercer University Press.

Brown provides a thorough analysis of the important contributions made by early champions of black education in central Georgia and the central role played by Ballard Normal School. Brown discusses the heated ideological debates on education and public life by Washington and Du Bois.

Cobb, A. J. 2000. *Listening to Our Grandmother's Stories: The Bloomfield Academy for Chickasaw Females, 1825–1949.* Lincoln: University of Nebraska Press.

Cobb illustrates the academy's history and unique situation under Native American, missionary, and federal control. This book offers a closer study of a particular culture and race taking control over their children's education. It is a part of history not often visited.

Cuban, Larry, and Michael Usdan, eds. *Powerful Reforms with Shallow Roots: Improving America's Urban Schools.* New York: Teachers College Press.

This book provides an in-depth case study of six urban school systems that underwent governance changes during the 1990s. The book theorizes that increased political and organizational effectiveness will increase academic achievement. The case study approach is useful for policymakers and educators who want to improve academic performance in urban schools.

Darder, A., D. Torres, and H. Gutierrez, eds. 1996. *Latinos and Education: A Critical Reader.* New York: Routledge.

This book challenges the common notions of culture, identity, and language, establishing a clear link between educational practice and the structural dimensions that shape institutional life. The editors achieve a balance of theory and practice, as they discuss multiple issues, both historical and contemporary.

Delpit, Lisa. 1996. *Other People's Children: Cultural Conflict in the Classroom.* New York: The New Press.

Delpit suggests that many of the academic problems attributed to children of color are actually a result of miscommunication as schools and "other people's children" struggle with the imbalance of power and the dynamics of inequality plaguing our system.

Dickenson, Thomas S., ed. 2001. *Reinventing the Middle School: Transforming Teaching.* New York: Routledge/Falmer Press.

The contributors to this work propose that middle schools reinvent themselves by returning to the original concept of the middle school and implementing all aspects of it in an integrated fashion.

Evans, Dennis. 2001. *Taking Sides: Clashing Views on Controversial Issues in Secondary Education.* Irvine: University of California Press.

Topics debated include:

1. Should school attendance be voluntary?
2. Is citizenship education working in the public schools?
3. Should all secondary school students experience the same curriculum?
4. Is ethnocentric education a good idea?
5. Should secondary schools emphasize education for the workplace?
6. Should religious content and concepts be more evident in our schools?
7. Do school uniforms cause improvements?
8. Are zero-tolerance policies necessary and effective?
9. Is achievement-level tracking of students a defensible educational practice?
10. Is high-stakes testing defensible?
11. Should teacher pay be tied to measures of student learning?

12. Is the school principal indispensable?
13. Is block scheduling better than traditional scheduling?
14. Is homework beneficial to students?
15. Does the practice of grading students serve useful purposes?
16. Can technology transform education?
17. Should service learning be a high school graduation requirement?
18. Is the emphasis on globalization in the study of world history appropriate?
19. Should classical works be the emphasis of the literature curriculum?
20. Should we be cheering for high school sports programs?

Fine, M., and J. Sommerville, eds. 1998. *Small Schools, Big Imaginations: A Creative Look at Urban Public Schools.* Chicago: Cross City Campaign for Urban Schools Reform.

According to Hugh B. Price, president and CEO of the National Urban League, this book provides a "road map for leaders in our urban communities who are struggling to develop schools where equality, justice and opportunity are common practices."

Fine, Michele, ed. 1994. *Chartering Urban School Reform: Reflections on Public High Schools in the Midst of Change.* New York: Teachers College Press.

A collection of essays written by school reformers discusses the reform movement and examines the partnership that inspired the creation of charter schools.

Foster, Michele, and Lisa Delpit. *Black Teachers on Teaching.* New York: New Press Education Series.

Foster provides a straightforward account of the politics and philosophies involved in the education of black children since 1950.

Gatto, Taylor J. 2000. *The Underground History of American Education: A Schoolteacher's Intimate Investigation into the Problem of Modern Schooling.* New York: Oxford Village Press.

From a teacher's perspective, this is a passionate critique of American education. He provides history through lived experience and suggestions for reform.

Gay, Geneva. 2000. *Culturally Responsive Teaching: Theory, Research, and Practice.* New York: Teachers College Press.

Gay attempts to answer the question of why students of color are unsuccessful in school and suggests ways in which minority student underachievement can be addressed.

Grant, Carl A., and Christine E. Sleeter. 1999. *Turning on Learning: Five Approaches for Multicultural Teaching Plans for Race, Class, Gender, and Disability.* Indianapolis: John Wiley and Sons.

This book is the practical, lesson-based companion to *Making Choices for Multicultural Education: Five Approaches to Race, Class, and Gender.* It grew out of the requests of teachers and preservice education students for specific illustrations of how to work with diversity and excite their students.

Greene, Maxine. 2000. *Releasing the Imagination: Essays on Education, the Arts, and Social Change.* San Francisco: Jossey-Bass.

Greene argues for schools to be restructured as places where students reach out for meanings and where the previously silenced or unheard may have a voice.

Hamann, E., S. G. Worthman, and E. T. Murillo. 2001. *Education in the New Latino Diaspora: Policy and the Politics of Identity.* Westport, CT: Greenwood Publishing Group.

This book discusses new social relations and cultural identities that have emerged in the United States as a result of new immigration, and it illustrates how schools have struggled to meet student needs.

Herbst, J. 1996. *The Once and Future School: 350 Years of American Secondary Education.* New York: Routledge.

Herbst traces the beginning of secondary education in colonial America to the present day, presenting a clear understanding of past, present, and future directions.

Hilliard, Asa G., III. 1995. *Testing African American Students.* Chicago: Third World Press.

"When we see a dramatic decline in the number of African American teachers, a dramatic decline in the number of African American students in colleges and universities, a dramatic reduction in the number of teachers being prepared at black colleges and a continuing disproportion in the numbers of African American children in special education classes, standardized testing seems to play a key role. Therefore we have a special interest in assuring that testing instruments and practices are valid measures for African Americans" (9).

Hubbard, Lea, and Amanda Datnow. 2002. *Gender in Policy and Practice: Perspectives on Single Sex and Coeducational Schooling.* New York: Routledge.

These authors examine how schooling shapes and is shaped by the social construction of gender in history and in contemporary society.

Irvine, Jacqueline J., ed. 1997. *Critical Knowledge for Diverse Teachers and Learners.* Washington, DC: American Association of Colleges for Teachers.

This monograph offers insights into the knowledge required for preservice and in-service teachers who teach children of diverse backgrounds.

Jones, Tricia, and Randy Compton. 2002. *Kids Working It Out.* San Francisco: Jossey-Bass.

This book provides tools for educators, administrators, and policymakers to implement conflict-resolution education programs in school systems.

Kozol, Jonathan. 1992. *Savage Inequalities: Children in American Schools.* New York: Crown.

Kozol offers an exposé of the extremes of wealth and poverty in the American public school system and the devastating effect they have on poor children.

Ladson-Billings, Gloria. 2001. *Crossing over to Canaan: The Journey of New Teachers in Diverse Classrooms.* New York: John Wiley & Sons.

The author, a professor of education at the University of Wisconsin, studies the habits of mind required of beginning teachers who are prepared to support diverse classrooms. She defines multicultural education and raises the expectations for teacher education programs.

Ladson-Billings, Gloria. 1997. *The Dreamkeepers: Successful Teachers of African American Children.* San Francisco: Jossey-Bass.

Ladson-Billings challenges readers to envision intellectually rigorous and culturally relevant classrooms that have the power to improve the lives of not just African American students, but all children.

Latham, Bob. 1998. *The Invisible Minority: GLBTQ Youth at Risk.* Point Richmond, CA: Point Richmond Press.

This self-published text provides basic information on sexual orientation plus handouts for presentations to high school classes or for faculty and administrators at any grade level.

Leistyna, P., A. Woodrum, and S. A. Sherblum, eds. 1996. *Breaking Free: The Transformative Power of Critical Pedagogy.* Cambridge, MA: Harvard Educational Review Reprint Series.

This volume provides the reader with a clear introduction to the field of critical pedagogy, including central debates and insights of the field, explaining key concepts, and defines basic terminology.

Maher, M., Jr. 2001. *Being Gay and Lesbian in a Catholic High School: Beyond the Uniform.* New York: Harrington Park Press.

This book provides youth's stories in their own words. Sister Jeanine Gramick says, "This is a book to be taken seriously by all who are concerned about high school youth, whether in Catholic schools or not."

Meier, Kenneth J., and Joseph Stewart Jr. 1991. *The Politics of Hispanic Education: Un Paso Pa'lante y Dos Pa'tras.* Albany: State University of New York.

This is the first systematic study of the politics of "second generation discrimination" against Hispanic students.

Mortimer, Jeylan T., and Reed W. Larson, eds. 2002. *The Changing Adolescent Experience: Societal Trends and the Transition to Adulthood.* New York: Cambridge University Press.

This book examines the social, economic, political, and technological changes in the twenty-first century that will affect children as they grow into adulthood.

Nieto, Sonia. 2000. *Affirming Diversity: The Sociopolitical Context of Multicultural Education.* 3rd ed. New York: Longman.

The author explores the meaning, necessity, and benefits of multicultural education for students of all backgrounds. Nieto looks at how personal, social, political, cultural, and educational factors relate to the success or failure of students in today's classrooms.

Nieto, Sonia. 2000. *Puerto Rican Students in U.S. Schools*. Mahwah, NJ: Lawrence Erlbaum Associates.

This book is helpful for anyone who wants to learn why Puerto Rican students are systematically left behind in our public education system or are dropping out.

Olsen, L., A. Jaramillo, Z. McCall-Perez, J. White, and C. Minicucci. 1999. *Igniting Change for Immigrant Students: Portraits of Three High Schools*. Oakland, CA: California Tomorrow.

Three schools partnered with California Tomorrow to demonstrate an equity-centered approach to education.

Orenstein, Peggy. 1994. *Schoolgirls: Young Women, Self Esteem, and the Confidence Gap*. New York: Anchor Books.

This is a follow-up to the 1990 American Association of University Women (AAUW) study of adolescent girls and educational methods. Orenstein's findings support the study and confirm the messages that girls receive from teachers, schools, and boys that scholarship for girls is irrelevant.

Pollack, William, Todd Shuster, and Jim Trelease. 2001. *Real Boys' Voices*. New York: Penguin.

This work takes us into the daily world of boys, not only to show how society's outdated expectations force them to mask many of their true emotions, but also to let us hear how boys themselves describe their isolation, depression, longing, love, and hope.

Reese, W. J. 1999. *The Origins of the American High School*. New Haven, CT: Yale University Press.

Reese discusses the story of the American high school and analyzes social changes and political debates that shaped these institutions.

Sadker, Myra, and David Sadker. 1994. *Failing at Fairness: How American Schools Cheat Girls*. New York: Touchstone.

Twenty years of research documents gender bias and sexism pervasive in schools from kindergarten through higher education.

Salomone, Rosemary C. 2003. *Same, Different, Equal: Rethinking Single Sex Schooling.* New Haven, CT: Yale University Press.

Salomone, a professor at St. Johns University School of Law, presents an objective assessment of the educational and legal issues surrounding single-sex education.

Sapon-Shevin, Mara. 1999. *Because We Can Change the World: A Practical Guide to Building Cooperative, Inclusive Classroom Communities.* Boston: Allyn and Bacon.

This book brings together issues of inclusion, cooperative learning, conflict resolution, social justice teaching, and community-building.

Sawyer, Don. 1993. *NESA Activities Handbook for Native and Multicultural Classrooms.* Vol. 3. Vancouver: Tillacum Library.

This collection of activities is designed for teachers who want to provide meaningful and culturally based learning strategies for high school students.

Schneidewind, Nancy, and Ellen Davidson, eds. 1998. *Open Minds to Equality: A Sourcebook of Learning Activities to Affirm Diversity and Promote Equality.* Boston: Allyn and Bacon.

This is a practical book for teachers for building multicultural, gender-fair classrooms and for teaching students about both discrimination and approaches to equality. Grounded in theory but fully accessible to teachers, the book is a teacher-friendly resource that opens teachers' and students' minds to equality.

Sehr, D. T. 1997. *Education for Public Democracy.* Albany: State University of New York Press.

This book examines democratic public and private education, particularly focusing on two high schools, their structure, organization, curriculum, and pedagogy.

Shapiro, Arthur K., ed. 1999. *Everybody Belongs: Changing Negative Attitudes toward Classmates with Disabilities.* New York: Garland Publishing.

Shapiro offers practical guidance to schools that are struggling with how to mainstream children with disabilities.

Sleeter, Christine E., and Carl A. Grant. 1999. *Making Choices for Multicultural Education: Five Approaches to Race, Class, and Gender.* New York: John Wiley and Sons.

This book offers the educational community a way of thinking about race, language, culture, class, gender, and disability in teaching.

Smith, Stephanie, and Jean G. Thomases. 2001. *CBO Schools: Profiles in Transformational Education.* Washington, DC: Academy for Educational Development Center for Youth Development and Policy Research.

This collection provides information on eleven community-based organization (CBO) schools that help those young people who have been unsuccessful in mainstream schools to become engaged, challenged, and supported so that they find ways to succeed educationally and, in the process, change their lives and communities.

Stern, Deborah. 2000. "**Practicing Social Justice in the High School Classroom.**" In W. Ayers et al., eds. *A Simple Justice: The Challenge of Small Schools.* New York: Teachers College Press, Columbia University.

Using a Chicago alternative high school as a model, the author encourages the practitioner to see the connections between injustice and schooling and between justice and education.

Swisher, Karen Gayton, and John W. Tippeconnic, eds. 1999. *Next Steps: Research and Practice to Advance Indian Education.* Charleston, WV: Eric Clearinghouse/Rural Education and Small Schools.

This book provides definitions for "Indian education" and a discussion of its future. The editors and twelve other Native American scholars help readers explore two important themes: (1) education for tribal self-determination and (2) the need to turn away from discredited deficit theories of education to an approach that builds on the strengths of native languages and culture and the basic resilience of indigenous peoples.

Tatum, Beverly D. 1997. *Why Are All the Black Kids Sitting Together in the Cafeteria? and Other Conversations about Race.* New York: HarperCollins.

Author Tatum explains that these students are in the process of establishing and offering their racial identity—free of negative stereotypes.

Totten, S., and J. E. Pedersen. 1997. *Social Issues and Service at the Middle Level.* Boston: Allyn and Bacon Press.

This is a resource book full of actual implementation of integrated social issues, community service, and service learning. Students are actively involved intellectually, emotionally, and physically. Service learning is further explained in ways that can be directly implemented into the middle-level classroom.

Wallace, Adams D. 1997. *Education and Extinction: American Indians and the Boarding School Experience.* Lawrence: University Press of Kansas.

Adams offers a comprehensive account of the effort to assimilate and colonize Native American children. He provides a poignant description of the comprehensive experience at the boarding school, as well as an analysis of policy and resistance.

Walley, W. C., and G. W. Gerrick, eds. 1999. *Affirming Middle Grades Education.* Boston: Allyn and Bacon.

The book explores the environment of the middle school in relation to early adolescence. It discusses the necessity of middle school and challenges stereotypes of its education and youth.

Watkins, William H. 2001. *The White Architects of Black Education: Ideology and Power in America, 1865–1954.* New York: Teachers College Press, Columbia University.

This book offers an examination of the historical relationship between white philanthropy and black education, which led to the structuring of segregated education.

Weis, Lois, and Michele Fine, eds. 1993. *Beyond Voice: Class, Race, and Gender in U.S. Schools.* Albany: State University of New York.

This volume addresses race, class, and gender in the United States. The contributors debate issues of institutional power and privilege and the policies, discourse, and practices that silence powerless groups.

Wilson, Bruce L., and H. Dickson Corbett. 2001. *Listening to Urban Kids: School Reform and the Teachers They Want*. Albany: State University of New York Press.

Authors spoke to kids, not teachers or administrators, about the key characteristics of effective teachers to determine if the reform efforts for urban education were demonstrated in the classroom.

Wooster, M. M. 1993. *Angry Classrooms, Vacant Minds: What's Happened to Our High Schools?* San Francisco: Pacific Research Institute for Public Policy.

This is an informative history of American secondary education with suggestions and applications for contemporary reformers.

Journals

American Legacy: The Magazine of African American History & Culture
www.americanlegacymagazine.net
(212) 367-3143

This magazine covers a variety of historical and contemporary issues for a wide audience on African American knowledge, contributions, and possibilities inclusive of information relating to education at all levels.

American School Board Journal
www.asbj.com

The journal chronicles change, interprets issues, and offers readers practical advice on a broad range of topics pertinent to school governance and management, policymaking, student achievement, and the art of school leadership. In addition, regular departments cover education news, school law, research, and new books.

American Secondary Education Journal
(419) 289-5334

This is a quarterly journal on a variety of issues in secondary education. It is based at Ashland University, Ashland, Ohio.

Assessment in Education: Principles, Policy, and Practice

This journal offers a wide range of perspectives and ideas on various assessment strategies. It is a rich resource for any educator seeking direction in the area of assessment and evaluation.

Democracy and Education: The Magazine for Classroom Teachers
www.ohiou.edu/ide/journal_cover.htm

This magazine for teachers explores both theoretical and practical issues. The topics range in diversity and scope, addressing democracy from much needed perspectives.

Education Policy Analysis Archives
http://epaa.asu.edu/epaa/

A peer-reviewed journal of education policy topics, it is published by the College of Education at Arizona State University.

Home Education Magazine
www.home-ed-magazine.com

Home Education Magazine is one of the oldest, most respected, and most informative magazines on the subject of home schooling.

Journal of American Indian Education
http://jaie.asu.edu/abstracts/abs1999.htm

The *Journal of American Indian Education* offers excellent resources for students and teachers. Special issues from the journal are dedicated to "the wisdom and perspectives of recognized Native and non-Native elder leaders and scholars in the field of American Indian Education."

Middle Ground
www.nmsa.org/services/midground.htm

A quarterly magazine, *Middle Ground* celebrates the exciting leaps in learning and the energy of young adolescents. Like a trusted colleague, it gives practical advice, keeps up with new developments in middle-level education, and speaks from the heart of experience.

Middle School Journal
www.nmsa.org/services/midjournal

It is a refereed journal, an official publication of the National Middle School Association. The journal publishes articles that promote middle-level education and contribute to an understanding of the educational and developmental needs of youth between the ages of 10 and 15.

Phi Delta Kappan

www.pdkintl.org/kappan/kappan.htm

This is a professional print journal for education that addresses policy issues for educators at all levels. An advocate for research-based school reform, the *Phi Delta Kappan* provides a forum for debate on controversial subjects. It has been published monthly since 1915.

Rethinking Schools

www.rethinkingschools.org

An educational newspaper, *Rethinking Schools* is committed to informing and challenging public education practice, theory, and policy.

Teacher Magazine

www.edweek.org/tm

This is a magazine for educators at all levels, containing challenging discussion, commentaries, and opinions on a wide spectrum of educational issues.

Teaching Tolerance Magazine

www.tolerance.org

Teaching Tolerance supports the efforts of K–12 teachers and other educators to promote respect for differences and appreciation of diversity. *Teaching Tolerance* serves as a clearinghouse of information about antibias programs and activities being implemented in schools across the country. The ideas presented on the website and in this semiannual magazine represent some of the most innovative, useful initiatives found to date.

Urban Education Journal

www.urbanedjournal.org

This journal provides an interactive forum to investigate critical issues in urban education. This is an electronic journal fostering conversation about the complexities of urban education among practitioners, researchers, policymakers, and graduate students, who often work in isolation from one another. The intent is to foster collaboration and understanding among all interested individuals and groups.

NONPRINT RESOURCES

Almanac of Policy Issues: Elementary and Secondary Education
www.policyalmanac.org/education/el-sec.shtml.

This site provides information on critical secondary education issues (for elementary education as well), including government policies, news, directories, articles, and education-related organizations.

American Federation of Teachers (AFT). **Doing What Works: Improving Big City School Districts**
www.aft.org

AFT and some media accounts in recent years have reported significant achievement gains in individual schools that have adopted a "what works" approach to school improvement. This AFT policy brief illustrates a more widespread phenomenon: entire districts, by doing what works—and by working in cooperation with their local AFT unions and the community—are posting significant gains, many for the third to fifth year in a row. The brief, *Doing What Works: Improving Big City School Districts,* outlines commonsense, research-proven reforms that school staff, unions, families, community groups, district administrators, school boards, and policymakers can implement to ensure that all schools have the commitments and resources needed to do what works for all children.

American Federation of Teachers (AFT). **Trends in Student Achievement for Edison Schools, Inc.: The Emerging Track Record**
www.aft.org

An October 2000 report from the American Federation of Teachers finds that, five years after their first schools opened, students in Edison schools mostly perform as well as or worse than students in comparable public schools; occasionally they perform better. These findings, based on state and district student achievement data, contradict Edison's own reports on student achievement in its schools, which suggest performance in Edison schools is better than objective data bear out. The report advises school districts interested in hiring a private education management company to independently assess the company's track record of raising student achievement.

American Federation of Teachers (AFT). **Venturesome Capital: State Charter School Finance Systems**
www.aft.org

The first report of the National Charter School Finance Study examines the laws, regulations, and state practices governing charter school finance during the 1998–99 school year in twenty-three states and two cities. Topics include facilities funding, the role of negotiations with funding authorities, grade-level funding differentials, special education funding, federal funding, the financing of schools focusing on at-risk youth, financial accountability, and other elements of the eclectic charter school finance systems. This study also includes estimated dollar amounts that states allocate to charter schools based on the types of students enrolled and numerous other factors central to charter school funding. (This study was contracted to the AFT Educational Foundation in conjunction with Policy Studies Associates, Inc., and Fox River Learning, L.L.C., and funded by the U.S. Department of Education in December 2000.)

Annual Survey of America's Charter Schools
www.edreform.org

Surveying 481 of the nation's 2,357 charter schools, the Center for Education Reform found that charter schools are enrolling fewer students on average and leaving more on waiting lists than they were a year ago. A large number of charter schools are reaching out to minority and at-risk populations.

Antioch Leads Statewide Effort to Benefit Native American Education as Part of National Program
www.antiochsea.edu/earlycollege/index.html

This is a national initiative to create seventy "early college high schools" with the collaboration of Washington State tribes, schools, and Antioch Washington University. This initiative changes the structure of high school and the first years of college in order to secure success for Native American students. This program has the potential to improve high school and college graduation rates and to prepare underserved students for entry into professional careers. This is funded by the Bill and Melinda Gates Foundation, Carnegie Corporation, Ford Foundation, and W. K. Kellogg Foundation.

Blue Web'n
www.kn.pacbell.com/wired/bluewebn

Blue Web'n is an online library of over 1,200 Internet sites categorized by subject, grade level, and format (lessons, activities, projects, resources, references, and tools). One can search by grade level, broad subject area, or specific subcategories. Each week five new sites are added.

Busy Teachers
www.ceismc.gatech.edu/BusyT

This is an award-winning site created to help teachers find direct source materials, lesson plans, and classroom activities. Information is divided into nineteen categories, such as English, math, guidance counseling, and even recess.

The Catalyst
www.catalyst.org

This site has been developed specifically for the high school–level teacher as a resource for finding relevant information for use in the teaching of chemistry. Moreover, students and other visitors interested in the topic of chemistry will find The Catalyst to be a valuable Web resource for finding the information or answers they are seeking, and are encouraged to take advantage of this site as well. This site is updated frequently.

Charter Friends National Network
www.charterfriends.org

Connects and supports state-level charter school initiatives through online communications, publications, conferences, grant programs, and multistate projects, among others. The Charter Friends National Network is a project of the Center for Policy Studies in cooperation with Hamline University in St. Paul, Minnesota.

CNN Student News
http://fyi.cnn.com/fyi

CNN Student News provides a comprehensive look at news and information for students and resources for teachers.

Committee for Education Funding. January 23, 2003. **Protecting Public Education from Tax Giveaways to Corporations**
www.cef.org

An NEA-commissioned report to advise states on ways to protect and enhance funding for public education.

Committee for Education Funding. February 2003. **A Tale of Three Cities: Urban Perspectives on Special Education.**
www.cef.org

During 2002, the Center for Education Policy reviewed the operations of special education programs in Chicago, Cleveland, and Milwaukee, and conducted interviews and on-site forums with the major stakeholder groups in those three cities. The report presents general observations about special education and describes common concerns for revising the Individuals with Disabilities Education Act (IDEA) to address these concerns.

Cooper, Laura. 2002. **Listen Up: The Role of Relationships in the Success of Students of Color.**
www.gse.harvard.edu./news/features/cooper02012002.html.

Cooper offers reflections on an urban high school program that featured a "panel of successful students of color who shared their perspectives about the barriers they've encountered and supports they've received in their own efforts to achieve academically."

Council of Educators for Students with Disabilities
www.504idea.org

This site provides training and resources for educators, as well as conference information and other events of interest to educators.

Discovery Channel School Online
www.school.discovery.com

This site includes a wealth of resources and ideas. It provides information related to science, social studies, language arts, and the humanities for kindergarten through twelfth grade teachers. Educators can search the database by grade level or subject matter.

Education Week
www.edweek.org

This site provides educational articles from newspapers around the country and abroad. The site is updated daily.

Education World
www.education-world.com

This is a free resource with numerous lesson plans, articles, links, and references on a wide range of topics, content, and contemporary concerns. People in a variety of education positions contribute to this site. It contains a weekly 'zine and database.

Educational Resources for Native American Studies, First Nations Studies, Indigenous Studies, and Aboriginal Studies
www.GoodMinds.com

This is a Native American–owned and –operated business located in the Six Nations of the Grand River Territory in Ontario. Their dedicated team is committed to providing educators with a comprehensive, one-stop site for the very best in native educational resources.

Educational Resources Information Center/AskERIC
http://ericir.syr.edu
www.askeric.org

This is a federally funded collection of education-related resources including Ask ERIC, a question-and-answer service, a virtual library, a research and development team, and constantly updated materials.

Eduhound
www.eduhound.com/

This website with a wide range of topics on education and resources for the practicing teacher offers a prescreened directory of over twenty thousand links in more than fifty categories. This website also provides useful resources on how to build free Web pages.

Edutopia
http://glef.org/index.html

George Lucas Educational Foundation is a nonprofit organization that documents and disseminates stories about exemplary practices in K–12 public education through the creation of media, such as films, books, newsletters, and CD-ROMs. This site provides a variety of resources for educators and great examples of schools making important and significant changes for the betterment of young people's education.

Eisenhower National Clearinghouse (ENC)
www.enc.org

It is a catalog of curriculum resources providing users with detailed information and a wide selection of K–12 math and science resources.

Exploring Middle School Reform
www.middleweb.com

This site provides a wealth of resources for schools, districts, educators, parents, and public school advocates working to raise achievement for all students in the middle grades.

Global SchoolNet Foundation
www.gsn.org

Global SchoolNet focuses on collaborative learning. It provides online opportunities for teachers to collaborate, communicate, and celebrate shared learning experiences. It also has links to numerous worldwide projects.

Harvard Educational Letter
www.edletter.org/

This bimonthly education publication summarizes and synthesizes pre-K–12 education research and practice. It provides concise, accurate, and thought-provoking coverage of the most pressing issues and debates in education and practical suggestions to put to use in classrooms and schools.

The Homeless Project's Education Program, Common Cents
Campaign: Educating Youth about Homelessness
www.homelessinfo.org.

This guide for teachers describes comprehensive ways to educate students about homelessness. It also has reading discussion exercises, activities, service-learning plans, and resources for both teachers and students.

IEDX: Internet Education Exchange
www.iedx.org

This site offers the latest news, information, and tools to help educators take action to improve schooling, teaching, and learning in communities across America.

Index of Native American Education Resources on the Internet
www.hanksville.org/NAresources/indices/NAschools.html

This is a virtual library replete with different resources for teachers and anybody interested in Native American education.

Learning Webs
www.learnweb.com

This site focuses on curriculum resources for all levels of instruction from the Arizona Environment and Education Network.

MIT Council on Primary and Secondary Education
http://web.mit.edu/cpse/

The Council on Primary and Secondary Education (CPSE) develops programs that bring the strengths of MIT to bear on the American K–12 educational system. The projects sponsored by the CPSE include the MIT/Wellesley Teacher Education/Certification Program, Teacher Sabbaticals, and Educational Outreach Programs.

National Alliance to End Homelessness
www.endhomelessness.org

Let's End Homelessness! is a collection of fact sheets that provides information about homelessness activities and ways in which students can help. It is divided into four different age-appropriate sections, ranging from kindergarten through high school. It provides a list of resources, including websites, age-appropriate books, videos, and teaching guides.

National Association of School Psychologists. **Position Statement on Gay, Lesbian, and Bisexual Youth**
www.nasponline.org/information/pospaper_glb.html.

National Association of School Psychologists supports equal access to education and mental health services for sexual minority youth in public and private schools.

National Coalition for the Homeless. June 1999. **NCH Fact Sheet #10.**
www.nch.ari.net/edchild.html.

This fact sheet examines the barriers to public education faced by homeless children and youth, the progress states have made in removing those barriers, and current policy issues.

NPR Special Report. 2002. **Educating Latinos: A Five-Part Series on the Crisis in Education**
www.npr.org/programs/atc/features/2002/nov/educating_latinos/resources.html

This is a five-part series on the crisis in education. It provides a variety of resources on Latinos in education, bilingual education, teacher shortages, mothers and daughters, and the assimilation experience.

Out for Equity
www.stpaul.k12.mn.us/outforequity

Out for Equity's comprehensive Safe Schools Manual contains a collection of materials and resources to aid educators and other staff members in combating homophobia and developing safer, more inclusive school climates for lesbian, gay, bisexual, and transgendered individuals. It can be downloaded for free at the Out for Equity website.

Premack, Eric. 2003. **The Charter School Development Guide.** Revised.
www.cacharterschools.org/pubs.html

This comprehensive how-to guide is an invaluable source on the process of planning and starting a California charter school. Though developed for a California audience, the concepts and principles underlying its practical advice have proven useful to charter developers and charter-granting agencies across the country. Detailed appendixes provide the actual text of California's Charter Schools Act, sample charter petition documents, and a preoperations start-up checklist.

Public Education Network
www.publiceducation.org

This site provides a variety of tools and publications for the educator who is interested in improving public education through school reform. Public Education Network (PEN) is a national association of local educators and individuals working to advance public school reform in low-income communities across our country. PEN seeks to build public demand and mobilize resources for quality public education for all children through a theory of action that focuses on the importance of public engagement in school reform. PEN believes community engagement is the missing ingredient in school reform and that the level of public involvement ultimately determines the quality of education provided by public schools.

Quality Counts 2003: If I Can't Learn from You . . . January 9.
www.edweek.com/sreports/Qc03/

Education Week's review of federal data shows there are fewer qualified public school teachers in low-income than in moderate- and high-income areas. Teachers in high-poverty areas report more difficult working conditions, less satisfaction with their pay, and less cooperation from parents. Recruitment efforts to find qualified teachers are lagging in low-income areas.

Second Nature Resource Center
www.secondnature.org

Originally known as Starfish, this center disseminates sustainability and environmental education resources.

StarkNet: A K–99 Education Network
www.stark.k12.oh.us/DOCS/units/homeless/lessons

Individual Subject Area Lesson Sequence: Homelessness.

This lesson sequence for teachers breaks down a comprehensive curriculum on homelessness by specific themes and issues about homelessness to be discussed daily while teaching the unit.

T.H.E. Institute
www.thejournal.com/institute

T.H.E. Institute, an innovative model for professional development, offers educators a range of professional development services. In addition, T.H.E. offers educators—and businesses serving education—an array of consulting services. Headed by Geoffrey H. Fletcher, a nationally known expert in education and technology in education, T.H.E. Institute brings the highest-quality professional development and consulting possible to educators and businesses around the world through years of experience in the classroom, central office, university, and state department of education.

Transformational Education
www.tedweb.org

This online community is for people interested in advancing alternative and transformational education. TEDweb is extremely valuable for educators interested in the progressive educational movement. TEDweb is run by the Academy for Educational Development.

Trimble, Susan. **What Works to Improve School Achievement**. National Middle School Association. Center for Education Reform. www.nmsa.org/research/summary/studentachievement.htm

This report provides interesting data in response to the new federal educational policies. It pays particular attention to the many ways that assessment is working in schools across the nation.

Voice of the Shuttle
http://vos.ucsb.edu/

Its mission has been to provide a structured and briefly annotated guide to online resources that respects the established humanities disciplines in their professional organization and points toward the transformation of those disciplines as they interact with the sciences and social sciences and with new digital media. VoS emphasizes both primary and secondary (or theoretical) resources, and defines its audience as people who have something to learn from a higher-education, professional approach to the humanities (which in practice has included students and instructors from the elementary school, high school, and general population sectors).

Web66
http://web66.coled.umn.edu/

This is a K–12 project that focuses on using the Web across disciplines and grades. The developers of this project see the World Wide Web as a catalyst that will integrate the Internet into K–12 school curriculum. This is a project by the University of Minnesota.

Woodward, Tali. 2002. **Edison's Failing Grade**.
www.corpwatch.org

This article argues that investors and school districts are rethinking and ending ties with the nation's leading public education privatizer.

⚡ Index

⚭ About the Author

Leila E. Villaverde is assistant professor of cultural foundations in the Educational Leadership and Cultural Foundations Department at the University of North Carolina, Greensboro. She is the coeditor of *Rethinking Intelligence: Confronting Psychological Assumptions about Teaching and Learning* and *Dismantling White Privilege: Pedagogy, Politics, and Whiteness.* She lectures on social foundations, curriculum studies, feminist theory, and aesthetics. She teaches both undergraduate and graduate courses to preservice teachers, teachers, administrators, and future professors. Dr. Villaverde considers secondary education a crucial cultural space for youth to create meaningful lifelong commitments to learning and activism. Professor Villaverde strongly believes middle schools and high schools are potentially transformative environments for the development of ethics and social consciousness.